WHAT IN THE
WORD
?

CHARLES HARRINGTON ELSTER

WHAT IN THE
WORD
?

WORDPLAY,
WORD LORE,
AND ANSWERS TO
YOUR PESKIEST QUESTIONS
ABOUT LANGUAGE

A HARVEST ORIGINAL
HARCOURT, INC.
Orlando Austin New York
San Diego Toronto London

www.HarcourtBooks.com

The introduction to "The Grandiloquent Gumshoe"
appeared, in slightly different form, in the "On Language"
column of *The New York Times Magazine,* August 29, 1999. The
introduction to "A Civil Tongue" appeared, in slightly different form,
in *The Wall Street Journal,* April 23, 1999. The discussion of
the word *resistentialism* in "The Grandiloquent Gumshoe" is
derived from an "On Language" column the author published in
The New York Times Magazine, September 21, 2003. The segment
"New Yawk Tawk" in "Born in the USA" appeared, in slightly
different form, in the Spring 2005 issue of *Verbatim.*

Library of Congress Cataloging-in-Publication Data
Elster, Charles Harrington.
What in the word?: wordplay, word lore,
and answers to your peskiest questions about language/
Charles Harrington Elster.—1st ed.
p. cm.
A Harvest Original.
Includes bibliographical references and index.
1. English language—Etymology.   2. English language—Usage.
3. English language—Style.   4. Play on words.   5. Americanisms.
I. Title.
PE1574.E57   2005
422—dc22   2005008899
ISBN-13: 978-0156-03197-4   ISBN-10: 0-15-603197-3

Text set in Stone Serif
Designed by Kaelin Chappell Broaddus

Printed in the United States of America

First edition
C E G I K J H F D B

*In memory of Dorothy Carr Morris,
my beloved aunt Dot*

CONTENTS

ACKNOWLEDGMENTS

For assistance with several questions dealing with elusive American expressions, I thank Joan Houston Hall, chief editor, and Leonard Zwilling, general editor, of the *Dictionary of American Regional English*. For their clever contributions to the I-could-have-been game, I am indebted to my punderful friends Norm Storer and Gregg Brandalise. And for her enthusiasm, keen ear and eye, and staunch support, I am grateful to my editor, Jen Charat.

Thanks to my favorite Yiddish maven, Sol Steinmetz, for being helpful, as always. Thanks to Arthur Salm, Cory J Meacham, Leo Diesendruck, William Weldon, Jim Means, Joe Freeman, DeeAnne Williams, and Karen Skullerud for permission to reprint their words, and to Toni Michael both for permission to reprint her words and for suggesting the terrific word *hyphos*. Thanks also to Daniel Reveles and the scores of other folks who asked me the questions I have answered in this book. Though your words have been changed to protect your innocence, you're still in the book in a sense.

If you've got a question about language,* I welcome your queries and theories, questions and indigestions, especially when accompanied by a generous check. You may snail-mail me c/o Gelfman Schneider Literary Agents, Inc., 250 West 57th Street, Suite 2515, New York, NY 10107, or email me at

words@members.authorsguild.net.

I also invite you to visit my website at

http://members.authorsguild.net/chelster.

*If you're wondering about using *have got* for *have*, see page 66.

INTRODUCTION

Wherever there is language, there will be questions—lots and lots of questions. Where does it come from? Is this correct? Should I write it this way or that way? What's the proper pronunciation? What's the difference between? Is there a word for that?

This book is for people who want ready answers to those questions, who expect to be entertained as well as informed, and who like to have some fun with words.

For more than twenty years—as a writer, editor, and radio commentator—I have made it my business (and sometimes my whole waking existence) to learn everything I could about words. I have studied what they mean, where they come from, and how they should and should not be used. I have communed with the works of eminent authorities, past and present, and taken the measure of their counsel. I have lain by the fireside of English and listened to its words tell their wondrous tales. I have spent countless hours combing the pages of dozens of dictionaries, looking for the glittering gem of enlightenment.

I have become, in short, a wordwise guy. (And a bit of a wise guy with words.)

Over the years people have asked me hundreds of questions about all aspects of language, and herein you will find my answers to a great many of them—from FAQs like "What's the origin of *okay*?" to urgent pleas like "Can you tell me the correct plural of *cactus*?" to unusual queries like "Is there a word for when inanimate objects conspire against you?"

I even tackle the most maddening question of our time, one that has plagued us since the dawn of the digital age: What idiot programmed my spell-checker?

Throughout this book I clear up confusions, clarify distinctions, and sort the tall tales from the truth. I calm your word-jangled nerves and dispel your lingering verbal doubts. I tell you how to avoid common mistakes and when it's a mistake to avoid something that's common. I settle your bets and debates before they become lawsuits.

As your verbal *chef de cuisine,* I have concocted in these pages a salmagundi, gallimaufry, and olla podrida of word lore, wordplay, and advice aggressively seasoned with spicy opinion and a generous pinch of salty humor. My menu was inspired by people like you—people curious, confused, or plumb crazy about words—so I think you'll find it savory, nutritious, and a whole lot cheaper than a meal at most restaurants.

Here's a tantalizing sample of what you'll be tasting at this feast.

In "Once Upon a Word" you'll discover why prose is purple and why you mind your p's and q's. You'll find out who put the corn in *corned beef,* who put the *X* in *Xmas,* and who was the first peeping Tom. And you'll learn some unflattering words—like *Oslerize,* to kill all men over forty—that have come from some unlucky people's names.

In "A Slough of Solecisms" I deliver you from unwitting error and misperception by explaining, for example, the difference between *i.e.* and *e.g.;* why you should never, ever write *'til;* whether you are *done* or *finished;* what's up with *What it is, is;* and why *to beg the question* doesn't mean what you may think it does.

In "The Grandiloquent Gumshoe" I patch holes in your vocabulary, recover your lost locutions, and track down the missing pieces in your verbal picture of the world. Here you'll find terms for a host of word-needy concepts, including the snappy comeback that you think of too late, the stuff that people attach to their car aerials, the female counterpart for *phallic,* when a trademark becomes generic, and a person who has an annoying habit of dropping in uninvited at mealtimes.

In "The Elegance of Style," while you (w)rack your brains about *(w)rack* and the meaning of *bimonthly* (is it every other month or twice a month?), your wordwise guide will save you from apostrophe catastrophes, opine on the plural of *octopus,* tell you how to distinguish *people* and *persons,* and rule on whether it's *Welsh rabbit* or *Welsh rarebit.*

In "A Civil Tongue" I show you that becoming a better speaker is a lot less daunting than losing weight or learning French. I give you sound advice on why *primer* rhymes with *swimmer,* why you should pronounce the *t* in *tsunami,* where the stress should fall in *patina* and *formidable,* how to handle French mouthfuls like *cache* and *denouement,* how not to pronounce *mischievous* and *heinous,* and how to pronounce oft-misspoken names like *Brontë, Coleridge, Halley's comet,* and *Ayn Rand.* You'll also learn how *colonel* came to be pronounced like *kernel,* why the *b* in *debt* is silent, and what it's called when people say *ath-uh-lete* and *drown-dead* for *athlete* and *drowned.*

In "Born in the USA" you'll be sitting in the catbird seat and happy as a pig eating pancakes as I serve you up a heaping plate of all-American words and expressions. Your mojo will be workin' in a New York minute as you discover the amusing origin of *schmuck,* find out why we call a bathroom the *john,* and learn where the *H* comes from in *Jesus H. Christ.* You'll have a bitchin' time, I guarantee.

Finally, in "The Wonder of Words" you'll learn about mondegreens like *José can you see,* lost positives like *gruntled,* and palindromes like *Was it Eliot's toilet I saw?* I'll expose the great *-gry* hoax, treat you to a taste of Cockney rhyming slang, and teach you the word for words like *brunch, guesstimate,* and *palimony.*

And that's not all, as the marketing wonks are wont to say.

These chapters are liberally garnished with even more delicious verbal diversions. In the "Quote Unquote" feature you'll encounter an eclectic selection of my favorite wise and witty words. In the "Fascinating Fact" feature you'll discover priceless curiosities like words in which *q* is not followed by *u*, the three earlier names of Scrabble, and the real title of the painting known as "Whistler's Mother." And if your taste turns to fun and games, there are oodles of Bodacious Brainteasers—like "Tasty Toponyms," "Are You Brandiloquent?" and "The Brobdingnagian Rubicund Saxiphage"— designed to test your verbal mettle.

But don't just take it from me. See for yourself. Thumb through the book and sample the fare. I think after a few bites you'll agree that your wordwise guy and wise guy of words is also a wise word guide.

Well, what are you waiting for? Turn the page and get an edge in wordwise.

WHAT IN THE
WORD
?

ONE

ONCE UPON A WORD

Word Histories, Mysteries,
Hoaxes, and Hype:
Sorting the Tall Tales
from the Truth

Breathes there anyone who has not wondered, from time to time, about the origin of a familiar word or expression? For those of us who are naturally curious about the English language, hardly a day goes by without the question arising: Where does that dadblamed thing come from, anyway?

Although words are human creations, few of us know the stories behind them. Most of our discussions about word and phrase origins are limited to speculation. And in these days of instant Internet communciation, when we are bombarded with all manner of linguistic information, some of it trustworthy and much of it not, few of us possess the means to detect the etymological tall tales and hoaxes that circulate in cyberspace.

A friend tells you that the word *handicapped* comes from disabled beggars using their caps to panhandle, another friend asserts that *Xmas* is insulting to Jesus, and a coworker claims that *jiffy* is an actual unit of time. Can you believe any of it?

You receive an emissive (my proposed word for an email message) from an ostensible authority calling for a boycott of the word *picnic* because its origin is presumably linked with the lynching of African Americans. Could such a disturbing etymology be true?

Another emissive floats in informing you that a certain well-known four-letter word in fact stands for *ship high in transit*. It seems plausible, but how can you know for sure?

Then there are the etymological mysteries that suddenly occur to you as you're going about the business of life. You're eating a corned beef sandwich and you wonder, Why do they call it *corned* beef? You're minding your p's and q's and it hits you: What the heck are *p's and q's*? You're watching an old movie when somebody says, "Your goose is cooked," and you think, How in the world did that culinary phrase come to mean "It's curtains for you, buster"?

The answers to these, and many other original questions, await you in the following pages.

Worm Words

Q. *I am going stark raving mad trying to find out where the phrase* as the worm turns *comes from and what it means. I've searched the Web and scoured my library to no avail. Please help!*

A. *The worm turns* comes from an old proverb, "Tread on a worm and it will turn," meaning that even the most defenseless creature will, when sufficiently provoked, attempt to defend itself. Shakespeare used it in *Henry VI*, where he wrote, "The smallest worm will turn, being trodden on / And doves will peck in safeguard of their brood." Today it usually means that the loser or oppressed party is now (or will become) the victor. The expression usually appears as *the worm turns* or *the worm will turn*, not *as the worm turns* (which strikes me as a confusion with "as the world turns").

⇥ I could have been a writer

De Goostibus

Q. *Criminals are often told by the good guys,* Your goose is cooked. *What is the origin of this phrase? Is there a historical connection between geese and crooks?*

A. Goose-cooking apparently has nothing to do with criminals etymologically. It just means to ruin someone's plan or project, to rain on somebody's parade.

There are several oddball theories about the origin of the phrase. One says that some folks in a besieged town in the sixteenth century hung a goose from a tower as a symbol of contempt for the town's attackers, the goose being a proverbial "symbol of stupidity and futility," explains one etymological dictionary. The attackers, enraged, redoubled their efforts and burned the town to the ground, thus fully cooking that goose.

Another colorful but dubious theory connects the phrase with the fable about the goose that laid the golden egg. My sources agree, however, that this locution probably doesn't have such a fabulous origin and that it isn't particularly old. The earliest record of it is from 1851, in a London street ballad attacking the pope for appointing a certain cardinal: "If they come here we'll cook their goose, / The Pope and Cardinal Wiseman."

Straight Eye for the Queer *Gay*

Q. *I'm interested in knowing how the word* gay *went from meaning "merry" or "lively" to "homosexual."* The gay 1890s *has a totally different connotation from* the gay 1990s.

A. The transformation occurred in the 1960s and 1970s and took root in the dictionaries in the 1980s. The usage note in *The American Heritage Dictionary* points out, among other things, that "*gay* is distinguished from *homosexual* in emphasizing the cultural and social aspects of homosexuality."

Some people resent that a "special-interest group" has appropriated *gay* and made it difficult, if not impossible, to use the word

but it seemed like a life sentence. 🖙

in its traditional sense. But no thinking person could misinterpret the historical use of *gay* (as in *the gay nineties*), and the appropriation of a word—especially one with plenty of common synonyms—is a small price to pay to fill such an obvious need.

Plane English

Q. *Obviously, the expression* pushing the envelope *has nothing to do with the United States Postal Service. But I haven't a clue where it* does *come from. Do you know?*

A. *Pushing the envelope* comes from aviation. The *envelope* is aviation engineering jargon for the limits within which an aircraft can perform. When a pilot attempts to make the aircraft perform at or beyond those limits, it is called *pushing the envelope.* The expression traveled from aviation into other technical contexts, and by the 1980s it had entered the general vocabulary, where it is used of any attempt to push something to the limit, go beyond the expected or the norm, take risks—not something the Postal Service is known for doing.

What's a *Petard*, and Why Does It Get Hoisted?

Q. *What is the origin of the expression* to hoist with his own petard*? Is it* hoist with *or* hoist by*? When it's used in the past tense, is it* you were *hoist or* hoisted with/by *your own petard? And what the heck is a* petard, *anyway? Can you tell I'm royally confused about this one?*

A. These are all legitimate questions, and you are not alone in your confusion. Let me try to sort out this royal mess for you.

A *petard* was a case containing an explosive, used in warfare to blow open a door, a gate, or create a hole in a wall. The word comes from the Latin *pedere,* to break wind. When you are hoist (or hoisted) with (or by) your own petard, you are blown up by your own bomb (or flatus). The expression first appeared in Shakespeare's *Hamlet* as *hoist with his own petar* (the form without *d* is an archaic spelling). It is used figuratively today to mean that your own scheming against others backfires and hurts you instead.

❧ I could have been an accountant

Should it be *hoist* or *hoisted,* and what should follow it, *with* or *by*? There's some wiggle room here. "The usual renderings are *hoist with his own petard* and *hoisted by his own petard,*" says *Garner's Modern American Usage.* If you want to sound literary and show that you know your Shakespeare, stick with *hoist with his own petard.* However, notes Garner, because *hoisted by his own petard* "is nearly four times as common, it shouldn't be labeled incorrect." And neither should *hoisted with his own petard,* which also seems respectable to me.

How Can Prose Be Purple?

Q. *One of my students recently inquired about the derivation of the term* purple prose, *meaning "overwrought composition." I had no answer. Do you?*

A. I do. The idiom was originally a *purple passage* or *purple patch,* and the earliest citation in the *Oxford English Dictionary* is from 1598. The rhetorical sense in English comes from the *Ars Poetica* of Horace, specifically from the phrase *purpureus pannus,* a purple garment or raiment, the color purple symbolizing royalty, grandeur, power.

Purple prose doesn't seem to have become wholly pejorative until the twentieth century, when steep declines in the vocabulary and reading comprehension of college-educated Americans caused a panic in the education establishment and the newspaper industry, which together launched a campaign against prose that displayed royalty, grandeur, and power. This led to the disappearance of the semicolon, the invention of the sentence fragment, and a marked increase in the use of words like *methodological.*

Deck Orate

Q. *The last time I got all decked out—to attend a wedding—the question popped into my head: What do decks have to do with dressing up? Does this expression perhaps come from sailing? Or decks of cards? Or maybe baseball's* on deck?

but it just didn't add up. 🖙

A. Three strikes and you're out. Sorry, but this *deck* is an archaic verb that means "to clothe, adorn" and dates from 1513. It was a borrowing from the Dutch *dekken,* to cover. *Deck* replaced the Old English *theccan,* to cover, with which it is cognate. I suspect that, as in *dress up,* the *out* of *deck out* was added later to denote exceptional elegance or finery in one's adornment.

BODACIOUS BRAINTEASER

COLORFUL LANGUAGE

In this game the clues lead to familiar words, phrases, expressions, names, and titles that incorporate the name of a color. For example, what Bing Crosby dreamed of (a white Christmas); another name for jealousy (the green-eyed monster); you're not supposed to shoot until you see this (the whites of their eyes); and an extremely rare lunar event (a blue moon, as in once in a blue moon).

1. The object of the question "Have you any wool?"

2. What you follow to get to the Emerald City.

3. A famous George Gershwin composition.

4. A colorful novel by Nathaniel Hawthorne.

5. An infamous dungeon in Bengal, India.

6. In the Peanuts comic strip, Snoopy's nemesis.

7. The colors of Harvard and Yale.

8. It was all around 1960s rock star Jimi Hendrix.

9. A poetic name for Ireland.

Governor Gubernator

Q. *Why is* gubernatorial *the adjective corresponding to the noun* governor *instead of* governatorial? *Wouldn't the latter be more logical?*

A. You have the French to thank for the confusion. *Governor* comes from the Latin *gubernator,* governor, through the French *governeor* or *-eur,* and dates back to the thirteenth century (when

⇥ I could have been a firefighter

the Normans were governing England). *Gubernatorial* is an early American (c. 1725) inkhorn term coined directly from the Latin *gubernator.*

Memo to self: Notify Arnold Schwarzenegger—aka the Terminator—that there's a Latin word he may want to revive now that he's governor of California.

10. A colorful novel by Anthony Burgess.

11. One of the four bodily humors in medieval medicine, known also as melancholy.

12. A powerful, toxic defoliant used in the Vietnam War.

13. A name for a member of Hitler's Nazi Party.

14. When writers overwrite, this can be the result.

15. A colorful name for Vermont.

16. What some say an inebriated person sees.

17. Activists for the elderly.

18. Sensationalism and unscrupulousness in the media.

19. Another name for England's King William III.

20. *Random House Webster's College Dictionary* defines this two-word epithet as "a person who wields unofficial power, esp. through another person and often surreptitiously or privately."

Answers appear on page 263.

Puzzled by POSSLQ

Q. *A recent* New York Times *crossword puzzle had the hint "unmarried partner, in modern lingo," and the answer turned out to be* POSSLQ. *What does that mean?*

A. For many years now, people have struggled to find a word for a live-in lover who is not a spouse. Suggestions have ranged

but I was too burnt out. 🖙

FASCINATING FACT 🖜

Q. *Scrabble* is not the original name of the famous word game. It had three earlier names. Do you know what they were?

A. *Lexiko* was the original name. Later it was called *It*, then *Criss-Cross*, and finally *Scrabble*. 🖜

from *significant other,* which is cloyingly trendy, to *quasi-conjugal dyad,* which exudes a clinical aroma. *POSSLQ,* pronounced PAH-sul-kyoo, is an acronym invented by the U.S. Census Bureau (c. 1980) to designate a person of the opposite sex sharing living quarters. Upon its arrival it was ridiculed, quite understandably, by journalists and literati.

One of the best of the many terms proposed to fill this gap in the language is *covivant.* But I think my favorite is *amari,* coined by poet Cynthia MacDonald. It combines the Greek privative *a-,* not, with the Latin *maritare,* to marry, with a suggestive similarity to the Italian *amore,* love.

Green Room **in the Limelight**

Q. *I once heard a story about how the theatrical terms* green room *and* limelight *are related. Before the use of floodlights there were green limelights positioned at the foot of the stage. The room where the actors put on their costumes and makeup was painted green so they could get used to the green light before going onstage "into the limelight."*

A. Nice theory, but I have found no evidence to support it. Besides, those early limelights weren't green; they were an intense and brilliant white. Brewer's *Dictionary of Phrase and Fable* claims that it is "so called because at one time the walls were coloured green to relieve the eyes affected by the glare of the stage lights."

The *Oxford English Dictionary* and several other dictionaries I checked note perfunctorily that the green room is so called "probably" because such rooms were originally painted green, although they do not say why. In *Seeing Red or Tickled Pink,* Christine Ammer explains that "the 'green room,' where performers rest between

🖜 I could have been a cook

acts and receive admirers, has been so called since the late seventeenth century. Playwright Colly Cibber mentioned it in his 1701 play *Love Makes the Man*. Presumably the term came from a tradition of painting the walls of these rooms green, perhaps, as some suggest, because this color is restful to the eyes, which have been exposed to bright footlights. Today's green rooms can be painted any color, but the term survives."

Get Sirius

Q. *Why are the hottest days of summer called* dog *days? Because you sweat like a dog?*

A. You may sweat like a dog during the dog days, but dogs don't. They pant. The *dog days* are so called because this was the time of year when the poets of yore convened at literary festivals where they competed to see who could improvise the best doggerel. (Yeah, right.) Actually, explains the *Morris Dictionary of Word and Phrase Origins, dog days* dates back to Roman times, when the hottest weeks of summer were known colloquially as *caniculares dies*. The Romans' theory "was that the dog star Sirius, rising with the sun, added its heat to the sun's and thus the period — roughly from July 3 to August 11."

The Birth of *Hospice*

Q. *I am a professor of medicine, and my students have asked me about the etymology of the word* hospice. *Can you please help?*

A. *Hospice* is a loanword from French, coming ultimately from the Latin *hospitium*, hospitality, lodging. The word entered English in the early nineteenth century (the earliest known citation is from 1818) and was used of a house, especially one belonging to a religious order, where pilgrims and other travelers could rest. By the 1890s it had taken on its current sense, "a nursing-home for the care of the dying or the incurably ill" (*Oxford English Dictionary*).

but it didn't pan out. ☞

Gone Missing Link

Q. *Everywhere I turn these days I see the expression* gone missing *or* went missing. *Where did it come from? And why are people using it when they simply mean vanished or disappeared?*

A. *Gone missing* and *went missing* are originally British, and have been documented in print since at least the 1870s. For no discernible reason (other than novelty) these phrases have lately enjoyed great vogue in the American press and have been repeated ad nauseam in broadcast news. Yet two respected language columnists, William Safire of *The New York Times* and Jan Freeman of the *Boston Globe*, have pronounced them acceptable and useful, and I tend to agree. They say that *gone/went missing* expresses a shade of meaning that *vanish* and *disappear* cannot — that whatever has gone missing has done so under mysterious and probably suspicious circumstances, and although it is missing it is still somewhere to be found. But you're right that this nuance doesn't justify merely substituting *went missing* for *vanish* or *disappear* or using it to mean "to cease to exist": *my golf ball went missing* and *funding for that program has gone missing this year* are not felicitous applications.

FASCINATING FACT 25

Did you know that by derivation *pumpernickel* means "bread that makes you fart"? In the dialectal German of Westphalia, from which it comes, *pumpernickel* was "originally an abusive term," says *The Barnhart Dictionary of Etymology*, "a compound of *pumpern* to break wind + *Nickel* goblin, rascal."

Hanky Pinkie

Q. *How did we come to call the little finger the pinkie finger? Why* pinkie?

A. *Pinkie* (sometimes *pinky*) hails from the Dutch *pinkje*, the diminutive of *pink*, the little finger. How the Dutch came to use *pink* for the little finger is not known; two competing theories—

I could have been a chef

wholly unsubstantiated—claim that the digit in question was used either for dike plugging or for olfactory exploration. *Pinkie* was originally a Scottish colloquialism, first recorded in 1808 in John Jamieson's *Etymological Dictionary of the Scottish Language.* It was recorded in American usage by 1860, and in the twentieth century it became widespread.

Optical Allusion

Q. *In several of her books Martha Grimes uses the word* optics *in contexts that pertain to ordering drinks in an English pub. I can't find this* optics *in a dictionary or anywhere. Can you tell me what it means?*

A. In England an optic is "a measuring device fastened to the neck of liquor bottles in pubs," explains Norman W. Schur in *British English, A to Zed.* "The device is called an *optic* because the liquor flows out of the upside-down bottle into a transparent vessel and is thus visible to the naked eye. In this fashion, not a micron over one-sixth gill [the legal standard measure in England, like a one-and-a-half-ounce shot in the United States] escapes into the waiting glass."

Schur refrains from remarking that only in the land of Scrooge (the bar owner) and Oliver Twist (the customer) would they invent such a diabolically stingy device.

Differently Handicapped

Q. *In a discussion of the origin of the word* handicapped, *a friend explained that it's a shortening of the phrase* hand in cap, *implying that disabled persons were often begging on the street. Is the word still acceptable and not degrading to the disabled community?*

A. Your friend is right that *handicap* comes from *hand in cap,* but his explanation about disabled beggars is fanciful. A *handicap* is "a contest in which the better contestants are given certain disadvantages, or the poorer ones certain advantages," says *The Barnhart Dictionary of Etymology.* The word has been traced back to the

but my goose was already cooked. 🔙

1650s. The *hand in cap* phrase referred to an old wagering game in which bets were placed in a cap. The use of *handicap* in horse racing dates from the 1750s, and has been used of other races and contests (such as golf) since 1875. "The general sense of encumbrance or disability is first recorded in 1890," says Barnhart, ". . . and the transferred sense of put at a disadvantage, disable, cripple, in 1864."

The participial adjective *handicapped* meaning "disabled, crippled" dates from 1915. Today, *crippled* is generally considered pejorative, and the preferred terms in good usage are *disabled* and *handicapped,* which are used interchangeably. *Differently abled,* promoted by some as a more neutral term, is a wee bit too PC for most folks and about as likely to catch on as *differently cabled,* the polite way of describing people like me who don't subscribe to cable TV and don't give a damn about what they're missing.

FASCINATING FACT 🐚

Did you know that the brand names *Nike* and *Adidas* are eponymous (formed from names)? *Nike* is the name of the Greek goddess of victory (called *Victoria* by the Romans). *Adidas,* says *The Barnhart Dictionary of Etymology,* was fashioned from the name *Adi Dassler,* "a German manufacturer who in 1948 founded the company that produces the athletic equipment, especially footwear and garments." 🐚

Foiled Again

Q. *I once heard a story about aluminum that is much too good to be true. It seems (the story goes) that Reynolds* Aluminium *was just starting out, getting by on the proverbial shoestring, when someone in the firm made an error in a stationery order, instructing the printer to supply X number of envelopes, etc., reading Reynolds* Aluminum *instead of (the correct)* Aluminium. *Rather than eat the loss, the heads of the company decided that, since few people were as yet familiar with their product, they would go ahead with the stationery as printed, change the company's name (this is where the story gets wobbly), and, if questioned, boldly declare that aluminum is the* American *spelling. Is there any truth to this yarn?*

↤ *I could have been a chef*

A. Nope. It's complete poppycock. Sir Humphrey Davy coined *aluminum* in 1812, based on Latin *alumen, aluminis,* which meant "alum" (potassium aluminum sulfate). The variant *aluminium* with the additional *i* appeared that same year "as a deliberate alteration," one etymological source says, "on the analogy of other names of elements, such as sodium, potassium, magnesium, all coined earlier by Davy." (Kind of like *nucular* coming about because of false analogy with *muscular, molecular,* etc.) So the EC (etymologically correct) form is the American one. (Suck on that one, limeys.)

A Lot of Hot Air

Q. *I once had a high school science teacher who insisted that the correct name for the hot, dry winds we get in Southern California (typically in the fall) is* Santana, *meaning devil or devil wind. He was contemptuous of anyone (especially TV weatherheads) who called them* Santa Anas, *maintaining that this was a corrupt form perpetrated by ignorant Easterners and other transplants who had no knowledge of local geography or history. Years later I still wonder, was he right? Or are all those TV weatherheads who say* Santa Ana *in fact correct?*

A. It's a sad thing when teachers are intransigently wrong. Malleable minds can be deformed for life.

For once the broadcasters are right. Dictionaries agree that the preferred form is *Santa Ana,* with *The Random House Dictionary* labeling *Santana/santana* informal and the other major American dictionaries not listing this alternative at all. *Santana* does not, and cannot logically, mean "devil wind" because *santa/santo* in Spanish means "saint"; the word for "devil" is *diablo.* And *Ana* has nothing to do with wind; it's a name. Your teacher probably grew up hearing *Santa Ana* pronounced rapidly as *Sant'ana,* so he incorrectly concluded that it should be spelled as it was pronounced.

The Santa Ana (sometimes Santa Ana wind) comes from inland desert areas, descending upon the Los Angeles basin from the Santa Ana mountains—hence the name. The earliest citation in the

but the thought of it made me blanch. ☞

UNFORTUNATE EPONYMS

Sometimes having your name in lights is not a good thing. Of the hundreds of eponymous words in the language—words taken from names—a goodly number denote something unsavory. Here are some unusual eponyms whose sources would doubtless not be proud to have lent their names to the language in this way:

boswellize to write a detailed and overly adulatory biography, or to write a meticulous but wholly uncritical historical account. The word comes from James Boswell (1740–95), who wrote a detailed and adoring biography of Samuel Johnson.

bowdlerize (bow- as in take a bow) to delete material considered risqué, offensive, or obscene out of a squeamish sense of morality. Thomas Bowdler was an English editor who in the early 1800s published "morally cleansed" editions of the works of Shakespeare and Gibbon, from which he deleted (copiously) "whatever is unfit to be read by a gentleman in a company of ladies." His expurgations were so sweep-

ing, so prudish, and so annoying that people made a nasty word out of his name.

Comstockery strict, overzealous, and self-righteous moral censorship. Anthony Comstock (1844–1915) was the founder of the New York Society for the Suppression of Vice and "a self-appointed crusader against immorality in literature," writes Robert Hendrickson in his Dictionary of Eponyms. After helping to secure passage of the so-called Comstock Laws, which outlawed "objectionable matter from the mails," Comstock became a special agent of the Post Office, a position in which he "had the power of an inquisitor." According to Hendrickson, Comstock "is said to have arrested three thousand persons over a forty-odd year career," and destroyed "about 160 tons of books, stereotyped plates, magazines, and pictures" that he deemed obscene. "The crusader particularly objected to [George Bernard] Shaw's play, Mrs. Warren's Profes-

I could have been a waiter

sion, and [in 1905] Shaw coined the word making good clean fun of his name."

grangerize to mutilate books, especially by cutting out their illustrations.

Grangerism, noted *Saturday Review* in 1883, "is the pernicious vice of cutting plates and title-pages out of many books to illustrate one book." This practice, says the *Century Dictionary* (1914), "became popular when James Granger published, in 1769, his 'Biographical History of England,' which incited persons to mutilate other books to illustrate it." To this day Reverend Granger remains the bane of librarians everywhere.

grimthorpe to remodel a building badly, without regard for its original character or history.

The man behind this word is Sir Edmund Beckett, first Baron Grimthorpe (1816–1905), a lawyer and architect "whose restoration of St. Albans Cathedral, completed in 1904, aroused fierce criticism and controversy," says the *Oxford English Dictionary. Grimthorping* implies lavish expenditure without regard for skill, quality, or taste.

john brown to put to death by hanging. To *be john-browned* is to be hanged.

This gruesome bit of nineteenth-century American slang comes from the abolitionist John Brown, who was convicted of leading an armed uprising and was hanged in 1859.

martinet a strict disciplinarian, taskmaster.

Martinet comes from General Jean Martinet, a seventeenth-century French drillmaster who was infamous for subjecting his troops to harsh discipline and for his rigid adherence to military rules and regulations. He was "accidentally" killed by his troops during a battle.

Oslerize to kill all men over the age of forty.

Sir William Osler (1849–1919), a Canadian-born physician and professor of medicine, was the victim of a cruel misunderstanding. This distinguished medical

but I tabled that idea. ☚

UNFORTUNATE EPONYMS *continued*

researcher and historian once suggested, in a speech at Johns Hopkins University in 1905, that it would be an "incalculable benefit . . . in commercial, political and in professional life if, as a matter of course, men stopped work at sixty." Although Osler's plan for male retirement at sixty included a generous pension, his statement was widely misquoted and grossly misinterpreted as a proposal to kill all men over forty.

procrustean (pruh-KRUHS-tee-in) producing conformity by cruel or violent means.

Procrustes was a robber of Attica, says the *Century Dictionary* (1914), "who tortured his victims by placing them on a certain bed, and stretching them or lopping off their legs to adapt the body to its length." Many were maimed upon Procrustes' bed until the Greek hero Theseus tied the ruthless bugger to his own bedposts for a permanent snooze.

quisling (KWIZ-ling) a traitor who serves as a puppet of the enemy.

Vidkun Quisling, a Nor-wegian leader who collaborated with the Germans in World War II, is the source of this word. It was coined in 1940, at the beginning of the Nazi occupation of Norway.

Typhoid Mary someone or something that spreads disease, corruption, or disaster.

This epithet comes from Mary Mallon (d. 1938), an Irish cook who was a notorious disease carrier. In the early twentieth century she worked in the New York City area in various restaurants and in the homes of affluent citizens and was responsible for a deadly series of typhoid outbreaks.

Xanthippe (zan-TIP-ee) a henpecking shrew.

Xanthippe was the wife of the philosopher Socrates, and she has gone down in history as a quarrelsome, ill-tempered, nagging browbeater. But what most people don't know about this contentious couple is that Socrates was an ugly, arrogant runt who had it coming to him, for, as one etymologist puts it, he "was so unconventional as to tax the patience of any woman."

≫I I could have been a stockbroker

Oxford English Dictionary is from 1887, in the *Annotated Meteorological Review of California:* "The 'Santa Ana' wind receives its name because it frequently issues from the Santa Ana Pass."

Piece of Cake

Q. *Where does the* German *in German chocolate cake come from?*

A. It's eponymous, meaning it comes from a person's name. The original recipe, published in a Texas newspaper in 1957, called for "Baker's German's Sweet Chocolate." *Baker's* refers to the man who financed the first chocolate factory in the United States, Dr. James Baker, and *German's* refers to an employee of one of Dr. Baker's descendants, Samuel German, who developed the sweet chocolate in the recipe.

Over the Hill in a Fine Kettle of Fish

Q. *Young people look at me as if I'm crazy when I say, "Well, now that's a fine kettle of fish," meaning that a situation is not auspicious or something isn't in good shape. I'd like to know where this expression came from and whether I can still use it, or is it obsolete?*

A. Young people will always look at older people as if they're crazy, so my advice on that score is to just *fuggeddaboudit* and do your old-fogy *thang.*

Fine kettle of fish is not obsolete; it's just old-fashioned. It's what some have called an "over-the-hill expression," an idiom that survives in the language but belongs chiefly to an earlier generation. There are scores of these quaint sayings. Some of them survive because they have become cliché, like *bring home the bacon* and *in a pretty pickle,* which means much the same thing as *fine kettle of fish.* Some are now obscure and rarely used, like to *raise Old Ned,* to raise hell, and to *make bricks without straw,* to try to do something without the right tools or materials. Many are centuries old, like *don't look a gift horse in the mouth,* which goes back to before A.D. 400 when Saint Jerome called it a familiar proverb in those days (not in

but it was all inequity and bondage. ☞

English, of course). Your *fine kettle of fish* is one of these old ones, possibly going back as far as the twelfth century.

As Robert Hendrickson explains in the *QPB Encyclopedia of Word and Phrase Origins:*

> A *kiddle* or *kiddle net* is a basket set in the sluice ways of dams to catch fish, a device well known from the time of the Plantagenets. Royal officials had the perquisite to trap fish in kiddles, but poachers often raided the traps of fish, frequently destroying the kiddles in the process. Possibly an official came upon a destroyed trap and exclaimed, "That's a pretty kiddle of fish!" or something similar, meaning "a pretty sorry state of affairs!" and the phrase was born. Repeated over the years, *kiddle* was corrupted in everyday speech to *kettle,* giving us the expression as we know it today.

Kumbaya, My Lord

Q. *Ever since I was a child singing around campfires, I have been curious about the title and origin of that charming folk song and lullaby "Kumbaya." What does this word mean and what language does it come from?*

A. I'm glad you asked about this because I also learned the song, and the word, around the campfire at summer camp. It is spelled *kumbaya* or sometimes *kumbayah,* and it's "the title and key word of a Gullah spiritual, originating some time in the 1920s or even earlier," says Adrian Room's *Brewer's Dictionary of Modern Phrase and Fable.* "The word itself is Creole for 'come by here.'"

A fellow named Marvin V. Frey wrote the gospel chorus "Come by Here" in the 1930s, explains *Rise Up Singing: The Group Singing Songbook.* "A missionary couple learned [Frey's] song and used it in their work in Angola. When the song returned to the U.S., its original source had been lost." It "was revived in the folk-singing boom of the 1950s and 1960s," says Brewer, and has "been recorded by

⊲ᗅ I could have been a gardener

various singers, such as the American folk trio Peter, Paul and Mary, who included it in their album *Around the Camp Fire* (1998)." (I guess it was tailor-made for campfires, but I've sung it as a lullaby to my children.)

William Safire, the language columnist for *The New York Times Magazine,* once wrote that the song "epitomizes the gentle, peace-yearning spirituality (often derided as pot-smoking narcissism by hardhearted elders) of some of the hirsute youth of that generation." It is worth noting that the song is not in the public domain. It was copyrighted in 1957 and renewed in 1985.

Staked Out

Q. *I'm curious about the expression* beyond the pale. *It sounds as if something's missing at the end:* beyond the pale *(dawn, moon, etc.). Is there?*

A. The *pale* in *beyond the pale* is not the familiar adjective *pale,* meaning "dim or lacking color." This *pale* is a noun. It comes to us from Latin *palus,* a stake, and denotes a stake, post, fence, or other marker indicating the perimeter of a territory or district, historically one under the protection of some army or government. For example, in the fourteenth century *the Pale* referred to the areas in Ireland colonized by the British, and that which took place outside the Pale was beyond British jurisdiction. At first *beyond the pale* had this literal meaning, then later came to have the figurative meaning "out of bounds, unreasonable, unacceptable."

Pozzled

Q. *Is* sozzled *a real word? It's been in my family for a long time, but I've been told it doesn't exist, and I've never been able to find it in a dictionary.*

A. If by "real word" you mean a word that has been used by people who are not members of your family, then the answer to your question is yes. *Sozzled* appears in the *Oxford English Dictionary,*

but I didn't see any room in it for personal growth. 🖙

INTOXICATED ENGLISH

There are more synonyms for *drunk* than for any other word in the language. In his *Word Treasury* Paul Dickson collected 2,660 of them, a feat that earned him a world's record for synonyms from the folks at Guinness. Here are some of the most colorful and curious ones:

a guest in the attic
amiably incandescent
back teeth afloat
bar kissing
bitten by a barn mouse
boiled as an owl
Brahms and Lizst (Cockney
    rhyming slang for *pissed*)
breath strong enough to carry
    coal with
can't find his ass with both
    hands
can't see a hole in a ladder
chloroformed

clipped the King's English
conflummoxed
consumed a rancid oyster
crapulous
cupshotten
decks awash
discumfuddled
done a Falstaff
drunk as a brewer's fart
fed his kitty
floothered
flusticated
full as a state-school hat rack
gambrinous
gestunketed
getting an answer
got his snowsuit on and heading
    north
got kibbled heels
guarding the gates of hell
halfway to Concord
Harry flakers
has burned his shoulder

which traces it to a well-known slang dictionary of the 1880s. It means "drunk" or "drunken." There is also the word *sozzly*, which means "messy, sloppy," or "drunk." And *sossle*, or *sozzle*, is a noun meaning "mess, slop," or a verb meaning "to intoxicate."

Incidentally, *sozzled* is one of 2,660 recorded synonyms for *drunk*. That's the world's record for synonyms, says Guinness. You'll find all of them listed in Paul Dickson's *Word Treasury*.

⇥ *I could have been a mathematician*

has his head full of bees
has taken Hippocrates' Grand
    Elixir
has the yorks
iced to the eyebrows
in a vise
in the pulpit
ishkimmisk
ka-floot
killed his dog
kisky
laughing at the carpet
legless
lit up like Broadway
loaded to the Plimsoll mark
making a trip to Baltimore
moist around the edges
nimptopsical
oinophluxed
ossified
out like Lottie's eye
pigeon-eyed
plootered

pot-walloped
put to bed with a shovel
quilted
raised his monuments
reeling and kneeling
rockaputzered
saw Montezuma
seeing a flock of moons
seeing the French king
shellacked the goldfish bowl
smeekit
sniffed the barmaid's apron
spiflicated
staying late at the office
taken a segue
tight as a brassiere
too numerous to mention
upholstered
watching the ant races
wrapped up in warm flannel
zissified

Measuring Up

Q. I write about health and nutrition, and I have a diet-counseling website where I post a chart of various weights and measures. Recently someone asked me about "a knob of butter," wondering how much it was. I have never heard of "a knob of butter" and cannot seem to find it anywhere! Please help me "measure up" to her expectations.

but I hear that does a number on you. 🖙

A. Norman W. Schur, in his delightful book *British English, A to Zed,* says *knob* is the equivalent of the American *lump,* so it's an inexact measurement—like the better-known word *dollop,* which may mean a small or large portion or amount. I suppose it depends on how much you fancy butter.

Signifying

Q. *What is a* Sig Alert *or* Cig Alert? *I recently moved to Los Angeles and I hear this every morning during the traffic report on the radio. What does the* Sig *or* Cig *stand for? A signal? A cigarette? And if it is a signal, why don't they call it a* traffic alert *instead?*

A. Your immigrant ears have picked up on a genuine Southern California creation. *SigAlert*—so spelled—comes from the last name of Loyd Sigmon, an owner of KMPC in Los Angeles, who, as he himself put it, "came up with the idea that if the Police Department would press a button at the communications center, we could get a traffic report directly over the air." The first SigAlert was on Labor Day 1955. Today a SigAlert is defined as "a major accident that ties up traffic for over thirty minutes or bottlenecks traffic into one or two lanes."

Though *SigAlert* is commonly heard in traffic reports throughout Southern California, it has not spread to other regions, and it is not, to my knowledge, listed in any dictionaries.

No Picnic

Q. *I came across a shocking and horrifying story recently—it was circulated via email by some professor of history, I think—explaining that the word* picnic *originated in the gruesome practice of lynching African Americans. Can this sickening etymology be true?*

"This email is being sent to you as a public service announcement and as information in the form of a little known Black History Fact," begins the message I received. "The term 'picnic' derives from the acts of lynching African Americans. The word 'picnic' is rooted from the whole theme of 'Pick A Nigger.' This is where individuals would 'pic' a Black

❧ I could have been an actor

person to lynch and make this into a family gathering. There would be music and a 'picnic.'"

A. This story is viciously apocryphal, a pernicious etymological rumor, yet another example of the many falsehoods being disseminated on the Internet and swallowed whole by the credulous public. It is all the more regrettable that this preposterous canard was promulgated as a "Black History Fact." Such wrongheaded, unsubstantiated rabble-rousing does a grave disservice both to black Americans and to the language.

The word *picnic* has no connection whatsoever to lynching or to African Americans; it is not pejorative in any way. It dates from 1748 and is borrowed from the French *piquenique*, a word of uncertain origin that comes perhaps from *piquer*, to pick, and *nique*, a worthless thing. People may have attended "lynching picnics" in the days of Jim Crow, but etymologically *picnic* has nothing to do with lynching or with "picking" someone to lynch. Calling upon us to banish the word *picnic* from the language is as crazy as asking us to boycott the words *final* and *solution* because together they denote Hitler's diabolical program of genocide. Whoever is responsible for spreading this lie is guilty of lynching an innocent word.

Cop: An Attitude

Q. *How did police officers come to be called* cops?

A. The two stories you hear or read the most, that *cop* is short for *copper*—a reference to the big brass buttons on the uniforms of London bobbies—or that it's an acronym for *constabulary of police* or some such thing, are both unfounded. (Acronymic etymologies, in particular, are always suspect.)

The true source of *cop* meaning a police officer appears to be the verb *to cop*, which in northern England was used to mean "to capture, catch, lay hold of, 'nab,'" says the *Oxford English Dictionary*, whose earliest citation for this sense is from 1704. This verb *cop* probably goes back in turn to the Latin *capere*, which meant to

but I couldn't get past the first stage. 🖗

catch, seize, take possession of by force. By the mid-nineteenth century, says the *QPB Encyclopedia of Word and Phrase Origins*, the verb was "adopted as a name for a policeman, who, of course, caught or captured crooks." The old-fashioned variant *copper* has nothing to do with the metal or with buttons. It simply tacks the agent suffix *-er* onto the verb to form a noun meaning "one who cops."

Charlie Cracks *Corned*

Q. *I was having lunch at my favorite greasy spoon and I got to wondering why they call it* corned *beef. The waitress didn't know. The manager didn't know. And even the manager's father, who had been a butcher in a Jewish deli, didn't know. They started asking other people in the restaurant and nobody knew. Some guessed that the cows may have been* corn-fed, *but that didn't seem right. Do you know the answer to this?*

A. "Originally a *corn* was any small substance or particle — especially a seed or kernel," explain William and Mary Morris in their *Dictionary of Word and Phrase Origins*.

When beef was laid down in a brine to cure, it was sprinkled with *corns* of coarse salt. So the process came to be known as *corning* the beef and the end product was *corned beef.* The same use of *corn* to mean a grain or particle remains in words like *peppercorn*—whole black peppers—and *barleycorn.*

Incidentally, though the "corn-fed" conjecture does not apply to corned beef, it is the source of the adjective *corny,* meaning "hackneyed" or "sentimental." *Corny* is first recorded in the early 1930s, though it is probably considerably older, and is thought to have come from the lingo of jazz musicians. When performers left the big cities for the backwaters, they took to calling their rural audiences *corn-fed,* then *corny,* because these rural folk, in the eyes of the performers, were unsophisticated and preferred standard material over anything new.

I could have been a firefighter

Where'd You Get Them Peepers?

Q. *Where do we get the expression* peeping Tom*? Was there somebody named Tom who was caught peeping?*

A. There was, at least according to Anglo-Saxon legend.

As the story goes, this epithet comes from the famous story of Lady Godiva. Her husband Leofric, the Earl of Mercia and Lord of Coventry, was mercilessly taxing his subjects. Lady Godiva, who cared for her subjects, thought this unjust and implored him repeatedly to lower the taxes. To shut her up, Leofric said he would relent only if she rode through the town in her birthday suit. To his amazement, she accepted the challenge and issued a proclamation ordering everyone to stay indoors with their shutters closed while she passed. Because it was merry old England and not merry old MTV, the townspeople actually obeyed and closed their shutters — all except Tom the tailor, who bored a hole in his shutter through which he ogled the naked lady as she trotted through town on a white horse. Lady Godiva got her way and Leofric lowered the taxes. But Tom was struck blind for his transgression and his bad deed lives on in the language.

Cheating the Devil

Q. *Does* what the dickens *come from the famous writer Charles Dickens?*

A. It does not. *What the dickens,* like *what the deuce,* is a euphemism for *what the devil.* Other euphemisms of this type (and there are many) include *what in tarnation* for *what in damnation* and *what the Sam Hill* for *what the damn hell.* This kind of thinly disguised swearing is called "denatured profanity" or, more colorfully, "cheating the devil."

And that's my dadblamed, doggone, ding-busted answer to your goldurn, goshdarn, cotton-pickin', chicken-pluckin' question!

but that plan went up in smoke. 🖛

The Spin on English

Q. *When I was young and learning to play pool, my friends would tell me to put some English on it, meaning to put some spin on the ball by hitting it a little off-center. I've heard this expression applied to some other sports, but it seems to me to be most closely associated with pool. Where does this expression come from?*

BODACIOUS BRAINTEASER

THE BROBDINGNAGIAN RUBICUND SAXIPHAGE

Muster your powers of deduction and decode the bombastic answers to these familiar riddles:

1. What kind of dog knows how to tell time? *A canine that possesses an analog or digital chronological measuring device.*
2. What time is it when an elephant sits on your fence? *It is time to reinstall the vertical*

vicinal barrier on the periphery of your curtilage.

3. Why do birds fly south? *Because the distance they must traverse makes ambulation inadvisable.*
4. Why does a baby pig eat so much? *In order to facilitate the endogenous creation of an adult domestic swine.*
5. When are cooks bad? *When*

A. Pool, or billiards to be more precise, is indeed the source of this expression, which has spread to other sports, especially baseball. The earliest citation in the *Oxford English Dictionary* is from *The Innocents Abroad* (1869) by Mark Twain, a noted billiards enthusiast. "You would infallibly put the 'English' on the wrong side of the ball," he wrote, and the quotation marks he placed around *English* show that at the time the expression was still wet behind the ears.

Why *English* for "spin"? "It doesn't stem from any derogatory American reference to the affectedness or tricky ways of English-

⇥ I could have been a dentist

men, as has often been proposed," writes Robert Hendrickson in *Grand Slams, Hat Tricks and Alley-oops: A Sports Fan's Book of Words.* "It was probably suggested by *body English,* the way the body gestures or 'speaks' when words cannot be found to express an action." The English call it *English side,* a term that, according to the *OED,* arose at about the same time.

---

they engage in the fustigation of the edible contents of an oviform object.

6. What holds up a train? Maleficent male members of the species Homo sapiens.

7. What do you call something that's big and red and eats rocks? *A brobdingnagian rubicund saxiphage.*

8. Why is an egg not like an elephant? *If you are not cognizant of the distinction, or do not possess a sufficiently refined faculty of discrimination, then it would be imprudent to entrust you with the task of retrieving the diurnal ovoid expulsions of Gallus gallus.*

Answers appear on page 263.

I'm not sure Hendrickson's right that *English* came from *body English.* The *OED* has a 1959 citation from the *Times* of London that recounts an old story about "an enterprising gentleman from these shores" who traveled to the United States and impressed the Americans with a masterly display of side. "His name was English," says the *Times* account. I have no doubt that this story is apocryphal and there probably never was a side-winding pool shark named English. But I am inclined to believe that nineteenth-century American billiard players like Twain, being American and therefore

but I couldn't do the drill.

fiercely independent in their choice of words, turned up their noses at the English *side* and decided to call it *English* instead. I guess you could say they wanted to put their own spin on the word.

Can You Say *Help* in French?

Q. *What is the origin of the aviation term* mayday?

A. The term *mayday* (often *Mayday*, probably by association with the month of *May*) has nothing to do with the first day of May. It comes from the French *m'aider* in the phrase *venez m'aider*, which means "come help me." The spelling *mayday* represents the French pronunciation.

Mayday is an oral distress signal (as opposed to *SOS*, which is visual or aural Morse code). Since 1927 it has been the official international radio call for help in aviation and navigation. Why did we adopt a French term for this? Probably because French was the language of international communication until English supplanted it in the late twentieth century.

Buy Buy

Q. *How did* he bought the farm *come to mean "he died"? I knew it was hard to make a living as a farmer, but I fail to see how buying a farm could be lethal.*

A. *Bought the farm*—also *bought a plot*— comes from World War II U.S. Air Force slang, an American extension of the British Royal Air Force *buy it*. Originally it meant to die in a plane crash; now it just means to die. As the story goes, American training bases were in rural areas, and when a pilot crashed on a farm, the farmer would often sue the government for damages, demanding enough to pay off the mortgage and own the farm. Crashes that resulted in such lawsuits were usually fatal, so the deceased pilot was said to have *bought the farm* (regardless of the outcome of the lawsuit). The expression is idiomatically used in the past tense (*bought the farm*), not the present (*buy the farm*).

⇥ *I could have been a dentist*

X Mess

Q. *What is the origin of the abbreviation* Xmas *for* Christmas*? A friend once complained that it's an insult to Jesus and that if people knew that they'd stop using it. Is that true?*

A. Your friend must be exceptionally intimate with Jesus to know whether he is offended by any given word. In this case, however, your friend got his divine signals crossed, for *Xmas* is as innocent as a lamb and not an insult to anyone or anything.

Xmas for *Christmas* "has a long and honorable history," says the *Morris Dictionary of Word and Phrase Origins*. The *X* is the twenty-second letter of the Greek alphabet, *chi,* and stands for *Christ.* "This is not a modern, commercial invention," note Bergen and Cornelia Evans in *A Dictionary of Contemporary American Usage.* "*X* has been used in this way in English . . . since at least the year 1100." The *OED* traces *Xmas* in print to 1551, when it appeared in a treatise on British history.

P's and Quriosity

Q. *What are your* p's and q's *and how can you possibly mind them?*

A. Fair question. It is impossible to mind something if you don't know what it is. Trying to do so would drive you out of your mind.

Like many an old expression, *mind your p's and q's* has inspired a variety of stories about its origin, but nobody knows for sure where it came from. The least likely answer is that it is related to the powdered queue (ponytail or pigtail) of sixteenth- and seventeenth-century dudes that might soil the collar of the pea (as in jacket). Then there's the pub story, in which your tab was kept on a chalkboard with *p* standing for *pint* and *q* for *quart*—and you'd better mind that board or the proprietor could rip you off. That's a nifty explanation that has everything going for it but evidence.

Experts generally agree that the least interesting and most obvious explanation is the most likely—that the letters in fact stand for letters, and the expression originated in the teaching of

but it was too boring. ⟨

ENGLISH IS A SPANISH OMELET

The olla podrida of English is heavily spiced with Spanish. From California to Texas to Florida (all Spanish names), English is a Spanish omelet. People live in cities and towns with Spanish names like San Antonio, Santa Fe, Las Vegas, and Los Angeles. They drive along streets with Spanish names and live in Spanish-style houses in developments with (unfortunately often mangled) Spanish names. They admire Hispanic flora and enjoy Hispanic food. Spanish surrounds them and, whether they realize it or not, they speak it every day.

In the sixteenth century, when Spain was exploring and conquering the New World, Spanish exerted its earliest influence upon English. By 1600, English had acquired *alligator, anchovy, banana, cannibal, cocoa, hurricane, mosquito, potato, sassafras, sherry, sombrero,* and *tobacco.* By 1700, English had adopted *cargo, barricade, escapade, siesta, matador, toreador, tomato, chocolate, vanilla,* and *cockroach.* By 1750, English had gained the geological term *mesa,* and by 1780, the word *stevedore* (from *estibador,* one who packs or loads cargo), which preceded *longshoreman,* its Anglo-Saxon equivalent, by more than twenty years. By 1850, English had appropriated the now-familiar *canyon, bonanza, loco,* and *vigilante.*

As nineteenth-century American pioneers pushed west into

penmanship. The letter *q* follows *p* in the alphabet, and in lowercase their bulges are reversed, so they are easily confused by fledgling writers. Thus generations of teachers admonished their young scribes to *mind their p's and q's.* Though the expression originally meant "to be very careful and precise," it has come to be used more often to mean "to be on one's best behavior."

Your Lawyer Is an Avocado

Q. *I'm curious about the word* avocado *coming to us from the Aztec language Nahuatl. In Spanish, avocados are called* aguacates. *Did we*

✒ *I could have been a dentist*

territory long dominated by Spain and, later, Mexico, the idiom of the cowboy grew out of the vernacular of his counterpart, the vaquero. From the vaqueros the cowboys adopted the words *ranch, rodeo, lasso* and *lariat, chaps, poncho, serape, stampede, desperado,* and *buckaroo,* an anglicization of *vaquero.*

The buckaroos learned new names for creatures: *burro* for a donkey, *pinto* for a piebald horse, *cinch* for a bedbug, and *coyote* for a wild dog. They ate *frijoles, chiles, tamales,* and *enchiladas.* And if a buckaroo drank too much *mescal* or *tequila,* he might wind up in the *calaboose* or *hoosegow*—the jail. Other well-worn borrowings from the heyday

of the Old West include *hacienda, patio, arroyo, hombre, amigo,* and *pronto.*

"The Spanish contributions to the American vocabulary are far more numerous than those of any other Continental language," observes H. L. Mencken in *The American Language.* Think about that the next time you're sitting on the patio of your hacienda sipping sherry, taking a siesta, eating some vanilla ice cream with sliced bananas, or gazing at a cloud of mosquitoes in the canyon and a desperado cockroach the size of a stevedore goes loco and starts playing matador on your ankle.

---

get the word from Spanish speakers a long time ago and then they stopped using it in Mexico?

A. In Nahuatl the word was *ahuacatl,* which meant literally "fruit of the avocado tree" and figuratively "testicle." The Spaniards who conquered Mexico had some trouble pronouncing *ahuacatl;* for them it came out as *aguacate.* Other Spanish speakers in the New World translated *ahuacatl* as *avocado,* which at that time was the word for a lawyer. Clearly a similarity in sound explains this substitution, but one has to wonder if there were any other reasons to associate lawyers with testicles.

but it wouldn't have been fulfilling. 🖙

❧ QUOTE UNQUOTE ❧

"Many authors write like amateur blacksmiths making their first horseshoe; the clank of the anvil, the stench of the scorched leather apron, the sparks and the cursing are palpable, and this appeals to those who rank 'sincerity' very high . . . Virtuosity, so much admired in some other arts, is at present unfashionable in literature."—Robertson Davies

At any rate, modern Spanish kept *aguacate* for the fruit and changed *avocado* to *abogado*, while English adopted *avocado*, which first appeared in print in 1697, for the fruit. Incidentally, *guacamole* is a portmanteau (or blend) word of *aguacate* and *mole*, derived from the Nahuatl *ahuacamolli*, meaning "avocado soup or sauce."

A Load of Bull

Q. *Somebody emailed me a story about the origin of a certain four-letter word. The story goes like this.*

In the sixteenth and seventeenth centuries, when a great deal of cargo was transported by ship, it was common to ship large amounts of manure for use as fertilizer. The manure was shipped dry because it weighed a lot less (and smelled a lot better) than when it was wet. However, if the manure was exposed to seawater it would begin to ferment and release highly flammable methane gas. Bundles of manure stored well belowdecks often did get wet, and if someone came below with a lantern—boom!—the manure hit the fan, so to speak. When people finally figured out what was causing these mysterious explosions, they began stamping the bundles of manure with SHIP HIGH IN TRANSIT *so that the sailors would stow this potentially dangerous cargo well above any water in the hold. That phrase was later shortened to* SHIT, *which became the word for excrement that we use today.*

❧ *I could have been a dentist*

So tell me, is there any truth to this?

A. All acronymic etymologies are suspect—especially the ostensibly funny ones and the ones having to do with taboo words. (Commit that to memory.) Yet you see these canards all the time, continually promulgated in newspapers and on the Web. For the record, *tip* does not mean *to insure promptness* (it should be *ensure,* anyway); *posh* does not stand for *port out, starboard home;* and this silly manure story is bull. *Shit* was around long before ships sailed in the sixteenth and seventeenth centuries, and its etymology is so boring that you'd fall asleep if I recounted it. (Check your local dictionary.) That's generally the way it goes with taboo words that have been part of the language for ages. Maybe it's because the etymologies are so dull, obscure, or circuitous that people feel the need to embellish. And I suppose that as long as other people fall for it, they will continue to embellish.

Jiffy Rube

Q. *Where does* jiffy *come from? Someone once told me it's a unit of time. If that's true, then is that* jiffy *the source of the expression* in a jiffy, *meaning "in a small amount of time"?*

A. You can't believe everything you hear, and you can't believe everything you read—even when the source seems reputable. According to *The New York Public Library Desk Reference,* "a 'jiffy' is an actual unit of time. It is 1/100 of a second." But this statement appears with no further explanation, and I have not found any evidence to substantiate it.

The earliest occurrence of *jiffy* in print dates from 1785. It appeared in a book called *Baron Munchausen's Travels* by Rudolph Raspe, where it was used as if it were an actual unit of time ("six jiffies"). It's not, of course, and the word was probably fabricated by the author. The phrase *in a jiffy* (also *in a jif*) first appeared in Francis Grose's *Classical Dictionary of the Vulgar Tongue* in 1796, so it

but I knew I'd never be a crowning success. 🔏

could very well have migrated from Raspe's book into the general vocabulary, or perhaps Raspe simply set down an expression already established in the vernacular.

The Wizard of *-oid*

Q. *This has been bugging me major. If the suffix* -oid *means "akin to" or "resembling," and the word* asteroid *is formed from the Latin* aster, *star, and* -oid, *why do we use the word* asteroid *when they're more like planets than stars? Shouldn't we call them* planetoids? *Also, why call it a* meteoroid *if it doesn't resemble a meteor?*

A. What I gather from my sources is that historically the terms *asteroid* and *planetoid* have been more or less interchangeable. The only difference I can discern is that *asteroid* is more commonly used of the so-called minor planets revolving around the sun between Mars and Jupiter and is not used, as *planetoid* sometimes is, of something resembling a planet.

. A scientist named Sir John F. W. Herschel coined *asteroid* in 1802 for those minor planets, and *planetoid* was coined for the same thing in 1803. That year Herschel wrote, "It is not in the least material whether we call them asteroids, as I have proposed, or planetoids, as an eminent astronomer, in a letter to me, suggested." Perhaps *planetoid* is the more precise word, but it didn't win the popularity contest, which is usually all that matters, and in this case people decided they liked Herschel's word better.

You ask, "Why call it a *meteoroid* if it doesn't resemble a meteor?" This seems to be an interesting case of the cart coming before the horse. When the word *meteor* entered English in the 1400s (our modern spelling dates from 1576), we couldn't detect meteoroids. When meteoroids finally were detected, they were so named because they looked like meteors that hadn't yet entered the atmosphere and ignited. H. A. Newton, writing in the *American Journal of Science* in 1865, coined the word: "The term 'meteoroid'

⇥ I could have been a dentist

will be used to designate such a body [namely, a meteor] before it enters the earth's atmosphere." The *Oxford English Dictionary* explains that a meteoroid is a body "of the same nature [there's your *-oid*] as those which when passing through the earth's atmosphere become visible as meteors."

Got the Bug

Q. *When did the word* bug *come to mean "something wrong, a flaw or a problem"? Did this sense come from computer science lingo or is it older than that?*

A. Your instincts are good: It's a lot older.

In *Wired Style*, Constance Hale and Jessie Scanlon report that "tech trivia buffs" love to recount "the apocryphal story of naval officer, Harvard scientist, and Cobol inventor Grace Hopper, who discovered that a moth stuck in her Mark II had fouled her computer." Although Hopper didn't coin *bug*, those techies were on the right track, just a couple of innovative generations late. The sense of "a defect or fault in a machine, plan, etc.," says *The Barnhart Dictionary of Etymology*, "appeared in 1889, probably from the idea of a small insect getting inside machinery and interfering with its action." So insects rule after all.

Synonyms for *bug* include *undocumented feature, issue*—the annoying buzzword these days for *problem*, as in "I have issues with that"—and of course *glitch*.

Headed Your Way

Q. *Can you tell me the origin of the word* towhead *and why it means "light blond hair"?*

A. The *tow* in this word refers to certain fibers—flax, hemp, or jute—that have been prepared for spinning on a spinning wheel. These fibers are very light blond, almost white. Thus, a person with hair the color of this tow was called a *towhead*.

but it seemed like a bridge to nowhere. ☚

Towhead may also mean "a sandbar, shoal, or small island in a river, especially one with cottonwood trees on it." Both senses of the word date from the nineteenth century.

Just a Skosh

Q. *Where and when did we get the word* skosh, *meaning a "little bit"?*

A. It entered English in the early 1950s, during the Korean War. It comes through Korean pidgin from Japanese *sukoshi,* which is pronounced like "skoshy" and means "a small amount."

Who Put the Foot in *Pedagogue*?

Q. *I know that* ped- *means "foot." We see this foot in words like* pedestrian, *one who goes on foot,* pedestal, *the foot or bottom support of something, and* pedal, *something you press with your foot. So what I want to know is, who put the foot in* pedagogue? *A pedant with his foot in his mouth?*

A. I'm afraid you're pedaling down the wrong path. *Pedagogue* and *pedagogy* have nothing to do with feet. These words come from the Greek *paidagogos,* a tutor of children, which in turn comes from *pais, paidos,* a boy or child, and *agein,* to lead or conduct, and it means literally "a leader or conductor of youngsters." "Among the ancient Greeks and Romans," says the delightful but sadly forgotten *Century Dictionary* (1914), "the pedagogue was originally a slave who attended the younger children of his master, and conducted them to school, to the theater, etc., combining in many cases instruction with guardianship."

This servile tutor of classical antiquity eventually rose to become the modern pedagogue, a teacher or schoolmaster, but a stigma of pedantry—meaning "a slavish attention to rules and minor details of learning"—remained. Perhaps that's why, when certain members of the teaching profession wanted to find a more elegant word for themselves than *teacher,* they eschewed *pedagogue*

↤ I could have been a train conductor

and settled on three terms: *educator,* which is a good alternative; *educationist,* which is a pompous one; and *educationalist,* which is preposterous. But unless you happen to be a pedagogue, that's neither here nor there, and being the verbose pedant that I am, I digress.

Incidentally, the word *pedant* may be related both to *ped-,* foot, and to *pedagogue. Pedant* has been traced to the Italian *pedante,* a teacher, schoolmaster. The origin of *pedante* is uncertain, but it may come from the Greek *paideúein,* to teach, which may have had the earlier sense of "foot soldier." According to *The Barnhart Dictionary of Etymology, paideúein* was "humorously identified" with *paidagogos* "in allusion to the fact that a teacher of children is always on his feet."

A Reply to a Cutting

Q. *What exactly is "the quick" in the expression* cut to the quick?

A. I can give you a quickie answer. *Quick* originally meant "alive or living," as in the biblical phrase "the quick and the dead." In *cut to the quick, quick* retains its original meaning, and the expression means "to hurt deeply," literally "to wound the living tissue that bleeds."

Murder, She Smoked

Q. *Are the words* assassin *and* hashish *related? Seems unlikely to me.*

A. Hard as it may be to believe that a drug associated with laidback hippie culture could have something to do with murderers, it's true: These words are indeed related and the connection between them is well attested.

Although *assassin* didn't become an English word until the sixteenth century, the *Oxford English Dictionary* shows how it goes back to the time of the Crusades, when "certain Moslem fanatics . . . were sent forth by their sheikh, the 'Old Man of the Mountains,' to murder the Christian leaders." The Arabic *hashshāshīn,* explains

but it was beyond my station. 🖙

The Barnhart Dictionary of Etymology, means "literally, hashish eaters," and referred to "a religious and military order located chiefly in the mountains of Lebanon, who were remarkable for their secret murders in blind obedience to their leader, a condition brought on because the members selected to commit a murder, especially of a king or public figure, were first intoxicated with hashish."

I don't know about you, but I'll take the stoners at a Grateful Dead concert over the ones from the Crusades any day.

TWO

A SLOUGH OF SOLECISMS

*Wherein the Author Leads You
Safely Out of a Morass of Mistakes
and Misperceptions into the Clear,
Comforting Light of Correct English*

Descriptive linguists are fond of accusing prescriptive language mavens like me of being "opposed to change." That's just silly. I'm not opposed to change in language any more than I'm opposed to change in the weather. You can't be against change, and you can't be in favor of it. Change is inevitable.

But language, unlike weather, does not change by itself. Language is a human creation subject to human influence. It is a work in progress, and we are all party to its development. We change the language, for better *and* for worse.

Generally speaking, change keeps a language vital. But not all change serves the best interests of all the people who use a language. Change that springs from creativity, that is advanced by need, and that is reinforced by utility is unobjectionable. But change that results from ignorance, pomposity, eccentricity, a mania for fashion, or a desire for novelty is suspect. That's the kind of change we prescriptivists are concerned about.

I'm not some zealot who wants to take away your language license just because you've made a few mistakes. You don't need to be a language expert to use language competently. But I think people who consider themselves educated have a responsibility to know something—or at least to try to know and remember something—about the words they choose to use. Does the person who says "I have infinitesimal respect for you" deserve your respect? If you don't know enough about the word *infinitesimal* to avoid a gaffe like that, then you shouldn't use that word. Unfortunately, too many people lack the requisite qualifications in too many instances. (And I mean *instances*, not—as you too often hear—*incidences*.)

When people use the word *reticent* (which means reluctant to speak) to mean *reluctant*, when they use *everyday* and *every day* interchangeably, when they misspell *minuscule* as *miniscule*, and when they use *i.e.* when they mean *e.g.*, what do we gain? (And, for that matter, what have we lost?) There is no justification for these changes. There is no legitimate need for them. They have no utility. They muddy the waters of our discourse. To embrace them would be like installing a sink with two taps for cold water and calling it home improvement.

The polemical question is often posed: "What difference does it make as long as we communicate?" I think that sets the bar for all communication at the level of a boor. It's like taking someone out to dinner and then announcing, as the food arrives, "Who cares what your meal tastes like as long as it fills you up."

There is something to be said for aspiring to eloquence, even on a practical level. If we all had richer and more versatile verbal toolboxes, we could spend less time deciphering sloppy, inarticulate communication and more time understanding and enjoying each other.

I could have been a train conductor

In this chapter I offer you some advice (with attitude!) on how to enrich your verbal toolbox and, in your own inimitable fashion, aspire to eloquence.

Till, We Meet Again

Q. *The word that really rubs me the wrong way is* till, *as in "Make no payments till next year." Doesn't that* till *mean to plow the ground? Shouldn't it be* 'til *instead?*

A. No, a thousand times no! *Till* is an entirely acceptable (though less formal and less common) variant of *until.* The forms *til* (bad), *'til* (worse), and *'till* (worst) are substandard and deserving of your scorn.

Want a second opinion? "*Till* is, like *until,* a bona fide preposition and conjunction," says *Garner's Modern American Usage.* "Though less formal than *until, till* is neither colloquial nor substandard . . . If a form deserves a *sic,* it's the incorrect *'til.* Worse yet is *'till,* which is abominable."

Kate White, editor in chief of *Cosmopolitan* magazine, and her three-martini editor get a Major Bozo-no-no Award for titling her mystery novel *'Til Death Do Us Part.*

Ill Literally

Q. *Consider the word* literally *in a sentence like this: "His jokes literally kill me." To avoid a rather grim interpretation, shouldn't it be "His jokes figuratively kill me"?*

A. Although I might snicker silently to hear someone say "His jokes literally kill me"—or if I was feeling especially petulant, I might say "Congratulations on your resurrection"—I would laugh out loud if I ever heard someone say "His jokes *figuratively* kill me." It would be so ridiculously self-conscious and pedantic. The solution, of course, is to eliminate *literally.* Most of the time the word is superfluous, anyway, and it's easily replaced with another adverb if such hyperbolic emphasis can't be resisted.

but it wasn't my ticket to success. ☚

A Plea for *Pleaded*

Q. *These days I constantly hear the word* pled *on radio and TV, as in* he pled not guilty *and* they pled their case. *I was taught that* pleaded *was the correct past tense. Has that changed?*

A. No, it hasn't—or not quite yet, anyway. I'm all for holding the line on *pleaded,* as is *The New York Times Manual of Style and Usage,* which says "the past tense is *pleaded,* not *plead* or *pled.*"

Pleaded is "still the predominant form" in both American English and British English, notes lawyer-lexicographer Bryan A. Garner in his *Dictionary of Modern Legal Usage,* and *pled* has long been condemned by usage experts. In England, where *pleaded* is preferred, *pled* is considered an Americanism, which is to say a vulgarism. For the record, however, *pled* did not originate in America; it is as old as *pleaded* and came to American English via Scottish immigration.

Garner concedes that *pled* has "gained some standing" in American English, and though it may not be the best usage, it cannot still be "condemned as horrible." All right, fair enough. Let them use it on radio and TV, but you won't catch it coming out of this maven's mouth.

Control Alt[ernative] Delete

Q. *Are* alternate *and* alternative *interchangeable?*

A. In strict usage—which I choose to follow here because this distinction strikes me as useful—*alternate* and *alternative* are not interchangeable. I was gently taught this lesson many years ago by the syndicated columnist James J. Kilpatrick, a usage connoisseur if there ever was one, when he read the manuscript of my first book and saw that I had used the phrase *alternate pronunciations* throughout, rather than *alternative pronunciations.*

The trouble occurs chiefly when these words are adjectives and *alternate* gets used in place of *alternative.* The adjective *alternate* means "by turns, first one and then the other." The adjective *alter-*

⇥ I could have been an astrologer

native means "providing a choice between one thing and another." Thus we may work on *alternate* days but we take an *alternative* course of action.

Another Alternative

Q. *A common error my students make is saying* many alternatives *or* a number of alternatives. *When they do this, I hasten to point out that while there may be many options there are only two alternatives.* Alternative *should be restricted to situations where there are only two choices, right?*

A. Wrong. Your students are using *alternative* appropriately— so stop harassing them. Here are the rulings of three modern authorities on usage, among many I could cite:

"Since, therefore, 'alternatives' in the sense of a choice among several possibilities fills a want," says Theodore M. Bernstein in *The Careful Writer* (1965), "it may be respectably used in that way, as well as in its stricter meaning."

"The idea that *alternative* may apply to a choice between two and no more is a pedantry discountenanced by no fewer than nine authorities," says Roy H. Copperud in *American Usage and Style: The Consensus* (1980).

"Etymological purists have argued that [*alternative*] should be confined to contexts involving but two choices," says *Garner's Modern American Usage* (2003), but this contention "has little or no support among other stylistic experts or in actual usage."

Are you convinced yet?

The Skinny on *i.e.* and *e.g.*

Q. *What is the difference between the abbreviations* i.e. *and* e.g.*? I get them confused.*

A. You are not alone. Many people have trouble with *i.e.* and *e.g.*; the usual mistake is using the former in place of the latter. Both abbreviations stand for Latin phrases: *i.e.* for *id est,* meaning "that

but it wasn't in the stars. 🖘

is (to say)"; *e.g.* for *exempli gratia,* meaning "for example." We use *i.e.* to reword, clarify, or specify something ("the real estate agent's mantra—i.e., 'location, location, location'"). We use *e.g.* to introduce one or more examples ("I like to read all kinds of fiction, e.g., mysteries, thrillers, and mainstream novels.")

Two other points should be noted. First, as you can see from the two previous examples, in regular text these abbreviations are not italicized; they are also followed by a comma. Second, usage experts generally frown on using them in regular text (as opposed to footnotes, lists, etc.) and advise using the more comprehensible English phrases instead: *that is* or *namely* for *i.e.* and *for example* or *for instance* for *e.g.*

Evil Ways

Q. *This morning I heard an NPR reporter end a story with the line, "They have a long ways to go." Is that correct, or should it be "a long way to go"? Or are both "ways" okay?*

A. *Ways* is at best casual English. Some experts call it dialectal. However you slice it, it is not standard English.

William and Mary Morris, in the *Harper Dictionary of Contemporary Usage,* second edition (1985), don't mince any words in their condemnation of *a long ways.* Calling it "a fairly common usage in rural dialect," they charge that it is "used mostly by people of little education. 'A long way' is the accurate form and the one used by literate, educated persons." That pronouncement's a bit stuffy even for me, but the fact remains that *a long ways* is not appropriate in professional journalism or any formal writing.

You'll get a different story, though, from *Merriam-Webster's Dictionary of English Usage* (1994), which takes a descriptive and unapologetically permissive approach to style: "*Ways* has been used as a synonym of *way* in such expressions as 'a long ways off' since at least 1588. The *OED* includes citations for this use from Henry

◁ I could have been a boxer

❧ QUOTE UNQUOTE ❧

When Andrew Turnbull, the fifteen-year-old nephew of F. Scott Fitzgerald, wrote to ask the famous writer how he might go about building his vocabulary, this was Fitzgerald's reply:

"Dear Andronio: Upon mature consideration I advise you to go no further with your vocabulary. If you have a lot of words they will become like some muscle you have developed that you are compelled to use, and you must use this one in expressing yourself or in criticizing others. It is hard to say who will punish you the most for this, the dumb people who don't know what you are talking about or the learned ones who do. But wallop you they will and you will be forced to confine yourself to pen and paper.

"Then you will be a writer and may God have mercy on your soul!"

Fielding, Lord Byron, and Stephen Crane, among others . . . It occurs widely . . . and is by no means limited to the spoken language . . . Such usage is standard in American English."

What should you conclude from this disagreement among authorities? Probably just what the lenient but circumspect *Merriam-Webster's* concludes—that it is best to avoid the appearance of evil and eschew the evil *ways:* "Its occurrence in writing is still frowned upon by a number of commentators. [No joke!] *Way,* of course, occurs more commonly, and without any stigma."

Havoc My Way

Q. *I often hear members of the media say* wreaked havoc. *This sounds wrong to me. Isn't* wrought *the past tense of* wreak?

A. *Wreaked* is the proper past tense of *wreak,* which means "to cause, bring about." *Wrought* is an archaic past tense of the verb to

but it didn't have the right ring to it. ❧

work. In case you're wondering, *wrought iron* is iron that has been manufactured in such a way that it can be readily worked.

Everyday Errors

Q. *I like to shop at Whole Foods Market — which my friends and I call Whole Paycheck — where they use the words* every day *in the slogan on their store-brand products:* Every Day Value. *I've also seen them use it as one word,* everyday, *in phrases like* food you can trust everyday. *What's the rule for using* every day *versus* everyday, *and did Whole Foods get it right or wrong?*

A. Whole Foods has good food (I like to shop there too) but flawed usage. *Every day* is an adverbial phrase, meaning it modifies a verb. So when you see a verb lurking somewhere nearby, use two words: *Every day I have the blues; she used it every day; food you can trust every day.* The single word *everyday* is an adjective, and it always precedes the noun it modifies: *an everyday event; hardly an everyday accomplishment.* So the slogan should be *Everyday Value,* not *Every Day Value.*

Under the Whether

Q. *Is it all right to use the phrase* whether or not, *or is the* or not *redundant? Shouldn't we say "I don't care whether it rains" instead of "I don't care whether or not it rains" (or "I don't care whether it rains or not")?*

A. I am happy to answer your question in the affirmative. Yes, it is all right to use the phrase *whether or not,* but yes, the *or not* is usually redundant and superfluous.

"Usually the *or not* is a space waster," says Theodore M. Bernstein in *The Careful Writer,* as in this sentence: "Whether the terrorist statement was true or not was not known." But if your intended meaning is "regardless of whether," then you must use the whole phrase or your sentence will sound funny. Change your *I don't care whether it rains* to *I will go whether it rains* and you can see immedi-

⊰ I could have been a manicurist

ately how in the former *or not* is padding while in the latter it is necessary.

Whatever you do, don't follow the example of Senator Christopher Dodd of Connecticut, who was clearly under the weather when he asked secretary of state nominee Condoleeza Rice "whether or not you consider [the incidents at Abu Ghraib prison] to be torture or not." No wonder Condy had trouble answering the question.

Nobody Doesn't Like Supposedly

Q. *I'm trying to determine the difference between the words* supposably *and* supposedly. *Can you please help?*

A. *Supposedly* (suh-POH-zid-lee) is the proper adverb corresponding to the adjective *supposed* (suh-POHZD) in the usual sense we hear and read: "as is supposed or assumed to be true, presumably." The word *supposably* is much less common and means "conceivably, imaginably." It's hard to imagine where you would have a need to use *supposably* outside of some narrow academic context, but *supposedly* is an everyday word. Your confusion is probably the result of the regrettably common mispronunciation of *supposedly* as *supposably*. A similar mispronunciation is *unequivocably*—which is not a legitimate word, though you sometimes see it in print—for *unequivocally.*

No Ifs, Ands, or Buts

Q. *I once had a supervisor who told me it was improper to begin a sentence with* and *or* but. *Is that true?*

A. No. It is a foolish superstition devised by well-meaning but wrongheaded teachers as a way to prevent their pupils from composing breathless, run-on prose. But it has no basis in logic or in our literature.

Modern authorities all agree that it is perfectly respectable and proper to begin a sentence with *and* or *but,* just as it is perfectly

but I couldn't nail down a job. ☚

FASCINATING FACT ☺

Crucial Information

Q. Whenever I look at a representation of Jesus on the cross, I wonder what the letters *INRI* stand for and why they were placed above his head. Can you explain?

A. *INRI* is an initialism that stands for *Jesus Nazarenus, Rex Judaeorum*, the capital *I* being the Latin way of writing *J*. Translated it means *Jesus of Nazareth, King of the Jews*. John 19:19ff. tells how Pontius Pilate "wrote a title, and put it on the cross. And the writing was, *Jesus of Nazareth the King of the Jews* . . . [A]nd it was written in Hebrew, and Greek, and Latin." ☺

respectable and proper to begin a sentence with *if, or, so, because,* and *since*. If there were in fact something wrong with using these words to launch a sentence, we'd have to toss out millions of sentences by all the best writers of English since Chaucer and revise about nine-tenths of the Bible, beginning with Genesis: *And the earth was without form . . . And God said, Let there be light . . . And God saw the light . . . And God called the light Day . . .* and so on.

A Wrench in the Works

Q. *Eeek! I just found out that a word I've been using forever isn't in a dictionary—and I checked a bunch of them because I'm a librarian. The word is* heartwrenching, *or maybe* heart-wrenching. *A friend ran a NEXIS search and found tons of citations for it in recent publications, some of them hyphenated and some not. Even though it's not in a dictionary, if other people are using it in print, am I justified in doing so?*

A. *Heartwrenching* is not in dictionaries yet but may soon be, given the frequency with which it has been appearing in print lately. My guess is that it came into being through a confused blending of the words *gut-wrenching* and *heartrending* (which is often miswritten and misspoken as *heartrendering*). Personally, I think it makes sense that guts are wrenched (twisted violently) and hearts are rent (torn or split), and we are better off leaving things that way. But if *heartwrenching* gains acceptance, no doubt we'll soon see the advent of *gutrending*.

➵ I could have been a doctor

All about *What It Is*

Q. *What's up with* What it is is . . . *? I hear this all the time now. It makes sense, in a weird sort of way, but it sounds really dorky. Why are people doing this?*

A. I am all too well aware of the dorky *what it is is,* and not long ago, on NPR's *Fresh Air,* I even heard a Hollywood screenwriter say, "What it was was . . ." Some of my friends—including writers— have taken to using this locution. You ask what this *what it is* is? What it is is that *what it is* is a tic that has been transmuted into a virus.

Garner's Modern American Usage observes that *what it is is* is (three *is*'s in a row!) "an ungainly construction" that is "much on the rise" not only in speech but also in print. He cites three examples: "What it is, is payback time . . ." (*Chicago Tribune*); "What it is, is unnerving" (*Sacramento Bee*); "What it is is very funny . . ." (*Omaha World-Herald*).

This strange, clumsy construction is yet another way we've come up with to stumble into a sentence without thinking about where we're going and how best to get there. It's a form of redundancy called pleonasm, the use of words whose omission would leave one's meaning intact. For example, *at this point in time* is a pleonasm for *at this time* or *now.* The problem here is that *what it is* is a noun clause that needs a verb to follow it, as you can see from how I've had to word this sentence. But the noun clause itself is pleonastic and superfluous, and the sentence is best begun straightforwardly: *It's payback time.* You could also divide the thought into a rhetorical question-and-answer: *You know what it is? [It's] payback time.*

And one more thing. This construction is still strange, clumsy, and pleonastic even if you try to disguise it by inserting some filler between the noun clause and the verb, as Bruce Handy did in a review of a biography of David Niven in *The New York Times Book Review* (January 10, 2005): "What he was, in fact, was a first-rate

but I lacked curiosity. ☚

personality." Make that "In fact, he was a first-rate personality" or, if you want *in fact* to create a pause in the middle, "Niven, in fact, was a first-rate personality."

Ones upon a Time

Q. *A friend told me I was wrong to say* these ones. *Am I?*

A. *These ones* is a perplexing usage. We say *this one* and *that one* and *the ones over there on the table,* and no one bats an eye. But why do some claim that if someone asks "Which ones do you want?" it's unacceptable to answer "These ones right here in the display case" or "Those ones up on the shelf"? If it's okay to say *I like this one,* why can't we say *I like these ones?*

Perhaps because many feel that *these* and *those* imply the presence of *ones* in some way that *this* and *that* do not. Yet who could possibly object to using *these ones* or *those ones* with a modifier in between, as in *I like these pretty green ones* and *I want those red ones over there?* It just doesn't add up.

Barbara Wallraff's advice in her book *Word Court* is, to me, right on the money: "Now, why we should deny the advantages of emphasis to a plural [*these ones*] when we grant them to a singular [*this one*], I don't know," she writes. "And yet I have to agree with you that *these ones* is often grating. My conclusion is that we should try not to use the phrase habitually but should also not object to its use where the special emphasis it imparts is wanted. ('Which programs did you say you liked?' '*These*—the ones this review is discussing.' 'What did you say? I wasn't paying attention.' '*These ones. These ones* here!')"

A Done Deal

Q. *My husband and I are at loggerheads over a point of usage. I often ask our two-year-old, "Are you done eating?" My husband says that's incorrect and I should say, "Are you finished eating?" Who's right?*

A. You are. It's okay to use *done* to mean *finished.* It's been used that way since the fifteenth century. In the nineteenth and twenti-

⇥ I could have been a doctor

❧ QUOTE UNQUOTE ❧

"Modern English, especially written English, is full of bad habits which spread by imitation and which can be avoided if one is willing to take the necessary trouble. If one gets rid of these habits one can think more clearly, and to think clearly is a necessary first step towards political regeneration: so that the fight against bad English is not frivolous and is not the exclusive concern of professional writers."—George Orwell, "Politics and the English Language"

eth centuries some people arbitrarily decided that only food could be done; everything else had to be finished. For a while that distinction was upheld by cultivated writers and speakers, but—because it was pointless and contrary to entrenched usage—it was eventually ignored and then repudiated.

Today all but the most hidebound authorities agree that using *done* as an adjective is acceptable as long as it is not ambiguous; in other words, *I'm done eating* or *the roast is done* is fine, but in a sentence like *The job will be done next week,* which may mean the job will be carried out next week rather than completed, the better word is *finished.* The only objection to *done* that can be reasonably made is that it's informal, which is hardly an objection at all considering that the colloquial has become our modern paragon of style and, to all but the most confident stylists, formality has become something of a sin.

The Defense Unrests

Q. *Why do sportscasters use* defense *as a verb when we already have the perfectly adequate verb* defend? *And why do they talk about an athlete's* quickness *instead of his or her* speed *or* agility?

A. All sports, especially football, are mock warfare, and sportsisms like *defense* are imitations of military jargon. Like war, jargon

but it was a prescription for failure. ❧

is best avoided. And the best way to avoid it while watching sports on television is to press the mute button on your remote.

I must disagree with you about *quickness*, however. That's like arguing that *calm* and *tranquillity* are somehow inherently better than *quietness*. *Quickness* is a fine, old, well-formed word. The *Oxford English Dictionary* traces it to Chaucer in 1369, and the sense of "speed, rapidity" dates from 1548.

Orient Expressed

Q. *I can't stand it when I hear someone say* orientate. *The correct verb is* orient *and* orientate *is just bad usage. Isn't it?*

A. I'm sorry, but you are wrong to assert that *orientate* is "just bad usage." It's true that contemporary usage experts do not favor it, and it can reasonably be dismissed as a needless variant, but as R. W. Burchfield (in *The New Fowler's Modern English Usage*) and the citations in the *Oxford English Dictionary* show, *orientate* has competed honorably with *orient* in educated usage since the nineteenth century. You and I may not like *orientate* and hope that by eschewing it ourselves we will encourage others to do the same, but, as Burchfield (who prefers *orient*) remarks, "one can have no fundamental quarrel with anyone who decides to use the longer of the two words."

When a House Is Not a Home

Q. *My pet peeve is the way Realtors use the word* home *instead of* house. *What if the buyer is not planning to live in the house?*

A. Using *home* for *house* is manipulative (they call those house peddlers "sales agents," don't forget), but it is entrenched. In the best usage, we call the building a *house,* and *home* is where the heart

I could have been a lawyer

is, where the family resides. But the distinction has long been blurred, and it's not just the fault of the real estate salespeople.

Homeowners (note *home*) buy in to it eagerly too, purchasing a *home* but selling a *house*. *Home* is personal and sentimental; *house* is neutral. That's why you hear the police say there was an intruder in a *house* but the occupants will say someone broke into their *home*. So what should we do? Go ahead and make the distinction when you see fit, but otherwise let idiom be idiom. I'm more concerned about getting people to pronounce *Realtor* properly: it's REE-ul-tur (like *real* + *tor*), not REE-luh-tur (like *relator*). Can you help me with that?

Grating to the Year

Q. *Using the word* anniversary *for an occasion that is not annual really rubs me the wrong way. For example, I recently saw* one-month anniversary *on the front page of my local paper, and I often hear people use* anniversary *of months and even weeks. Do you share this pet peeve, and is there any other word that could be used instead?*

A. I agree with you, and so do others. "Considering the word's tight association with 'year,'" says *Garner's Modern American Usage*, "the loose usage is subject to criticism and should be avoided if possible." *Milestone* is one possible alternative for an occasion of remembrance that is not annual, but the best word I can think of for that is *commemoration*.

There Oughtta Be a Law

Q. *I am a lawyer, and it has always been my understanding that the abbreviation* J.D. *stands for* Juris Doctor. *But lately I have witnessed the proliferating use of* Juris Doctorate *and* Doctorate of Jurisprudence *for* J.D. *Are these variants now acceptable?*

A. Categorically no, never, not in a million years. You are completely and unassailably right that *J.D.* stands only for *Juris Doctor,* and I encourage you to prosecute all offenders who use those bogus variants.

but it didn't suit me. ⬅

Theory Query

Q. *High on my list of pet peeves is the use of* theory *when hypothesis is the appropriate word. It bugs me that people use* theory *so indiscriminately, of any crazy notion or mere guess. The media constantly make this error. What is your opinion on this?*

BODACIOUS BRAINTEASER

AUTHOR ANAGRAMS

Can you unscramble these scrambled names of well-known writers?

1. dress us
2. me a nail
3. web he it
4. carlo swiller

5. dealer draw
6. pet rot exit bar
7. sin iron motor
8. we all make his praise

Answers appear on page 263.

A. The use of *theory* to mean "a hypothesis proposed as an explanation" (*Oxford English Dictionary*) is not an error—at least outside of science and philosophy. In those disciplines, the distinction between an untested explanation and a tested one is meaningful; in general discourse it is not. Consider, for example, what the noun *replica* means in fine art versus how the word is used generally: In fine art it is a copy, especially one made by the maker of the original, assumed to be of equal value; in general usage it is simply a facsimile or close copy.

Theory has been used in its general sense of "an idea or set of ideas about something; an individual view or notion" (*OED* again) since the late 1700s—the *OED*'s first citation is from Edmund Burke in 1792—and no modern authority I know of frowns on using the word in this sense. I don't doubt that some off-the-wall

I could have been a lawyer

ideas have been unjustifiably dignified by this word, but that's an error of judgment, not usage. Moreover, there have been some pretty wacky theories in the scientific, tested sense, too (take phrenology, for example), and some theories people thought were wacky but weren't (Copernican theory). Must an explanation or set of ideas now be judged useful or good to be a theory?

In short, only a scientist, engineer, philosopher, mathematician, et cetera, has a right to insist on your strict use of *theory,* and only in a technical context. To impose the distinction elsewhere — in journalism and literature, for example — is to fly in the face of long-established and unimpeachable usage.

A Hoi There

Q. *A friend told me I was wrong to say* the hoi polloi *instead of just* hoi polloi. *Am I? Seems to me I usually hear and read it with* the.

A. You're right — *the hoi polloi* is more common these days, and it has become acceptable to all but pedants and purists, who view it as redundant because the Greek *hoi* means "the," so technically *the hoi polloi* means "the the many."

This sort of punctilio doesn't bother most people, and I suppose it shouldn't (why should *hoi polloi,* the masses, be expected to know a little Greek?), but as an inveterate pedantic purist, I just can't bring myself to say or write *the hoi polloi.* It seems less elegant, less enlightened. For the same pedantic reason I prefer *the Sahara* over *the Sahara Desert* because *sahara* means *desert* in Arabic, and I call it the *Rio Grande* rather than the *Rio Grande River* because *rio* means *river* in Spanish.

The way I see it is this: If you're going to go to the trouble of using a hoity-toity locution like *hoi polloi,* it behooves you to know something about it, don't you think? Otherwise you might as well just stick with "the masses." But the urge to embellish, it seems, is irresistible, and *the hoi polloi* is now entrenched.

but it didn't appeal to me. 🖙

An Eye for an *I*

Q. *I have been noticing, with dismay, an increasing substitution of the pronoun* I *for the pronoun* me. *For example, I hear such abominations as "James gave the book to Fiona and I" and "Please join Margaret and I for dinner." I sometimes wonder if some of my friends have forgotten the word* me. *Do you agree that this error is more frequent now than it was twenty years ago?*

A. The *I* for *me* substitution is not a recent error. Usage commentators have been writing about it since at least the 1960s. It probably arose around the time when instruction in grammar was being phased out of the primary-school curriculum and one of the few remaining grammatical admonishments young people received was not to say things like "Me and my friend Johnny" and "Can Johnny and me go out and play?"—typical little-kid mistakes. As those young people grew older, they developed a phobia about *me* and began substituting *I* for it in all constructions. Thus, along with your examples, we often hear people utter abominations like *for you and I* and *just between you and I.* Language mavens call this kind of mistake hypercorrection, falling into a real error by bending over backward to avoid an imagined one.

Is the error more frequent today? you ask. Just listen to the evidence of your ears.

Keep Your Eyes on Comprise

Q. *I was taught that* comprise *means to contain, consist of, and that the whole comprises the parts. Yet again and again I read or hear, for instance, that a fence is* comprised of *wood or that cats* comprise *the largest group of animals seen by vets. I would have used* composed *and* constitute *in those examples. Am I right, or have the rules changed?*

A. You were taught correctly regarding the proper use of *comprise.* But for most of the twentieth century the word has been confused with and used in place of *compose* and *constitute,* so that today all dictionaries recognize this usage. In his *New Fowler's Mod-*

◆ I could have been a lawyer

ern English Usage, R. W. Burchfield objects to the parts comprising the whole but says "it cannot be denied . . . that the sheer frequency of this construction seems likely to take it out of the disputed area before long."

I, too, rarely see or hear *comprise* used in its traditional sense nowadays. (Alas!) But for the time being, you're still within your rights to eschew the "compose, constitute" usage and stick with the "contain, consist of" meaning. Although its use is on the wane, most modern authorities continue to defend the traditional meaning of *comprise.*

Begging to Differ

Q. *I'm wondering what your opinion is on the expression* to beg the question. *I see and hear people use it in different ways.*

For example, I heard Leslie Stahl on 60 Minutes *say, "The increasing influx of drugs into this country begs the question as to what we can do about it"; here it seems to mean simply to raise a question. And recently I found this sentence in a book called* E-Writing *by Dianna Booher: "Begging the question involves talking around the issue without addressing it . . . stating the obvious." I've always thought that* to beg the question *meant to continue arguing a point after it has been decided. Can you sort this out for me?*

A. Gladly. *To beg the question* properly does not mean any of the things you cite. The expression comes to us through law from the ancient art of rhetoric. It is a type of logical fallacy, formally called *petitio principii,* and it means "to assume as true what needs to be proved" or, as *Garner's Modern American Usage* puts it, "to base a conclusion on an assumption that is as much in need of proof or demonstration as the conclusion itself." When the lawyer asks the witness "Do you still have extramarital affairs?" before it has been proved that he ever committed adultery, *that* is begging the question. And the statement "Reasonable people are people who reason intelligently" begs the question, "What is intelligent reasoning?"

but life is too brief for that. 🖙

Lately, as your examples show, *beg the question* has been misused in a number of ways including "to raise a question," "to evade a question," "to invite an obvious question," and "to ignore a question or issue." Of these, the misuse of *beg the question* to mean "raise a question" has become so common that, as Garner notes, this sense "has been recognized by most dictionaries and sanctioned by descriptive observers of language." Yet Garner doesn't like it and neither do I, because using *beg the question* to mean *raise the question* is merely the result of a restless desire for elegant variation. Moreover, the consequence of this substitution is that we gain an imprecise variant that we do not need and lose a precise idiom that we sorely need. For if we relegate *beg the question* to a mere variant of *raise the question*, we will no longer have a simple, succinct way to describe the presumptuous logic of the young man in a public-speaking class who, in a speech intended to persuade his audience that music and art should be dropped from his high school curriculum, began by saying, "Since I know we all agree that taking music and art does nothing to prepare you for college, a career, or life, I'll start there."

Indecent Incidences

Q. *Have you noticed, as I have, the growing use of* incidences *when what is meant is* incidents *or* instances? *As my teenager says, what's up with that?*

A. What's up is that a lot of people out there are *incidunces.*

The word *incidence* means "rate or range of occurrence": *The incidence of crime in the city has decreased.* Because *incidence* sounds like *incidents*—the plural of *incident*, an event, occurrence, happening—some people turn it into a kind of homophonic double plural, hearing *incidents* as *incidence* and then making *incidence* plural: *A number of violent incidences between protesters and police.* The confusion with *instance*—a case, example—is a less-frequent but equally unfortunate blunder: *They found several incidences of mismanagement.*

◆ I could have been a printer

The best way to avoid this error? Toss *incidences* in your mental wastebasket.

Bacterial Infection

Q. *Is* bacteria *a singular or plural noun? I always thought it was plural, but these days I usually see it used with a singular verb.*

A. You're right, and it makes me freakin' sick!

In scientific writing and in careful usage, *bacteria* is a plural noun that takes a plural verb: *These bacteria cause disease.* The singular is *bacterium*, which takes a singular verb: *the bacterium that causes anthrax.* Is that so hard to remember, everybody?

The plural *bacteria* should not be used for the singular *bacterium* when the intended meaning is "a strain or variety of bacteria." This misuse appears with numbing frequency in newspaper writing: "Deadly Bacteria Begins to Infiltrate Fresh Fruit Juices and Produce" (*New York Times*); "And so the bacteria spreads" (*San Diego Union-Tribune*). The phrase *strain of bacteria* takes a singular verb because the noun *strain* is singular: *This strain of bacteria is a leading cause of infection.*

One last thing. Please, please, at all costs, avoid the anglicized plural *bacterias,* which is (and this is putting it nicely) nonstandard.

Get Your Back Up

Q. *My father used to lecture us kids about how it was wrong to say* in back of *and* back of. *Is that true? I hear people say things like "Let's go in back of the house" all the time.*

A. The phrases *back of* and *in back of,* meaning "behind," are long-standing Americanisms: *The car was parked (in) back of the house. Back of* was first recorded in the late seventeenth century; *in back of* was probably in common use by 1900. Today *in back of,* formed on analogy with *in front of,* is more usual than *back of,* especially in writing. Both phrases are standard, but some writers, editors, and teachers consider them casual or colloquial and prefer the succinct *behind* in formal prose.

but it wasn't my type of job. 🖙

NONE *IS* OR NONE *ARE?*
FOUR REPRESENTATIVE OPINIONS

"It is a mistake to suppose that the pronoun is singular only and must at all costs be followed by singular verbs."—H. W. Fowler, *Modern English Usage* (1926)

"If a rule is needed, a better one is to consider *none* to be a plural unless there is a definite reason to regard it as a singular."—Theodore M. Bernstein, *The Careful Writer* (1965) (Bern-stein was managing editor of *The New York Times* for many years.)

"The widely held belief that *none* must always be singular is a myth."—Bill Bryson, *Bryson's Dictionary of Troublesome Words* (2002)

"[*None*] may correctly take either a singular or a plural verb."—Bryan A. Garner, *Garner's Modern American Usage* (2003)

None the Wiser

Q. *Doesn't* none *mean "not one"? And shouldn't it be used with a singular verb? That's certainly what I was taught in school, but I often see* none *used with plural verbs in newspapers and magazines—even* The New York Times*!*

A. Despite what you were taught and what you may hear from certain soi-disant usage mavens, *none* with a plural verb is good English, and in fact more common in educated usage. Many authorities have noted this, unfortunately to little avail.

In short, it is idle to impose a strict rule that *none* must at all times be used with a singular verb because it is supposed to mean "not one." More often than not, *none* means "not any": *None of the answers were right.* Occasionally *none* means "no part," and when it does and the noun that follows *none* is singular, use a singular verb: *None of the debt has been paid.* But when the noun that follows *none* is plural, a plural verb is always better: *None of the weapons of mass destruction have been found.* And if your specific meaning is "not

I could have been a printer

one" you should use those words instead: *Not one of the seats was in its right place.*

Double Trouble

Q. *Why is it that you see—in major newspapers and magazines—the possessive form of a noun following a preposition, as in* I am a friend of Lisa's *rather than* I am a friend of Lisa? *Isn't that possessive* friend of Lisa's *redundant?*

A. This is called the "double possessive" or "double genitive." It may seem redundant, but it has been idiomatic since Middle English and is entirely standard. It may help to think how you'd say it with a pronoun: *I'm a friend of his,* not *I'm a friend of him; she's a friend of mine,* not *she's a friend of me.*

Losing Your Remind

Q. *One of the op-ed columnists for my local paper recently penned this phrase: "It reminds of the Anglo-French attack on Suez in 1956 . . ." Am I wrong or is* reminds of *missing something?*

A. You're right. Both the phrase and the op-ed columnist are missing something. As Theodore M. Bernstein reminds us in *The Careful Writer,* "Since *remind* means to recall to one's mind, it must be followed by an object that has a mind." Unless the columnist has lost his mind—a common affliction among columnists today—he should have written "It reminds me" or "It reminds one."

Grad You Asked

Q. *Which is correct:* I graduated from college *or* I graduated college?

A. Would that all college graduates knew the answer to this question! *I graduated from* is the accepted form today. *I was graduated from* is the older form, now passing out of use. *I graduated* (without *was* or *from*) is the new and still nonstandard form pressing hard against *I graduated from* and threatening to displace it. Though it may eventually gain acceptance, *I graduated college* is

but I didn't have an inkling of how to do it. ☞

THE DEVIL'S DICTIONARY

In 1906 Ambrose Bierce published a collection of satirical and epigrammatic definitions of common words that H. L. Mencken called "some of the most gorgeous witticisms in the English language." The best of them, I would add, are also timeless. Bierce addressed his *Devil's Dictionary* to those "enlightened souls who prefer dry wines to sweet, sense to sentiment, wit to humor and clean English to slang."

Here is a selection of some of the wittiest of his acerbic definitions:

Absurdity, n. A statement of belief manifestly inconsistent with one's own opinion.

Apologize, v.i. To lay the foundation for a future offense.

Applause, n. The echo of a platitude.

Bacchus, n. A convenient deity invented by the ancients as an excuse for getting drunk.

Battle, n. A method of untying with the teeth a political knot that would not yield to the tongue.

Bride, n. A woman with a fine prospect of happiness behind her.

Childhood, n. The period of human life intermediate between the idiocy of infancy and the folly of youth—two removes from the sin of manhood and three from the remorse of age.

Corporation, n. An ingenious device for obtaining individual profit without individual responsibility.

Cynic, n. A blackguard whose faulty vision sees things as they are, not as they ought to be.

Destiny, n. A tyrant's authority for crime and a fool's excuse for failure.

Discussion, n. A method of confirming others in their errors.

Erudition, n. Dust shaken out of a book into an empty skull.

Famous, adj. Conspicuously miserable.

Friendless, adj. Having no favors to bestow. Destitute of fortune. Addicted to utterance of truth and common sense.

I could have been a dry cleaner

Labor, n. One of the processes by which A acquires property for B.

Litigation, n. A machine which you go into as a pig and come out of as a sausage.

Longevity, n. Uncommon extension of the fear of death.

Love, n. A temporary insanity curable by marriage or by removal of the patient from the influences under which he incurred the disorder.

Misfortune, n. The kind of fortune that never misses.

Obsolete, adj. No longer used by the timid.

Opportunity, n. A favorable occasion for grasping a disappointment.

Painting, n. The art of protecting flat surfaces from the weather and exposing them to the critic.

Politics, n. A strife of interests masquerading as a contest of principles.

Positive, adj. Mistaken at the top of one's voice.

Precipitate, adj. Anteprandial.

Prevaricator, n. A liar in the caterpillar state.

Proofreader, n. A malefactor who atones for making your writing nonsense by permitting the compositor to make it unintelligible.

Reconsider, v. To seek a justification for a decision already made.

Riot, n. A popular entertainment given to the military by innocent bystanders.

Saw, n. A trite popular saying, or proverb. So called because it makes its way into a wooden head.

Self-evident, adj. Evident to one's self and to nobody else.

Selfish, adj. Devoid of consideration for the selfishness of others.

Tenacity, n. A certain quality of the human hand in its relation to the coin of the realm.

Urbanity, n. The kind of civility that urban observers ascribe to dwellers in all cities but New York.

but I felt pressed into it. ☞

AN OPEN LETTER TO NEWSPAPER EDITORS

"Countering the Republicans, Pelosi convenes Democratics to talk faith"—actual headline found in *The San Diego Union-Tribune*

In the box on page B4 today your newspaper reported that the 79th Assembly District is 53.3% *Democrat*. I hasten to point out that *democrat*, whether capitalized or lowercased, is a noun, never an adjective. The adjective is *democratic*, and the name of the party is the *Democratic Party*. You could have printed the adjective *Democratic* or the plural noun *Democrats*, but the singular noun *Democrat* is erroneous.

It's also politically charged. For several decades some Republicans have used the noun *democrat* as an adjective (*the Democrat*

unanimously frowned upon by usage authorities (and that *unanimously* includes me).

Conduct Unbecoming a Colleague

Q. *A colleague in my department (I'm a professor of medicine) continually uses* symposia *as a singular noun. He says,* this symposia is *and* conduct a symposia *and so on. Is this usage now acceptable?*

A. No way. You don't play basketball in *a gymnasia* or football in *a stadia*, do you? *A symposia* is a highbrow illiteracy. Your colleague probably also says *this is a crises* (instead of *crisis*, the singular form). *Symposium* is the proper singular, and the anglicized *symposiums* is the plural. (Although dictionaries list *symposia* for the plural, it is, as one authority puts it, "a pedantry.")

By the way, did you know that by derivation *symposium* means "a drinking party"? Maybe the next time your colleague blunderfully pluralizes the word, you should present him with a photocopy of a dictionary entry for it taped to a bottle of wine.

⇥ I could have been a hairstylist

Party, a Democrat majority) as a subtle form of derogation, and in recent years this has become regrettably common in print and broadcast reporting.

I urge you and your colleagues to keep a sharp eye out for this error and add a note about it to your stylebooks. *The Associated Press Stylebook* does not mention the erroneous and disparaging use of *Democrat* attributively, but *The New York Times Manual of Style and Usage* does. It says, "Do not use *Democrat* as a modifier (*the Democrat Party*); that construction is used by opponents to disparage the party."

Don't Compare and Contrast

Q. *I always thought that the phrase* compare and contrast—*a staple in classrooms and textbooks, and often used in exam questions—meant to look for both similarities and differences. But a friend recently claimed that we should use one word or the other, not both. Is she right, or is it all right to say* compare and contrast?

A. Take your friend's advice—avoid *compare and contrast.* It's a redundancy perpetrated by, of all people, English teachers, who perhaps were seduced into using it by textbook publishers, who perhaps borrowed it from the stilted language of examinations, which were probably written by earlier generations of English teachers, who may have picked it up from ... oh heck, I don't know!

All I know is that to *compare* is to examine for both similarities and differences; to *contrast* is to examine only for unlikeness or differences.

but the work was too cut-and-dried. ☞

Had It with *Would Have*

Q. *My question is about a way of using* would have *that I often hear today. For example: "If we would have known it was going on, we would have stopped it." Something tells me the first* would have *is wrong, but the second is correct. Also, is there a grammatical term for this construction?*

A. Your instincts are dead on. This is the past perfect tense we're talking about here, the one that uses *had* before a verb. It expresses the earlier of two past actions, something completed before an event in the past: *After I had studied* (past perfect) *Greek for two years, I studied* (past) *Latin.* It is also properly used in "if clauses" that express the earlier of two past actions, and this is called "progression of tenses." Thus, *If he had studied Greek, he would have done better with Latin,* not *If he would have studied Greek he would have done better with Latin.* False parallelism lures many people into using the erroneous *would have . . . would have* construction.

Another common misuse of this kind is using the past tense instead of the past perfect for an action completed in the past before another past event: *I suddenly remembered that I left my keys in the car* (wrong); *I suddenly remembered* (past) *that I had left* (past perfect) *my keys in the car* (right).

To Have and to Have Got

Q. *I've been trying to teach my grandson, without much success, that sentences like* Have you got a minute? *and* We've got to go *are incorrect, and that properly they should be* Do you have a minute? *and* We have to go. *Do you have any suggestions on how I can teach him to say it right?*

A. Here's my suggestion for you, Grampa: Give it a rest. Don't torture your poor grandson with a proscription against *have got.* It's idiomatic, standard, and especially common when special emphasis is intended: *You have got to be kidding. We've got to get out of here fast! Have we got a bargain for you.* Changing that last example to *Do*

◄▒ I could have been a sanitation worker

we have a bargain for you makes it sound like a question, not a pitch, and *We have a bargain for you* has all the enthusiasm of a road sign.

Unfortunately, *have got* has long been "foolishly criticized," as one usage guide notes. No modern authority with a reputation to lose cares if you use *have got* for *have* or *must,* and you needn't waste your own energy worrying about it either.

You Can Unquote Me

Q. *I prefer to say either* quote, end quote *or* quote, close quote, *but most people say* quote unquote. *To me that* unquote *negates the "quotedness" of the quotation. Am I just picky or am I right?*

A. Yes, you're being unnecessarily picky about *quote unquote.* Both *end quote* and *unquote* are acceptable, while *close quote* is editorese, useful in copyediting contexts but not normal in conversation. *Un-* may express reversal of an action (*undo, unsay*), removal (*unscrew, unveil*), or release (*unburden, unbend*). To *unquote* does not reverse the action of quoting nor deprive what has been quoted of its quotedness. It releases the speaker from the act of quoting, thus signaling an end to the quotation.

Unquote is merely short for *end quote,* and *quote unquote,* which arose in the era of cables and telegrams, is the far more common "formulaic pair." In political discourse *quote unquote* has come to be used chiefly in an ironic manner, indicating "That's somebody else's word for it, not mine," and usually the phrase precedes the matter quoted, especially when it is brief: *They call these policies, quote unquote, reforms.* Among those who dictate or read aloud it continues to be used neutrally.

Lie Down and I'll Lay It on You

Q. *When I hear people say, as so many people do, "I was laying in bed" or "Don't leave that laying around," I just know that's wrong but I'm not sure how to say it right. I've never really understood the difference between the verbs to* lay *and to* lie *and it would be a great relief to*

but it was all a bunch of garbage. 🖝

know how to use them correctly once and for all. Do you have a foolproof way a fool like me could remember this?

A. Congratulations to you for wanting to master this distinction. I would wager that most people today do not know how to conjugate these everyday verbs properly.

The first thing you must do is memorize this: *To lay is to put or place. To lie is to come to rest, recline.* If you are not putting or placing something, you cannot use *lay.* That's why *I was laying in bed* is wrong and makes you out to be a chicken who is depositing a fat fresh egg in the bed.

This is how the verbs are conjugated:

To lay *is to* put *or* place:
You lay the book on the table.
You are laying the book on the table.
You laid the book on the table.
You have laid the book on the table.

To lie *is to* come to rest, recline:
You lie on the bed.
You are lying on the bed.
You lay on the bed.
You have lain on the bed.

You see how the present tense of *lay* is the same as the past tense of *lie?* That's where all the trouble starts. You can't tell a dog to *lay down* (that means *put down*), but you can say you *lay* in bed (you reclined there in the past). Confused by this, people then compound the problem by using the past tense of *lay* (*laid*) for the past tense of *lie* (*lay*), for example, *I laid in bed last night.* There's that chicken again.

I know it's tough to keep these two verbs straight and remember all the conjugations, but it's well worth the effort because the

⇥ I could have been a proctologist

ability to properly distinguish *lay* and *lie* will distinguish you as a cultivated user of the language.

For Whom the Bell Told

Q. *I was taught that the adverbial phrase meaning "in all, with all taken into account" was* all tolled. *But I always see it in print as* all told, *and even my Microsoft Word spell-checker recognizes* all told. *Did the good sisters teach me incorrectly?*

A. Yes, the sisters done you wrong, my friend. It's *all told,* not *all tolled* (which would mean assessed a toll or having to do with the end of bell-ringing). Here *told* is the past tense of *tell* in the sense of to count or enumerate; thus *all told* means counting every-thing or everyone involved, with all said and accounted for.

Tell the good sisters, from me, "I told you so."

Wake-up Call

Q. *What do you recommend for the past participle of the verb* to wake up? *Is* had woke up *standard?*

A. Here's what I recommend and what most usage mavens pre-fer: *wake up* (present), *woke up* (past), and *had* or *have waked up* or *woken up* (past participle). If you don't like how that sounds for some reason, you may use *awake* (present), *awoke* (past), and *had* or *have awaked* or *awoken* (past participle). I have a predilection for the irregular or strong forms *woken* and *awoken* for the past parti-ciple; to me they sound more dignified and literary.

Rote Rooter

Q. *I've been hearing the phrase* rote memorization *a lot lately. Isn't it redundant?*

A. Indeed it is. *Rote* means memorization; specifically, as the fourth edition of *The American Heritage Dictionary* puts it, "a mem-orizing process using routine or repetition, often without full

but I didn't want to be the butt of jokes. ☞

attention or comprehension." We should say *rote learning* or *learning by rote*, depending on context.

Prevent(at)ive Maintenance

Q. *First a pet peeve, then a question.*

I think the expression preventive maintenance *is illogical and nonsensical. And an oxymoron. Maintenance is what you do to equipment that's in running condition to keep it in running condition.* Preventive maintenance *sounds like what you'd do if you wanted to sabotage the equipment, yet this idiotic expression is commonly found in technical manuals and used by doctors, politicians, and even my own mother.*

Now, sometimes you hear or read preventative maintenance *and* preventative medicine. *Why do we have two words,* preventive *and* preventative*? Where did this longer* preventative *come from?*

A. Yup, *preventive maintenance* is a dumb locution (my apologies to your mom), and unfortunately it's a very well-established dumb locution (at least your mom has lots of company).

My surmise is that it's a confusion and blending of *preventive measures* with *maintenance,* which of course amount to the same thing. When it comes to technical verbiage, though, stupidity and redundancy are de rigueur.

Authorities agree that the longer form *preventative* is "an irregularly formed doublet" and the shorter form *preventive* is preferable. One esteemed expert has this to say (and I agree): "*Preventative* never was useful, it being no more than an antique misreading of *preventive.* Because the imposter is centuries old, some dictionaries give it as a variant; no writer need give it a thought."

Couldn't Carelessness

Q. *Why do people say* I could care less *when they really mean the opposite:* I couldn't care less?

◈ I could have been a French teacher

A. Because they don't care at all, and that's sad.

Garner's Modern American Usage says that "although some apologists argue that *could care less* is meant to be sarcastic and not to be taken literally, a more plausible explanation is that the *-n't* of *couldn't* has been rubbed out in sloppy speech and sloppy writing." The folks who say *I could care less* are simply imitating other folks they've heard say it, without pausing to consider the faulty logic of the phrase.

Less Is Not Fewer

Q. *I have a question about the words* fewer *and* less. *I remember learning in school that* fewer *is to be used with numbers under one hundred and* less *is used for higher numbers, which would mean that the signs at the supermarket express lanes incorrectly state* fifteen items or less. *Have you heard of this distinction, and do I have it right?*

A. If we all learned our grammar from what we see in the grocery store, we'd all be in the express lane to illiteracy.

I have indeed heard of this distinction, and you are right that the express-lane signs have it wrong, but the rule you learned in school (or your memory of it) is way off. The distinction is not between lower and higher numbers but between things you can measure and things you can count. Careful writers and speakers use *less* with masses or quantities (*less sugar, less money, less energy*) and *fewer* with things you can count or itemize (*fewer dollars, fewer groceries, fewer ideas*). Thus, those supermarket express-lane signs should say *ten items or fewer,* not *less.*

Good Grief

Q. *When I ask almost anyone "How are you?" these days, the answer I get is "Good," or worse, "I'm doing good." To my ear this sounds dull and charmless, not to mention incorrect. Almost anything else (*fine, all right, so-so*) seems better to me. What do you think?*

A. If you ask a missionary "How are you?" no doubt the answer

but I lacked a certain je ne sais quoi. 🙾

SAY IT AGAIN, SAM!

Pardon me if I *repeat* myself *again,* but in the interest of *collaborating together* at this *particular point in time* to *completely annihilate* the odious verbal virus known as REDUNDANCY, here is a hit list of redundancies, every one of which I assure you I have heard on radio or TV or seen in print. I keep them in a file marked *Please RSVP.* *

Each and every day: Say "each day" or "every day," not both.

Fellow colleague: Your colleague is your fellow worker.

Completely annihilate: Annihilate means "to destroy completely."

Cooperate together and *collaborate together: Cooperate* and *collaborate* both mean "to work together."

Confer together: To *confer* means "to get together to exchange views."

Combine together: Combine means "to mix together."

Recur again: Recur means "to happen again."

Completely unanimous: Unanimous means "to be in complete harmony or agreement."

Completely surrounded: Can something be partially surrounded? To *surround* is already complete. Even worse is the redundancy *completely surrounded on all sides.*

Vacillate back and forth: To *vacillate* means "to waver, go from one side to the other or back and forth."

Report back: Eliminate *back.* To *report* means "to carry back information and repeat it to someone else."

Return it back: To *return* means "to give back." Eliminate *back* again.

Ascend upward: Ascend means "to go upward."

Descend down: Descend means "to go down."

Dwindle down: To *dwindle* means "to decrease or go down gradually."

Passing fad: A *fad* is a brief or passing fashion.

Hoist up and *raise up: Hoist* and *raise* mean "to lift up."

Real fact or *actual fact:* A fact is something real or actual.

Erupt violently or *explode vio-*

Please RSVP is redundant because *SVP* stands for *s'il vous plaît,* French for "if you please."

---

lently: Erupt and *explode* mean "to emerge or burst forth in a violent manner."

Mutual respect for each other: Mutual respect says it all because *mutual* means "for each other, given and received by each one."

Compete with each other: Compete means "to vie with another or others."

Final ultimatum: An *ultimatum* is a final demand.

Final completion and *final conclusion: Completion* and *conclusion* both imply finality, so the word *final* is superfluous.

Visible to the eye and *invisible to the eye:* What else but the eye can something be visible or invisible to—the nose?

Universal panacea or a *panacea for all ills:* A *panacea* is a universal remedy, a cure for all ills.

New recruit: A *recruit* is a newly enlisted person.

Temporary reprieve: Reprieve means "temporary relief."

Necessary requirement: A *requirement* is something necessary.

Opening gambit: A *gambit* is an opening move or a remark intended to open a conversation.

From whence: No need for *from* because *whence* means "from where" or "from what place."

Hot water heater: What else does a water heater do?

Artificial prosthesis: A *prosthesis* is an artificial device that replaces a missing body part, such as a leg.

Stonecut lithographs: A *lithograph* is an engraving made in stone.

An old antique: An *antique* is something old or old-fashioned.

Prerecorded earlier: Something *prerecorded* has been recorded earlier. Say *prerecorded* or *recorded earlier.*

Previous preconceptions: A *preconception* is a conception or opinion formed in advance, an opinion formed previously.

He was not physically present: Was he spiritually present? Did he have an out-of-body experience? Drop *physically* and say you were not present.

Omniscient knowledge of all things: Omniscient means "all-knowing, having knowledge of all things."

but I didn't have any animal magnetism. ☞

SAY IT AGAIN, SAM! *continued*

Current incumbent: An *incumbent* is a person currently holding an office. Don't say *present incumbent,* either.

Individual person: If a person is an individual and an individual is a person, then an "individual person" must be a person who is a person.

He wrote an autobiography of his own life: What other life could an autobiography be about but his own? The same goes for "She wrote a biography of his life." A *biog-* *raphy* is the story of another person's life.

He has an appetite to eat. She is one of two twins. They were dressed identically alike. We have a population of people to feed. She is quite popular with the people. It happened unexpectedly without warning. Given the current problems right now . . .

Are these redundancies *incredible to believe,* or are they simply incredible?

---

will be "I'm doing good." But seriously, you're right —*good* and *I'm doing good* are boring, clunky, and ungrammatical responses to "How are you?" but they are entrenched. Though *well* is the grammatically correct answer to the question, if it were the requisite reply it too would become dull over time. It also happens to sound rather stuffy. So I agree with you that variety is the spice of conversation in this instance. Let's leave *well* and *good* alone and give some other, more descriptive words a chance.

⇥ THREE ⇤

THE GRANDILOQUENT GUMSHOE

Words Recovered, Discovered, and Devised

When memory falters and friends cannot help, when the library has been scoured to no avail, when all avenues of investigation prove fruitless, they come to me. The lexically perplexed. The literally lost. The wordstuck.

I'm a word detective, a certified PVI (private verbal investigator). I recover your lost locutions and patch the holes in your vocabulary. "Grandiloquent Gumshoe" is my handle. My motto is "Reliable. Thorough. Discreet."

My job is to track down that missing piece in your verbal picture of the world, wherever it may be lurking—in the demimonde of dialect and slang, in the cobwebbed corners of cyberspace, in the benthic darkness of an unabridged dictionary.

The wordstuck wayfarers who find their way to my door complain of headaches, insomnia, and trichotillomania (a morbid compulsion to tear out one's hair). A shrink might say they suffer from denotative depression. All I know is they need a word and they don't know who to call—or *whom*, if you prefer to placate the god of grammar rather than the spirit of idiom.

"What do you call that tweed cap that Sherlock Holmes wears, the one with earflaps and visors in the front and back?" Elementary, my dear Watson. It's a *deerstalker*.

"Is there a word for a woman who keeps a man?" Yes, she's a *keeperess*. Samuel Richardson used it in his novel *Clarissa* (1748). You'll find it in the *Oxford English Dictionary.*

"What's that funny squiggle or flourish of the pen that people used in the olden days when signing their names?" It's a *paraph*, and its original purpose (back in the Middle Ages) was to discourage forgery.

"If a female ballet dancer is a ballerina, what's the comparable male word?" *Entre nous*, it's *danseur*, and because you asked, I'll also tell you that the twiddle he does with his feet when he leaps is called an *entrechat*.

"There has to be a word for the act of crossing oneself. Do you know it?" An amateur word detective might try to get away with *genuflection*, but the pro knows that is a bending (Latin *flectere*, to bend) of the knee (Latin *genus*, knee) in prayer or obeisance. The act of crossing oneself, which so often accompanies genuflection, is called *signation* (sig-NAY-shun).

"I have as yet been unable to unearth," wrote a wordstuck translator from Denmark, "a word pertaining to the time (if any such existed) before the creation of Earth, that is, before the Big Bang." Could I help him avoid "a dissatisfyingly verbose paraphrase"?

Could I ever. A dig through the dictionaries unearthed a translator's mother lode, something for every pre–Big Bang occasion: *precosmic*, "before the existence of the universe"; *pretemporal*, "before time began"; *precreative* and *pre-hexameral*, "before the Creation"; *preplanetary*; *pre-terrestrial*; and (my favorite) *antemundane*, "existing or occurring before the creation of the world."

⇥ *I could have been a bank teller*

Many clients want words about words. "I need the word that means 'a precise word for a precise situation.'" For that, *mon ami,* we must go to France and find my old friend *le mot juste.* "Is there a word for words that repeat themselves, like *mama, papa, bye-bye?*" They're called *reduplications* or *reduplicated words.* The term also applies to repetitive couplings in which the initial consonant or a vowel in the second element is changed: e.g., *hoity-toity, namby-pamby, ding-dong, dilly-dally.*

When clients ask me for a locution I suspect is nullibiquitous (not in existence anywhere), I hate to let them down, so I make something up. I've been asked to supply words for everything from bellybutton lint to the feeling of being small and irrelevant in this vast and awesome universe. Adding a few trinkets to the brimming treasure chest of English is a pleasant pastime, and in the following pages I'll display my collection of baubles and gewgaws.

Why do I do this crazy job? I do it because—and I'm not making this up—there's a poseur out there who calls himself "Mr. Language Person" and he must be stopped.* I do it because it gives me a glisk to think that I probably know a few more words than William F. Buckley Jr., who probably doesn't know the meaning of *glisk.* (It's a slight touch of pleasure or twinge of pain that penetrates the soul and passes quickly away.)

If you ever need my services, don't bother looking in the Yellow Pages or the classified ads. Check your local bookstore. I'll be hanging out by the reference shelf, belting down a few bons mots and swapping word stories with the other language mavens.

Log on to Logo-

Q. *A lover of books is called a bibliophile. What do you call a lover of words?*

A. Lucky—or maybe blessed. The general term for a word lover is *logophile* (pronounced like *log a file*), from the Greek *logos,* word,

*The humorist Dave Barry.

but I wasn't ready to make a change.

and *philein,* to love. If you are completely nuts about words, you are a *logomaniac.* And if you are so obsessed with words that you practically have seizures about them, you are a *logolept.*

Answer This ASAP

Q. *I know that in an acronym the initials make a word, like AIDS. But when the initials don't make a word, like HIV, is that also an acronym or is there a special term for that?*

A. They're called *initialisms* when you pronounce them as letters: ATM, SAT, URL, et cetera. They're *acronyms* when you pronounce them as a word: NASA, ZIP code, PIN (*PIN number* is redundant), and so on. Sometimes we can't decide whether the darn thing is an acronym or an initialism; for example, most people call the SAT, the college-entrance exam, an S-A-T, but some say it like *sat.*

Going Ripostal

Q. *Is there a term for that snappy comeback you think of when it's too late to use it—you know, that apt and cutting remark that would have put someone in his place or gotten you a big laugh?*

A. There are three terms, in fact, for the stinging rejoinder that comes to mind too late. One is a French phrase, *esprit de l'escalier* (es-PREE duh les-kal-YAY), that appears in the *Oxford English Dictionary* and dates from 1906. Its literal meaning is "spirit of the staircase," the idea being that the perfect riposte occurs to you while you're ascending the stairs to go to bed. The English equivalent, coined by Kirkpatrick Sale, is *stairwit,* a well-made word that has yet to catch on. And Bernard Cooper coined *retrotort* for any clever remark that comes to mind too late to be of use.

Shanghaied in Podunk

Q. *When the name of a place becomes a word—for example, to* shanghai—*is there a word for that?*

A. The word *toponym* may mean "a place-name" or "a name

◄ I could have been a concert pianist

derived from a place or region." In his book *Crazy English,* recreational linguist Richard Lederer says that "three of the most impressive categories" of toponyms "are alcoholic beverages, foods, and fabrics." Among the examples he cites are *bourbon* (a county in Kentucky), *champagne* (a region in northeastern France), and *gin* (from Geneva, Switzerland); *brie* (French district), *currants* (from Corinth, Greece), and *hamburger* (Hamburg, Germany); and *denim* (de Nîmes, France), *jeans* (Genoa, Italy), and *muslin* (Mosul, Iraq).

Other words that you might not suspect were toponyms include *tuxedo* (Tuxedo Park, New York), *marathon* (from the battle of Marathon, Greece, where the Greeks defeated the Persians in 490 B.C.), *limerick* (a county in Ireland), *spartan* (from Sparta in ancient Greece), *bikini* (an atoll in the Pacific where the atomic and hydrogen bombs were tested), *lyceum* (a gymnasium near Athens where Aristotle taught), and *solecism* (from Soloi, an Athenian colony in Cilicia, Asia Minor, whose inhabitants spoke a form of the Attic dialect that the Athenians considered barbarous and corrupt).

There are even toponyms from imaginary places: *utopian* from Sir Thomas More's *Utopia; Lilliputian* and *Brobdingnagian* from the island of Lilliput and the land of Brobdingnag in Jonathan Swift's *Gulliver's Travels;* and *Camelot* from the legend of King Arthur.

A Hole in the Language

Q. *Is there a companion word for* phallic, *something that means "resembling the female genitals"?*

A. This is a question I too pondered long and hard, so to speak, until one day the answer came to me between the salaciously parted pages of an unabridged dictionary. The companion to *phallic* is *yonic.* It comes from Sanskrit and has been used in English since the late eighteenth century. *Yonic* is the adjective corresponding to the noun *yoni* (YOH-nee), the

eureka shriek
that sharp, guttural exclamation you emit upon finding precisely what you didn't want to find.

but I couldn't get keyed up for it. ☞

Sanskrit word for vulva. *Yoni* is "a stylized representation of the female genitalia," says *Merriam-Webster's Collegiate Dictionary,* eleventh edition, "that in Hinduism is a sign of generative power and that symbolizes the goddess Shakti."

BODACIOUS BRAINTEASER

TASTY TOPONYMS

The word *toponym,* from the Greek *topos,* place, means "a place-name," so a "tasty toponym" is the name of something you eat that incorporates the name of a place. Tasty toponyms come in two forms: either as the actual place-name modifying a noun, as in *New York steak;* or, more commonly, as a place-name adjective modifying a noun, as in *French fries* and *Swiss cheese.*

Complete the following tasty toponyms by filling in the blanks.

1. _____ rabbit
2. _____ toast
3. _____ bean
4. _____ omelet
5. _____ clam chowder
6. _____ broil

Bearing Fruit

Q. *If there's a word for everything, this lexically perplexed person would like to know the word that describes the common practice, most often indulged in by fruit vendors, of loading baskets so the best fruit is on the top and the worst on the bottom, where it is invisible to the prospective buyer.*

A. If there were a word for everything, one of life's most pleasant pastimes—making up silly words—would not exist. And so I humbly offer you these tidbits with which to fill this lacuna in the language: *fructochicanery* and *fructodissimulation.*

Too polysyllabic, you say? Then how about *sleight of fruit?*

I can see you're still not buying it. Oh, all right. The word you

I could have been a musician

seek is the verb *to deacon*. It resides in the monumental *Dictionary of American Regional English* (*DARE*), which traces it back to 1855. It means "to make (something) appear better than it is, esp to arrange (produce) with the best on top."

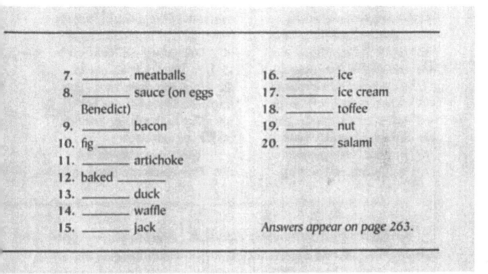

7. _____ meatballs		16. _____ ice	
8. _____ sauce (on eggs Benedict)		17. _____ ice cream	
		18. _____ toffee	
9. _____ bacon		19. _____ nut	
10. fig _____		20. _____ salami	
11. _____ artichoke			
12. baked _____			
13. _____ duck			
14. _____ waffle			
15. _____ jack		*Answers appear on page 263.*	

Things Are Against Us

Q. *I'm looking for a word that describes when inanimate objects conspire against you. Working in a research lab, I can assure you that this frequently happens.*

A. The word you seek is one of my all-time favorites: *resistentialism*, which Paul Hellweg's *Insomniac's Dictionary* defines as "seemingly spiteful behavior manifested by inanimate objects." The adjective is *resistentialist*. The English writer Paul Jennings coined *resistentialism* in 1948 in a parodic essay (a send-up of existentialism) of that title. In the philosophy of resistentialism, Jennings tells us, there is "a grand vision of the Universe as One Thing—the Ultimate Thing (*Dernière Chose*). And it is against us."

but I felt I wasn't noteworthy enough. 🙌

YOU HAVE ANOTHER THING COMING

Resistentialism has a long history in our literature. In his "Ode (Inscribed to W. H. Channing)" (1846), Ralph Waldo Emerson saw the resistentialist writing on the wall and proclaimed that "Things are in the saddle, / And ride mankind." In his autobiography, published posthumously in 1924, Mark Twain relates an anecdote about a recalcitrant burglar alarm in his ornate mansion in Hartford. It "led a gay and careless life, and had no prin-ciples," he says. "We quickly found out that it was fooling us and that it was buzzing its blood-curdling alarm merely for its own amusement." And in J. M. Barrie's *Peter Pan* (1911), Mr. Darling is fit to be tied over his "little brute" of a tie: "This tie, it will not tie . . . Oh yes, twenty times have I made it up round the bed-post, but round my neck, no! Oh dear no! begs to be excused!"

Reports of resistentialism abound in ephemeral literature as

The *Oxford English Dictionary* calls resistentialism a "mock philosophy." As you and I know, and as anyone who has ever had to call a plumber on a Sunday morning to unclog a refractory toilet will attest, there is nothing mock or sham about it. Resistentialism is real, and it is everywhere (especially when you least expect it).

Bellyacher

Q. *I am looking for a word to describe the material (lint) found in bellybuttons. This subject was a recent dinner conversation topic.*

A. First, let me say that I am delighted not to be a guest at your dinner parties. Second, let me suggest *omphalint,* from the Greek *omphalos,* the navel, the source of the word *omphaloskepsis* (ahm-fuh-loh-SKEP-sis), mystical contemplation of one's navel.

Wooden You Know

Q. *In many paintings and sculptures of Christ on the cross there's a little block or shelf of wood under his feet. Is there a word for that piece of wood?*

⇥ *I could have been an electrician*

well. The Peter Tamony Collection at the University of Missouri, Columbia, contains dozens of newspaper clippings documenting resistentialism in everyday life. Among them is a story about a lady in London whose telephone rang every time she attempted to take a bath. No matter what time she drew the bath, day or night, the phone always rang—and when she'd answer it, nobody was there. Things eventually got so bad that she stopped bathing altogether, which prompted her husband to investigate the problem pronto. The cause, he discovered, was a bizarre, electronically telepathic conspiracy between their water heater and the phone.

In the great scheme of things (think about that one!), Jennings tells us, we are no-Thing and Things always win. This is true, I believe, even in the ostensibly placid world of words—for, after all, words are themselves things that in turn signify Things.

A. There is, and I'm happy to foot the bill for it. That little block of wood is called a *suppedaneum,* which by derivation means "something under the foot." You'll find this crucial word, among other places, in the unabridged second edition of *The Random House Dictionary.*

Say Auncle

Q. *If* avuncular *means "pertaining to or like an uncle," is there a word that means "pertaining to or like an aunt"? All I can think of is* auntuncular, *but that sounds like it would pertain to both an aunt and an uncle.*

A. There are three corresponding adjectives for *aunt,* and all of them are as boring as bilgewater, which is probably why nobody uses them. The *Oxford English Dictionary* has two nineteenth-century citations for *auntly,* the best of the lot in my estimation, and *Webster 2* (1934) lists the also-rans *auntish* and *auntlike.*

Why is it, I wonder, that we have need of a word meaning "like

but I was shocked by the long hours. 🖎

an uncle" but we don't seem to need one that means "like an aunt"? If we did, we probably would have formed it the same way we formed *avuncular,* which comes from the Latin *avunculus,* a mother's brother. Had we done this, the companion to *avuncular* would no doubt be *amital* (AM-uh-tul), from the Latin *amita,* a father's sister.

And now, having created that word, I think I'm going to call my aunt Dorothy and solicit her amital opinions on a topic we both love to yak about: baseball.

Lapsing into a Dilemma

Q. *Can you supply a word for the dilemma one faces when trying to think of a word that escapes one's memory?*

A. I can. But first I must point out that, strictly speaking, when one cannot recall a certain word it is not a dilemma that one faces; it is a *lapsus memoriae* (LAP-sus muh-MOR-ee-ee), a slip of the memory. A dilemma is a choice between equally undesirable alternatives. *Lethologica* means "the temporary inability to recall a word," or "difficulty in recalling words in general." The combining form *letho-* means "forgetting" and comes from the Greek *lethe,* forgetfulness; *-logica* comes from the Greek *logos,* word.

Slippery Slope

Q. *What is the handwritten equivalent of a typo?*

A. Have you heard of the Latin phrase *lapsus linguae* (LAP-sus LING-gwee) for a slip of the tongue? Its counterpart in writing is *lapsus calami* (LAP-sus KAL-uh-my), a slip of the pen. A classics professor friend tells me that these phrases may be singular or plural.

Divide and Clunker

Q. *I'm sick and tired of reading my morning newspaper and finding, on practically every page and at least once in every article, an improperly hyphenated word. No, not just improperly hyphenated—*

❧ I could have been an electrician

ridiculously *hyphenated. The problem must be caused mechanically, because not even a dead-drunk journalist would hyphenate monosyllablic words like* worked *(work-ed) or misdivide words like* antishock *(antish-ock),* soonest *(so-onest),* long-standing *(longs-tanding), and* decried *(decr-ied). Is there a word for this kind of illiterate mangling? Maybe if I had a word for it, I wouldn't feel like shredding the paper before I've read it.*

A. Stop the shredders! I have breaking news from the front lines of language. Toni Michael, a writer and editor in San Diego, has proposed the perfect word for these misdivided words: *hyphos.* According to Michael, *hyphos* "cause a reader to stumble, back up, and re-parse the text in order to reconstruct the intended word." They are "an artifact of automated typesetting software . . . commonly and egregiously found in daily newspapers." Do you feel better now? I do.

offsprung
your grown-up child, or grown-up children in general.

offcling
a grown-up child who remains at home, refusing to leave the nest. The word may also be plural, meaning grown-up children who live with their parents.

intalksication
a sluggish, stuporous condition brought on by listening to talk radio, in which one is unable to think clearly, make reasonable judgments, or drive safely.

Cherchez la Femme

Q. *I am searching for the female equivalent of* womanizer. *Can you help?*

A. There is no morphologically congruent companion for *womanizer,* probably because *manizer* is a barbarism even more strange and repugnant than *womanizer.* But there are many words to describe a woman who seduces men and sleeps around.

Let's begin by dismissing the words *whore* and *slut.* They don't fill the bill for two reasons: first, because they are far more offensive than *womanizer;* second, because the former implies that the

but I wasn't emotionally grounded. ☚

❦ QUOTE UNQUOTE ❦

"The man who does not read good books has no advantage over the man who cannot read them." — Mark Twain

woman provides professional services while the latter suggests she submits freely and often rather than chasing or seducing.

The vulgar words *hussy* and *wench,* and the archaic *strumpet,* have also long been used of sexually promiscuous women, and *minx* went from meaning a wanton woman to meaning a saucy, flirtatious one. *Jade* and *biffer* are old terms for a woman who is wanton, disreputable, or feisty. And *temptress, seductress,* and *siren,* though somewhat literary, are unimpeachable female equivalents of *womanizer.*

Then we have the *flirt, coquette,* and *vamp;* all chase and tease men, but only the last connotes interest in having sexual relations. In fact, *vamp* may be your best bet because it so strongly suggests a woman bent on seducing and exploiting men—just as *womanizer* suggests lecherous pursuit, being "on the make." One dictionary defines *vamp* as "an unscrupulous, seductive woman who uses her sex appeal to entrap and exploit men." It's a clipped form of *vampire,* of course, and it's been used this way since the early 1900s.

As good as *vamp* is, however, my vote for the winner goes to *femme fatale,* which English borrowed from French, the language of lovers, in the early 1900s. For me, *femme fatale* perfectly combines the wiles of the temptress with the unscrupulousness of the vamp, then adds two other essential ingredients: mystery and irresistibility. The femme fatale is mysteriously charming, dangerously alluring, and irresistibly sexy.

Cherchez le Fogy

Q. *Is there a word for someone who is attracted to older people?*

❧ *I could have been a police officer*

A. Actually, there are several words pertaining to this idea, all formed from the Greek *gérōn*, old man, and *philein*, to love. The *Oxford English Dictionary* defines the adjective *gerontophil* as "loving or favouring old people, esp. old men; desiring sexual relations with old people." The first citation is from a tract on psychoanalysis published in 1918. The *OED* also lists two nouns: *gerontophilia*, attraction to older people, especially old men, and the very word you seek, *gerontophile*, a person who is attracted to old people.

Don't Look Back

Q. *Please end my decades-old nightmare. For years I've been trying to find a word that means "the fear of review, of revisiting a subject." Do you know of one?*

A. Alas, my friend, I've tracked down some six hundred phobia words, but not that one. But do not despair. Allow the word doctor to prescribe *repetiphobia* and *iteraphobia*. Take those two nonce words and call me in the morning. If you're not feeling better, we'll add two more concoctions to your word cocktail: *byrotephobia*, fear of rote learning or memorization, and *vapulequimortiphobia* (from Latin *vapulare*, to beat, *equus*, horse, and *mortuus*, dead), the fear of listening to someone beat a dead horse.

Diacritical Remarks

Q. *What do you call that little curl above the letter* n *in the Spanish language (as in* mañana *and* señor*)? And what do you call that squiggle under the letter* c *in French that you sometimes also see in the word* façade*?*

A. The curl above *n* is called a *tilde* (TIL-duh), and the squiggle under *c* is a *cedilla* (si-DIL-uh). The tilde indicates that the *n* is nasalized, so it sounds like the first *n* in *onion*. The cedilla indicates that the *c* is pronounced like *s* rather than *k*.

The Erase Is On

Q. *Is there an English word for pencil-eraser detritus?*

but I knew it would be a cop-out. ☞

A. I hope this doesn't rub you the wrong way but no, there isn't. However . . .

The best existing word I can think of for pencil-eraser detritus is *offscourings*. Although it doesn't specify rubbery rubbings, it does precisely denote the condition of the matter in question and how it came to be so. *Detritus* isn't such a bad choice either, though it does have a more pebbly, geological flavor. Then there's *offal*, which still has the off-putting aroma of the slaughterhouse clinging to it. You could also use the general term *leavings*, but it's so general. No, I think *offscourings* is your best choice—unless you'd prefer to invent something silly, like *squibbles*.

Wind Bagged

Q. *Would you please tell me the word for the sound of wind blowing through the trees?*

A. There are two words that cover the general semantic territory of a rustling sound, as of wind among leaves. *Psithurism* (SITH-yur-iz'm) is a whispering sound, particularly the sound of wind whispering in the trees, and *susurrus* (suh-SUR-us) and *susurration* (soo-suh-RAY-shin) can denote any soft rustling, whispering, or murmuring sound. Both these words are mouthfuls, though, so if you're after something poetic you're best off sticking with the simple but lovely *rustle, whisper,* and *murmur.*

Cosmoneology

Q. *I'm looking for a word for that vague feeling you sometimes get when you're looking up at the moon, stars, the totality of space. It's a feeling of being very small and irrelevant in this vast and awesome universe. Is there a word for that?*

A. There is now. The answer came to me as if from above: *cosmononplussation,* the vague, speechless awe one experiences upon gazing up into the cosmos and contemplating the pathetic minuteness of one's being. I have formed *cosmononplussation* from *cosmos* and the rare word *nonplussation,* the state of being nonplussed.

⇥ *I could have been a fisherman*

Phil- of Oneself

Q. *What's the word for a person who is in love with his or her own opinions?*

A. It's *philodox* (like *fill a docks*), from the Greek *philo-*, loving, fond of, and *doxa*, opinion. This uncommonly useful word, which the *Oxford English Dictionary* traces back to 1603, has yet to achieve the currency it so clearly merits. I urge you to use it freely and often—at home, at work, and especially at cocktail parties, where philodoxes abound.

There's a Word for At

Q. *Does the symbol @ have a name other than "the at sign"?*

A. Yes, it may be called a *logogram* or a *grammalogue*. Both words denote a symbol used to indicate a word. Other logograms or grammalogues include %, $, and & (ampersand). I'll admit that these two $20 words won't entirely free you from having to call @ "the at sign," but all things being =, if you ^ (caret) all about words, I think you'll agree that knowing them is a +.

Sick Transit

Q. *Pray tell, what is the word for someone with an insatiable desire to impersonate a transit employee so as to commandeer a bus or train?*

A. *Dangerous.*

As often happens with queries that are over the top, this one came to me with proof that it was a genuine hole in the language. In this case the proof was a clipping from the *New York Daily News* concerning one Darius McCollum, who had been arrested nineteen times over twenty years for taking city buses and subway trains on joyrides. Since we—or at least Mr. McCollum and his prison psychologist—now need a word for a transit employee impersonator, allow me to propose *locomotomaniac*.

cacospectamania
a compulsion to look at something repugnant (formed from the Greek kakos, *bad, Latin* spectare, *to look at, and* -mania, *compulsion).*

but it was too tough to tackle. ☚

Here's the logic: *locomoto-* suggests the vehicle (*locomotive* and *motor*), *loco* suggests someone who is nuts, and *maniac* denotes a person who is obsessed.

For the insatiable desire to commandeer a public transit vehicle, how about *cacoëthes transportandi*? I have formed this grandiloquent mouthful from the unusual Latin loanword *cacoëthes* (kak-oh-EE-theez), an insatiable desire, mania, incurable itch, and the Latin *transportare,* to convey across, transport.

Blackboard Jangle

Q. *There must be a word for the response one has to extremely annoying stimuli like fingernails on a blackboard—something highfalutin from medicine or psychology, perhaps?*

A. There are lots of slang and colloquial terms for such a response. Robert L. Chapman's *Thesaurus of American Slang* gives "the jitters, the all-overs, butterflies, the dithers, the fantods, the fidgets, the heebie-jeebies, the jeebies, the jimjams, the jumps, the leaping heebies, the quivers, the screaming meemies, the shakes, shpilkes, the willies, the wimwams."

Those are general. Then there are some words for uncomfortable, irritating, or unusually potent sensations. For example, *haptodysphoria* is the weird feeling some people get handling peaches, cotton, silk, or anything with a fuzzy surface. A *curglaff* is the shock felt when plunging into cold water. *Formication* is the sense that bugs (especially ants) are crawling over one's body. *Horripilation* is a bristling of the hair on the head or body, also known as *gooseflesh* or, more commonly, *goose pimples* and *goose bumps*. *Polystyrophobia* (my coinage) is a morbid dread of handling or hearing someone handle Styrofoam.

So is there a highfalutin term for an adverse reaction to fingernails on a blackboard? The closest ones I could find were *dysneuria,* a disordered state of the nervous system, and *dysacousia,* a condition in which a noise causes severe discomfort or pain in the ear.

◄ I could have been a fisherman

Car Talk

Q. *Is there a word for the paraphernalia that people attach to their car aerials so that they can find their vehicle easily in a crowded parking lot? If not, we could use one.*

A. I'm quite certain that we don't yet have a word for that, and I agree that one is sorely needed, especially by people whose sensible compact cars are continually lost from view because they are surrounded by Brobdingnagian SUVs.

Allow me to propose *aeriflamme* (AIR-uh-flam), which I have formed from *aerial* and the unusual (and nifty) word *oriflamme*. Originally the oriflamme was a red banner, associated with St. Denis, used as a military ensign and carried before the early kings of France. It comes from the Latin *aurea flamma,* golden flame, ultimately from *flammula,* a little banner. Later the word was used of any battle standard, and then any banner or pennant used as a literal or symbolic rallying point.

Since the original oriflamme had a patron saint, perhaps the aeriflamme could use one too. I nominate the Jack in the Box spokesclown for the job, for he has already been "aerialized" as a cult antihero, at least where I live.

Weed 'Em and Reap

Q. *What do you call it when the beginnings of successive words get spun around in a funny way—for example, if you say "keys and parrots" instead of "peas and carrots"?*

A. When you reverse the initial letters or syllables of two or more words, whether unintentionally or deliberately, you create a venerable bit of wordplay called a *spoonerism,* for which the technical term is *metaphasis,* a transposition of sounds. Sometimes these reversals are nonsensical, like *one swell foop* for *one fell swoop,* but many times they make perfect sense—except in their

smellfeast
someone who has an annoying habit of dropping in uninvited at mealtimes.

but I was concerned about my net worth. ☞

A SOUPÇON OF SPOONERISMS

Here are some other slippery transpositions attributed to William Archibald Spooner:

Is the bean dizzy? *for* is the dean busy?

In a dark, glassly *for* in a glass, darkly.

The weight of rages *for* the rate of wages.

Kinquering Kongs *for* Conquering Kings.

The Lord is a shoving leopard *for* the Lord is a loving shepherd.

Please sew me to another sheet *for* please show me to another seat.

You were fighting a liar in the quadrangle *for* you were lighting a fire in the quadrangle.

---

context. Some examples: *sweeter hitch* for *heater switch*; *blushing crow* for *crushing blow*; *well-boiled icicle* for *well-oiled bicycle*; and *a half-warmed fish* for *a half-formed wish*.

The word *spoonerism*, says *Merriam-Webster's Encyclopedia of Literature*, "is derived from the name of William Archibald Spooner (1833–1930), a distinguished Anglican clergyman and warden of New College, Oxford, who was a nervous man who committed many 'spoonerisms.'" Most of the amusing slips of the tongue attributed to Spooner are probably apocryphal, including two of the best-known: when he supposedly said to a lady in church, "Madam, I believe you are occupewing my pie," and when he reputedly toasted Queen Victoria with the words "Here's to our queer old dean." Another good one, almost certainly invented by Oxford undergraduates, is "You have hissed my mystery lectures and tasted a whole worm."

There are many funny spoonerisms, but my vote for the wittiest one ever goes to this quip attributed to Dorothy Parker of the famed Algonquin Round Table: "I'd rather have a bottle in front of me than a frontal lobotomy."

❧ I could have been a librarian

Capital Ideas

Q. *Lately I've noticed that the names of a lot of companies consist of two words or names made into one, but with the second word or name still capitalized—for example,* SwingLine, ChevronTexaco, DreamWorks, *and* HarperCollins. *Why are they doing that, and what is it called?*

A. I've noticed this too. When two names are combined, perhaps the idea is to signalize a corporate merger. When two words are combined, perhaps the unnecessary capital in the middle is supposed to imply that the company has lots of the other kind of capital.

It's possible that this trend was started by the obsessive innovators in the high-tech industry, where names like *JavaScript, QuarkXPress,* and *WordPerfect* are common. Whatever the reason for it, I suspect it's just a marketing gimmick, another not particularly clever way of giving a company or a product some imagined cachet. If we refuse to name it, maybe the fad will soon blow over and the suits will return to their senses. On the other hand, it may be a greater folly to expect corporate America to behave rationally, in which case we need a word for this because it's going to be with us for a while.

The practice of internal capitalization has been called *BiCapitalization,* and the internal capital letters themselves have been called *intercaps, incaps, midcaps,* and *BiCaps.* To these I humbly add my own creations. For the compound, overcapitalized corporate name, I propose *CorpoNym,* which combines the *corpo-* of *corporation* with the combining form *-(o)nym,* from the Greek *onoma,* name. (To the word maven, *corpo-* also slyly suggests another combining form, *copro-,* which means feces, dung.) For the trend of naming or renaming companies in this ostentatious way, I have two proposals: *upsizing* and *CapitalPains.*

And with that piece of *corp-,* I wash my hands of this dirty business.

but my schedule was already booked. 🙌

Tuft Luck

Q. *For more than twenty years I've been looking for a word. Seems to me a man's facial hair has three parts: mustache, beard, and ——, by which I mean that generally triangular patch beneath the lower lip. I realize some men don't have one. (I do.) For years I've been stopping men who have one and asking them what they call it. I've heard* imperial, stiletto, shiv *(my favorite and what I've taken to calling it), and even found several men who call it their* Zappa, *after rock-and-roll musician Frank Zappa. But what is it really called?*

A. You are asking, sir, for a pogonology (a treatise on beards), and since life presents few opportunities to use a rare and redoubtable word like *pogonology,* I am happy to oblige.

From the sixteenth century onward, there were several terms for it: *barbiche,* a French word that failed to gain entry in English dictionaries; *barbula,* the diminutive of the Latin *barba,* beard, which appears in a few unabridged dictionaries; *barbule,* an anglicized variant of *barbula;* and the colorful *pick-a-divant* (also *picke-divant, pick-divant,* and various other spellings), a word Shakespeare used in *The Taming of the Shrew* that the *Oxford English Dictionary* says is "apparently made up of French words, but itself unknown in French," and which appears to mean "peak(ed) in front." In Randle Holme's *Academy of Armory* (1688) we find this interesting citation: "The Barbula or pick-a-divant, or the little tuft of hair just under the middle of the lower Lip."

But that's all water under the beard. You say you've heard *imperial, stiletto, shiv,* and *Zappa* from modern men who sport sublingual hair. I'm glad they didn't call it a *goatee,* which is a tuft descending from the middle of the chin, just like the beard of a goat. People also incorrectly use *goatee* for a mustache and a chin beard, but this is properly called a *Vandyke. Imperial* is also a misnomer, for that denotes a rectangular mass of chin whiskers longer than a tuft or patch, much like the beard of a pharoah.

Stiletto and *shiv* have potential, suggesting pointiness along

◄I I could have been an erotic dancer

with a certain hip, minatory quality. Another word, preferred by a friend of mine who wears a small tuft, more horizontal than triangular, is *stinger*. (I suspect his wife may be the originator of this name for his hispid excrescence.) And given the distinguished role of eponyms in the language, calling it a *Zappa* makes sense, though technically *Zappa* should denote the straight mustache over a rectangular tuft that the musician wore, for which there already is another name: *Roman T.* Shakespeare sports a Roman T in that famous engraving on the title page of the First Folio (1623), where the Bard looks as if he's just stuck his bald head out of a hole in a painted board and is about to get pelted with pies.

But the one term you did not mention—which has been the most popular name for this itty-bitty beard since the 1990s, and which I'm surprised you didn't hear from one of the men you accosted—is *soul patch*, defined by *The Cassell Dictionary of Slang* (1998) as "a single tuft of hair worn beneath the lower lip."

In a terrific piece of pogonology called "Minds, bodies and soul patches" that I found at espn.com, Locke Peterseim discourses on the history and culture of the soul patch. In the 1950s, when trumpeter Dizzy Gillespie wore one, "it was sometimes called the 'jazz dab,'" he tells us. Other recent jocular names for it include *flavor-saver* and *cookie-duster*. "Unlike geometrically correct goatees, it doesn't say, 'I'm on Satan's team,'" explains Peterseim. "Instead, a soul patch says things like 'I'm cool' or 'I'm a little rebellious' or 'I'm sensitive' or 'I'm a little hung up on myself' or 'I can grow hair right there on that spot below my lip, and some of my friends can't.'"

Impacted **Redacted**

Q. *I am a freelance editor who has been hired to clean up a manuscript by a business executive. I seek a single word that means "negatively affected" (the author keeps using*

slimelight
bad publicity.

but I couldn't handle the grind.

impacted—*yuk!) and another that means "a negative effect." Do either or both exist?*

A. To my knowledge, there is no general, all-purpose term for "negatively affected." Perhaps that's why the lazy writer reaches for *impacted* instead of searching for a more precise word. Using *impact(ed)*, I am fond of saying, is like using a pile driver when a putty knife will do. The writer with more tools in the toolbox will consider the specific negative nuance intended and select the word best suited to the context.

And there are scores and scores of them: *harm, hurt, injure, ruin, impair, poison, vitiate, taint, damage, destroy, hamper, frustrate, limit, hinder, undermine, erode, subvert, corrupt, pervert, cripple, mar, wreak havoc*—well, you get the idea. The same goes for a noun meaning "a negative effect": *damage, loss, harm, hurt, failure, defeat, misfortune, mishap, downturn, deterioration, depletion, corruption, degeneration, limit(ation), hindrance, subversion,* and so on.

I realize this advice, if you choose to follow it, will make your job more difficult. The solution? Charge more. Rescuing people from the miasma of buzzwords and jargon is noble and dangerous work, and you should be duly compensated for it.

Celling Out

Q. *For some time I've been thinking that we really need a word for the havoc wreaked by the incessant and inconsiderate use of cell phones. Is there one, or can you make one up?*

A. Yes, the cell phone—which is fast turning into the more

◄ I could have been a tailor

compact *cellphone,* so we might as well get with it—has indeed become a public nuisance, almost as ubiquitous and annoying as
right-wing talk radio. Everywhere you go these days you see people
with a cellphone glued to their ear. They're discourteously jabber-
ing away, oblivious to the presence of others.

What shall we call this new and vexing brand of verbal pollution? In their *Dictionary of the Future,* Faith Popcorn and Adam
Hanft artfully dub it *secondhand speech,* the verbal equivalent of
secondhand smoke—"not as dangerous," the authors write, "but
more annoying, and definitely hazardous to your peace of mind."

Now that we know what to call the pollution, we need a word
for the polluters: those wireless public prattlers whose one-sided
conversations we are continually forced to share. Allow me to propose *cellfish,* which could also be employed as an adjective. And
what about those few sad souls who still don't possess the means of
instant and constant communication? How about *cellphless?*

Finally, we need something to describe the inattentive and
sometimes reckless way these cellfish drive while they're babbling
into their cranial appendages. For this I propose *celling out* (on analogy with *freaking out, dorking out, spacing out,* etc.).

"#"?

Q. *What do you call the symbol over the number 3 on your keyboard? It looks like this: #. I've heard it called a* cross hatch, *a* pound
sign, *and the* number sign *because it often precedes a number. I've even
heard it called the* tic-tac-toe *sign. What's the correct term?*

A. You may use any of those terms for # if you like, for they are
all legitimate, but if you are talking specifically about the # key on a
touch-tone phone, then the historically accurate locution is not
pound, which we commonly hear in recorded directions over the
phone ("press pound"). It is *octothorpe.* Though you'll have trouble
finding this word in a dictionary, several reliable sources attest to
its authenticity.

but the job didn't suit me. ✍

Here's the story behind it. In the early 1960s, engineers at Bell Telephone developed the # and * keys, originally intending to use them to access computer systems over a telephone line. Calling the * key "the star key" was a no-brainer (do you really think the general public was going to go for "the asterisk key"?), but deciding what to call the # key was another matter. An engineer named Don MacPherson is credited with inventing the word *octothorpe* for this new key. It was a whimsical coinage, created from the Greek and Latin combining form *octo-*, eight (because there are eight points on the symbol), and *Thorpe,* the last name of Jim Thorpe, a famous American athlete MacPherson admired.

Déjà Entre Nous

Q. *If* déjà vu *means the feeling of having experienced or done something before, is there a word or phrase that means the feeling of having read something before?*

A. Indeed there is. It's *déjà lu,* a loan phrase from French that means literally "read already." You'll find it in the *Oxford English Dictionary* between *déjà vu* and another loan phrase, *déjà entendu,* which denotes "a feeling that one has already heard a passage of music, etc., before."

Object Lesson

Q. *In the school where I teach, the students will be staging a kind of United Nations procession in which some of them will carry large fabric banners of different shapes, resembling shields, to identify various countries and their leaders. Is there a word for this object they'll be carrying, or do we need to coin one for it?*

A. There is no need to coin a new word for what you describe. Since the banners resemble shields and will display something akin to armorial bearings—symbols of locality, lineage, and leadership—then I think the word you need is *escutcheon,* from heraldry.

I could have been a painter

Place Time

Q. *I've been looking for a word that means "a person from a particular place." For example, the terms* New Yorker, Californian, *and* Canadian *are what? Is there a word for this?*

sialoquent
spraying saliva while speaking.

A. There is no established word (yet), but a number have been suggested. The best of them, most name specialists agree, is *demonym* (DEM-uh-nym, from Greek *demos,* the people), which is probably the word that will stick. Two well-regarded sources, Frank K. Gallant's *A Place Called Peculiar* and Paul Dickson's *Labels for Locals,* use *demonym.*

Spousal Arousal

Q. *For years now I have been searching for a counterpart to the word* uxorious, *excessively fond of one's wife. Is there a word that means excessively fond of a husband?*

A. You came to the right place, for there is indeed a word for this not necessarily unwholesome malady. The counterpart to *uxorious* is *maritorious,* from Latin *maritus,* husband. You'll find it in various books on unusual words (including my *There's a Word for It*) and in *Webster's New International Dictionary,* second edition (1934), a glorious repository of rare words that I keep on a stand by my left elbow while I work. Now that you know the word, please use it, especially in writing. If enough of us use *maritorious* then perhaps we can rescue it from oblivion and a current dictionary will see fit to list it.

Stage Plight

Q. *Is there an adjective to accompany the noun stage fright, something that means "affected or afflicted with stage fright"?*

A. How about *butterflied?*

but I gave up too easily. 🖘

Humor Me

Q. *I'm trying to recall a word that I think begins with* chacha *and has something to do with wild laughter. Can you help?*

A. If it begins with *chacha* chances are it has something to do with wiggly dancing, not wild laughter. I believe the word you seek is *cachinnate,* to laugh loudly and immoderately (in other words, to roll in the aisles). The corresponding noun is *cachinnation.* The *cach-* is pronounced *kak-*.

Moolah-lah

Q. *I am told there is a word that means "to make money in any way possible." What is it?*

A. How much are you willing to pay me to know?

Oh, all right, I'll tell you. It's *quomodocunquize,* a nonce word formed on the Latin *quomodocunque,* in whatever way. (Pronounce it KWOH-muh-doh-KUNG-kwyz, with primary stress on the penult.) You'll find it listed in the *Oxford English Dictionary,* with a single citation from Sir Thomas Urquhart in 1652: "Those quomodocunquizing clusterfists and rapacious varlets."

⇥ I could have been a pet groomer

Wardee You Want?

Q. *I have given up trying to find a word for a prisoner of a hospital. My sister suggested* wardee. *Will that do?*

> **deipnosophist**
> *an artful or learned dinner conversationalist.*

A. To me, *wardee* sounds more like an inmate in an insane asylum or a resident in an orphanage. There's an obscure word, *nosocomial*, that means "of or pertaining to a hospital," from the Greek word *nosokomeian*, hospital. Perhaps we should just take that Greek word and anglicize it to *nosocomian* and voila! there's your neologism.

Science Faction

Q. *Who coined the word* grok *and what exactly does it mean?*

A. Science fiction novelist Robert A. Heinlein coined it in *Stranger in a Strange Land* (1961). *Merriam-Webster's Collegiate Dictionary,* eleventh edition, defines *grok* as "to understand profoundly and intuitively." A more precise definition might be "to scan all available information regarding a situation, digest it, and form a distilled opinion." It's a nifty word, but outside of people who have read Heinlein, I don't think it has much currency.

Knee-Jerk Reaction

Q. *One night over a late dinner with friends after enjoying a play, it was suggested that we needed words for two things: (1) when sitting in a theater, church pew, baseball stadium, et cetera, the awkward pulling back of the knees we must perform to let someone get by; and (2) that peculiar sideways shuffle we use when moving down an aisle trying to get past people's retracted knees. No one could come up with anything satisfactory. Can you?*

A. I'll certainly try. For (1), allow me to offer *genusuction,* and for (2), *genufriction.* Both are formed from the Latin *genu,* the knee (as in *genuflect,* to bend the knee in worship or respect).

but I deferred that decision.

One day Noah Webster's wife caught her husband taking liberties with the housemaid. "Why, Noah," she exclaimed, "I'm surprised." To which Webster coolly replied, "No, my dear. You are astonished. I am surprised."

I've seen this (probably apocryphal) exchange attributed to other people, but I think it works best with Naughty Noah. It is a little-known fact that this Founding Father of the American language "was by all accounts a severe, correct, humorless, religious, temperate man who was not easy to like, even by other severe, religious, temperate, humorless people," writes Bill Bryson in *The Mother Tongue.* Webster was "short, pale, smug, and boastful," says Bryson, and he was hardly a paragon of scholarship. He took credit for coining words that had been in the language for centuries. He claimed to know twenty-three languages, yet he fabricated many etymologies in his famous dictionary of 1828. And he plagiarized a spelling book by an Englishman named Thomas Dilworth. (H. L. Mencken wrote that Webster was "sufficiently convinced of its merits to imitate it, even to the extent of lifting whole passages.") "It is hard to find anyone saying a good word about him," says Bryson.

Forget Me Not

Q. *When you know a word but you suddenly can't remember it when you need it, is there a word for that?*

A. Yes, there is, but doggone it, I can't remember it right now. (Just kidding.) It's *lethologica,* pronounced leeth-uh-LAH-ji-kuh. It's from *Lethe* (LEE-thee), the river of oblivion in Greek mythology, and the Greek *logos,* word, and it means "the inability to recall the precise word for something." The word for the tendency to forget people's names—especially ten seconds after you meet them—is *lethonomia* (leeth-uh-NOH-mee-uh).

Navel Exercises

Q. *Someone once told me about a word that meant "obsessed with*

⇥ *I could have been a hack writer*

looking at one's bellybutton" or something like that. Do you know this word?

A. The word you seek is *embellishment.* Actually it's *buttonholing.* Or maybe *dumbilical.* Oh, all right. "For reals," as my kids say, the word is *omphaloskepsis,* the practice of gazing at one's navel as a mystical exercise or, humorously, as a manifestation of or metaphor for self-centeredness. It comes from the Greek *omphalos,* navel, bellybutton, and *skepsis,* the act of looking.

Inanities

Q. *I'm a male nanny. Is there a word for that?*

A. How about *manny?*

But seriously, you could call yourself a *pedagogue,* a word now used as a fancy synonym for teacher but which descends from a Greek word for a slave charged with caring for the master's children, feeding them, taking them to school, and so on.

Men-*diss*-ity

Q. *If a misogynist is a hater of women, what do you call a hater of men?*

A. Justified? (Just kidding—sort of.) The word you seek is *misandrist* (stress on *-an-* or *mis-*), from *mis-,* hate, and *andro-,* man, male. The *Oxford English Dictionary* traces the corresponding *misandry,* hatred of men, from 1946.

Say No More

Q. *I've been losing sleep looking for a noun meaning a person who doesn't speak much, who uses very few words. Can you help me rest easy?*

A. I'll give you two for the price of one: *laconizer* (LAK-uh-ny-zur), from *laconic,* and *taciturnist* (TAS-i-tur-nist), from *taciturn.* Both appear in *Webster's New International Dictionary,* second edition (1934). That's all I have to say on the matter. Now go to bed.

ozoamblyrosis
loss of sexual appetite because your partner has wicked BO.

but I couldn't cough up any ideas. ☚

What Do You Do When You're Unbranded?

Q. *Is there a word for when a brand name becomes the everyday, generic word for something? For example, we xerox (photocopy) a document, put up sheetrock (drywall), and google (search electronically) stuff on the Internet.*

BODACIOUS BRAINTEASER

ARE YOU AN IDIOM SAVANT?

Below you will find the first part of various clichés. Can you provide the missing final piece of each well-worn expression?

1. the gospel . . .
2. once in a . . .
3. where there's smoke . . .
4. come hell . . .
5. pleased as . . .
6. hook . . .
7. the wrong side . . .
8. one good turn . . .
9. it's raining . . .
10. give it the old . . .
11. blood is . . .
12. in the twinkling . . .
13. a diamond . . .
14. like a bull . . .

A. "The practice, abhorred by lawyers, of using a trademark (like Kleenex or Xerox) as a generic term," says Erin McKean in *More Weird and Wonderful Words*, is called *antonomasia*. McKean is stretching the established meaning of this word quite a bit—dictionaries give two definitions for it: (1) the use of a title or epithet instead of a name, as in *Her Majesty* for a queen or *Prince of Darkness* for Satan; and (2) the use of a proper name to express a general idea, as in *Einstein* for a genius and *Sherlock* for a clever sleuth—but I think it's a reasonable and useful stretch.

If antonomasia becomes rampant, the trademark usually becomes generic. That's what happened with *aspirin, escalator, saran wrap, thermos, zipper,* and many other words. But *Xerox, Sheetrock,* and *Google,* as their lawyers will greedily inform you, have not yet

I could have been Lizzie Borden

become generic; they are daily victims of antonomasia that must still, by law, be capitalized. So is there a word for when a trademark finally succumbs to antonomasia and becomes generic?

Constance Hale, America's regnant digistylist and coauthor of *Wired Style: Principles of English Usage in the Digital Age,* may have

---

15. as plain as . . .	24. to gird (or gird up) . . .
16. to wear out . . .	25. to damn . . .
17. all's fair . . .	26. the show . . .
18. a wolf . . .	27. make hay . . .
19. like a bump . . .	28. face . . .
20. to throw out . . .	29. look a . . .
21. sitting in . . .	30. read (someone) the . . .
22. from soup . . .	
23. something is rotten . . .	*Answers appear on page 263.*

---

the answer. In email correspondence with me concerning whether to capitalize or lowercase the trademark *Listserv,* she argued that "Listserv's been kleenexed." That's a great coinage, and very catchy. The only problem is, *Kleenex* hasn't quite been *kleenexed.* So if you're worried about pesky lawyers hounding you for using a lowercase *k,* until antonomasia prevails you could say something's been *zippered* or *aspirined* instead.

Quoth the Ravin' Maven

Q. *What would you call a place where language mavens gather? A* mavenry, *perhaps?*

A. How about *heaven*? On second thought, that would imply that we've all gone to meet our word maker. I think your *mavenry,*

but I didn't have the chops. 🐦

like *citizenry,* would best refer to language mavens collectively, as: "Charles Harrington Elster is the cleverest maven in all mavenry!" It could also mean the act of a maven or the practice of being one: "Elster's mavenry is beyond compare!" For a place where language mavens congregate or rule, I would suggest *mavendom.*

BODACIOUS BRAINTEASER

ARE YOU BRANDILOQUENT?

Words that seem generic but are still trade names, and capitalized:

1. The owners of this word want you to say "photocopy" instead.
2. Does anyone ever really call this product "facial tissue"?
3. You can put it on a cut, on a scrape, or on diplomacy.
4. They clean ears and a lot of other things too.
5. Bill Cosby was a pitch man for this rubbery snack.
6. It took the skate out of roller skate.
7. It's the sport officially called "table tennis."
8. The plastic packing bubbles that replaced excelsior.
9. In the summer, kids love to lick this sweet, fruit-flavored, frozen treat.
10. It's sticky on one side, smooth on the other.
11. We use it to call attention to words printed on a page.
12. My mother calls them dungarees, but they are often called . . .
13. It looks like a flying saucer.
14. With this popular device, you can listen while you ambulate.

Talking the Walk

Q. *Please help me! I am seeking a word for the outlaw paths that crop up everywhere soon after official walkways have been laid out— the little shortcuts and cow paths that people make and take instead of the sidewalks and formal paths. Is there a term for these?*

I could have been a drummer

A. I have heard that *social paths* has been suggested for this, but that is dull as dog food. Since no single word exists for this, as far as I know—but what the heck do I know?—let's make one up.

How about *beelines*? Or maybe *commutions*? No, wait. I think they are best called *jayways*—a playful blend of *jaywalk* and *walkway.*

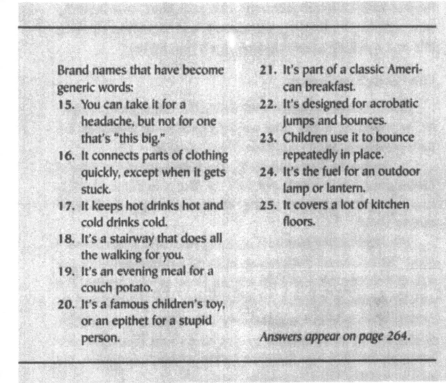

Brand names that have become generic words:

15. You can take it for a headache, but not for one that's "this big."
16. It connects parts of clothing quickly, except when it gets stuck.
17. It keeps hot drinks hot and cold drinks cold.
18. It's a stairway that does all the walking for you.
19. It's an evening meal for a couch potato.
20. It's a famous children's toy, or an epithet for a stupid person.
21. It's part of a classic American breakfast.
22. It's designed for acrobatic jumps and bounces.
23. Children use it to bounce repeatedly in place.
24. It's the fuel for an outdoor lamp or lantern.
25. It covers a lot of kitchen floors.

Answers appear on page 264.

Wipe That Smiley off Your Face

Q. *What do you call those funny "drawings" people use in email, which they create with various punctuation marks? For example, that sideways smiley face?*

A. These "treacly expressions of emotion," says *Wired Style:*

but I couldn't stick it out. 🖘

Principles of English Usage in the Digital Age, are called *emoticons* or, less often, *smileys.* "First created by Scott Fahlman . . . around 1980, these small graphical renderings, composed of ASCII characters, substitute for facial expressions and gestures." By 1990 both words had gone mainstream, and today most dictionaries list them.

Common emoticons include :-) the smiling face, ;-) the winking face, and :-(the face of dismay or chagrin. More esoteric emoticons include :-D a laughing person; <:/& a person whose stomach is in knots; and, my graphic favorite, (_x_) "kiss my ass."

Everybody's an Expert

Q. *I once came across a wonderful word that meant giving an opinion on something outside your area of expertise—or something like that—and I've forgotten what it was. Do you know it?*

A. You betcha. The word is *ultracrepidarian,* and you're right: It means going beyond one's sphere of knowledge or influence in offering an opinion, flappin' your gums about stuff you don't know nuthin' about.

Ultracrepidarian comes from the Latin maxim *ne sutor ultra crepidam,* "let not the cobbler overstep his last," a maxim pertaining to a story about a cobbler and the ancient Greek painter Apelles. The cobbler noticed a defect in a shoe Apelles had painted and remarked on it. Apelles was grateful for the advice, and the cobbler, encouraged by this, presumed to give his opinion about other elements in the painting. Annoyed by the cobbler's arrogance, the painter scolded, "Cobbler, stick to your last."

Naming Names

Q. *There's a word I'm trying to remember that means "a name that reveals something about a person or that corresponds with what they do." Do you know it?*

A. There are a couple of words that apply. An *aptronym* is an apt name, one that is especially descriptive of or suited to a person: for

◄ I could have been a golfer

example, William Wordsworth, the poet; Margaret Court, the tennis player; Gray Davis, the sober, gray-haired former governor of California; and Marilyn vos Savant, the *Parade* columnist who has the world's highest recorded IQ. Often the aptronym is humorously unsuitable—like Robert Coffin for an undertaker or Dr. Gas for a gastroenterologist—in which case I would call it a *distronym* or a *jocunym*. A *euonym* is an especially auspicious name, like Jesus, which means savior, or Harry Truman.

Bed-*read*-en

Q. *I love to read in bed. Is there a word for a person who does that?*

A. There is now: *librocubiculist.* I am coining it from the Latin *liber,* book, which when employed in English words often changes its spelling to *libr-*; the Latin *cubiculum,* a bedchamber; and the suffix *-ist,* which in this case denotes a person who performs a certain action. Pronounce it ly-broh-kyoo-BIK-yuh-list.

A Male Issue

Q. *I am trying to track down the word for a man who has only sons, no daughters.*

A. That word is *arrhenotokous,* pronounced ar-uh-NOT-uh-kus. It means "having only male offspring," and so could apply to a man, woman, or a couple. The word for "having only female offspring" is *thelyotokous* (thel-ee-AHT-uh-kus), and the word for "having both male and female offspring" is *ampherotokous* (am-fur-AHT-uh-kus).

Words into Word-Process

Q. *In the days of the typewriter, a letter or a document was typewritten. Is there a word—or words—that describes the same letter or document created on a computer?*

A. Dictionaries list the verb *word process,* which would apply, though it stinks so badly of jargon that I doubt it's used much

but I didn't know what for. ☞

outside of business gobbledygook. Can you imagine someone asking you how fast you can *word process* rather than type? Like *manuscript* (literally "written by hand"), *type, typing,* and *typewritten* have transcended their literal meaning and are applied to creating documents on computers.

A Pop-up Quiz

Q. *Is there a word for the experience of hearing or seeing something new and then, soon after, hearing or seeing it again, sometimes more than once? I'm sure this is a common experience, and so I thought there must (or ought to be) a word for it.*

A. Though the experience you describe is certainly common, I'm not sure anyone's come up with a word for it yet. But let me offer you some words that come close.

First, *synchronicity.* The Swiss psychologist Carl Jung coined this word for "a meaningful coincidence," as when you are thinking of an old friend you haven't heard from in a long while and then he or she emails you or calls you on the phone.

Closer than that, I think, is *meme* (rhymes with *seem*), which biologist Richard Dawkins coined in the final chapter of his book *The Selfish Gene.* The eleventh edition of *Merriam-Webster's Collegiate Dictionary* defines *meme* as "an idea, behavior, style, or usage that spreads from person to person within a culture." It's like a trend or fad, but more subtle, more telepathic.

Yet both of these words don't capture that kind of "déjà vu all over again" experience that most of us have had. (I have often had it with a new word; somehow it would find a way of popping up again once or twice a short time after I had learned it.) For that, I suggest that we resurrect a serviceable word that has fallen into disuse: *reperception* (from *re-*, again, and *perception*). I found *reperception* in the glorious *Century Dictionary* (I have the final 1914 edition), defined as "the act of perceiving again; a repeated perception." That's essentially what we're talking about, isn't it?

I could have been a tennis player

Taking Your Volumps

Q. *Many years ago I worked with a fellow who was a master at mangling the language. I especially remember one hilarious word he was fond of using for a shapely woman:* volumptuous. *I was shocked recently to hear this very word not once but twice on television. Is* volumptuous *a real word after all? Are people now going to start saying, "Get a load of the* volumps *on her"?*

agathocacological
composed of both good and evil, or pertaining to both good and evil.

horbgorble
to putter around aimlessly.

A. If used of a shapely and attractive woman, *volumptuous* is a corruption of *voluptuous* and a mistake, plain and simple. That said, I must tell you that *volumptuous* is in fact a word, though not one with any currency to speak of, and you won't find it in a dictionary. It's a joculism that appears in a delightful book of "words that don't exist but ought to" called *In a Word,* edited by Jack Hitt. It was coined by Colin Harrison, an associate editor at *Harper's* magazine, to describe a woman who is grossly overweight after having once been attractively buxom. In this sense, getting a load of someone's *volumps* would be another load altogether.

A Groovy Word

Q. *Is there a word for the vertical groove that runs from the nose to the upper lip?*

A. *Philtrum* is the word you seek. Interestingly, this anatomical term can be traced ultimately to the Greek *philein,* to love.

Your Pain Is My Pleasure

Q. *I understand there's a word for deriving pleasure from someone else's misfortune or misery. What is it, and is it from German?*

A. Yes, it is. The word is *schadenfreude,* from *Schaden,* harm, and *Freude,* joy. Though it has been used in English for a little over a century, it is still sometimes printed with a capital *S.*

but I had no love for the game.

LIT CRIT 101

Probably since the dawn of writing, writers have been practicing the not-so-gentle art of literary criticism—saying scathing things about each other. (Yes, I wrote *each other* and not *one another*. Although some still insist on using *each other* for two and *one another* for more than two, for years usage authorities have been telling us that the phrases are interchangeable and there is nothing to be gained by observing the distinction, which is not supported by actual usage.) Here are some of my favorite literary quips, gibes, and jabs:

"Reading him is like wading through glue."—Alfred, Lord Tennyson on Ben Jonson

"He was dull in company, dull in his closet, dull everywhere. He was dull in a new way, and that made many people think him *great*."—Samuel Johnson on Thomas Gray

"To me, Poe's prose is unreadable—like Jane Austen's. No, there is a difference. I could read his prose on a salary, but not Jane's."—Mark Twain

"The more I read, the less I wonder that they poisoned him."—Thomas Babington Macaulay on Socrates

"Mr. Henry James writes fiction as if it were a painful duty."—Oscar Wilde

"The nicest old lady I ever met."—William Faulkner on Henry James

"When you enter a Faulkner sentence, wave goodbye to friends and family. You won't be seeing them for a long time."—Frank McCourt

"Virginia Woolf's writing is no more than glamorous knitting. I believe she must have

---

Of *schadenfreude*, the nineteenth-century theologian and philologist Richard Chenevix Trench had this to say in *On the Study of Words* (1851): "What a fearful thing is it that any language should have a word expressive of the pleasure which men feel at the calamaties of others; for the existence of the word bears testimony to the existence of the thing."

I could have been a mason

a pattern somewhere."
—Edith Sitwell

"His style has the desperate jauntiness of an orchestra fiddling away for dear life on a sinking ship."—Edmund Wilson on Evelyn Waugh

"His careful and pedestrian and sometimes rather intelligent book reviews misguide one into thinking there is something in his head besides mucilage. There isn't."
—Raymond Chandler on Edmund Wilson

"Our only hippo-poetess."—Ezra Pound on Amy Lowell

"[Ernest Hemingway's] effect upon women is such that they want to go right out and get him and bring him home stuffed."—Dorothy Parker

"The greatest mind ever to stay in prep school."—Norman Mailer on J. D. Salinger

"For the reader who has put away comic books, but isn't ready yet for editorials in the *Daily News*."—Gloria Steinem on Jacqueline Susann

"If it were thought that anything I wrote was influenced by Robert Frost, I would take that particular work of mine, shred it, and flush it down the toilet, hoping not to clog the pipes."—James Dickey on Robert Frost

"That's not writing—that's typing."—Truman Capote on Jack Kerouac

"He has made lying an art. A minor art."—Gore Vidal on Truman Capote

"Every word she writes is a lie, including *and* and *the*."
—Mary McCarthy on Lillian Hellman

In contemporary America, where no opportunity to make a buck is overlooked, people have made a thriving business out of *schadenfreude*. From tabloids that revel in exposing the sorrows and foibles of celebrities to TV shows featuring home videos of embarrassing and often injurious mishaps, other people's pain has become our pastime.

but I can't make concrete plans. 🐾

Forget and Relive

Q. *I once heard that there's a word or maybe a phrase for a woman's ability to forget the pain of childbirth. Do you know what it is?*

A. It's a phrase: *parturient amnesia.* (*Parturient*, pronounced pahr-CHOOR-ee-int, means pertaining to childbirth.) Without this remarkable form of oblivion I suspect the human race would have become the human e-race, long before the advent of epidural anesthesia.

Unaligned

Q. *Do you know the word for an actor who comes onstage but doesn't speak, whose only job is to silently perform a task or accompany another actor with a speaking role?*

A. There are two words for this: *walk-on* may denote either an actor with a minor, nonspeaking role or the role itself, and *supernumerary*, an actor who plays a walk-on.

Gesture Kind of Word

Q. *I'm looking for a word for someone who gestures a lot (often in an annoying manner) while conversing. Do you know of one?*

A. To *gesticulate* means "to make gestures especially when speaking," says one current dictionary. But an even better word, I think, is *hypermimia,* which means "waving the hands a lot while speaking, gesticulating grandly or a great deal." A person exhibiting hypermimia would be a *hypermimic.* And a comedian who does impersonations of gesticulating celebrities would be a *hypermimic hyper mimic.*

Lip-Think

Q. *Is there a word for reading lips?*

A. I'm tempted to coin the verb to *lipthink* but there's already a noun for lip reading: *labiomancy.* This rare word—for which the

◄ I could have been a skier

Oxford English Dictionary has only two citations, from 1686 and 1812—unites the combining forms *labio-*, the lips, and *-mancy*,
from the Greek *mantéia*, divination. Now, I

periblepsis
*the wild look that ac-
companies delirium.*

don't think you have to be a *labiomancer* to know what I'm going to
say next:

   This chapter is over.

but that idea went downhill fast. 🖙

⊱ FOUR ⊰
THE ELEGANCE OF STYLE

Distinctions, Clarifications, Niceties,
and Other Little Things That
Make Your Language
More Polished and Precise

In this chapter I will help you find the worm in the apple of your expression and dig it out. I will share with you some useful tips and lessons that I have learned in more than twenty years as a writer, editor, and language maven—things that will help make your speech and writing more professional. I will wipe the dust off your diction, clean up your verbal clutter, and dispel the fog surrounding various perplexing questions of style.

I address your thoughtful questions about word choices, word distinctions, spelling, punctuation, and grammar, hoping to guide you not toward some crotchety vision of style but toward what is considered the best usage, as I have gleaned it, from the best authorities. And I do so hoping that you will come to share with me the vision of the English poet and artist William Blake (1757–1827), who wrote that "without minute neatness of execution the sublime cannot exist."

Minute neatness of execution. Therein lies the elegance of style.

"Skill in expression," writes Wilson Follett in *Modern American*

POMPOUS PROVERBS

This is a game of translation from the bombastic and grandiloquent to the simple and direct. Below you will find various well-known and well-worn sayings that have been translated into outrageously inflated, overblown diction. Your task is to decipher the highfalutin diction and translate these pompous proverbs back into plain English. For example, *precipitancy engenders prodigality* translates into *haste makes waste*, and *surveillance should precede saltation* means *look before you leap*.

1. Avian species of identical plumage congregate.
2. Male cadavers are unyielding of testimony.
3. The stylus is more potent than the claymore.
4. Lachrymation or ululation in response to accidentally effused lacteal fluid is inadvisable.
5. A plethora of culinary cognoscenti vitiates the potable concoction.
6. Hubris antedates a gravity-impelled descent.
7. Freedom from foul and nox-

Usage (1966), "consists in nothing else than choosing the fittest among all possible words, idioms, and constructions."

Let the choosing begin.

Dad Doesn't Have a Leg to Stand On

Q. *The other day I was reading a book about sea creatures to my four-year-old son. When he saw a picture of an octopus he pointed to it and said, "Mommy, why do octopuses have so many legs?" My husband,*

◄ I could have been a chiropractor

overhearing him, came into the room and told him the plural was octopi, *not* octopuses. *The dictionary gives both forms. Is one more correct?*

A. Clearly, your son gets his above-average intelligence from his mom, not his dad.

---

ious incrustations is proximate to rectitude and conformity with divine prescription.

8. Not every object that coruscates with resplendence will assay auriferous.

9. Eleemosynary activities have their incipience domestically.

10. Inhabitants of vitreous edifices of patent frangibility are hereby admonished not to jaculate petrous projectiles.

11. The existence of visible vaporous emissions from ignited carbonaceous materials confirms conflagration.

12. It is futile to endeavor to inculcate innovative maneuvers in a superannuated canine.

13. Abstention from speculatory undertaking precludes achievement.

14. Gramineous organisms are perpetually more verdant in an adjacent location.

15. Pulchritude possesses solely cutaneous profundity.

Answers appear on page 264.

There are three plurals for *octopus,* one obsolescent, one standard, and one unacceptable. The classically correct plural, rarely used today, is *octopodes,* pronounced ahk-TOP-uh-deez; I say "classically correct" because it exactly follows the Greek. But the standard form nowadays is the anglicized *octopuses,* formed with -*es* like other regular English plurals. Now, because *octopus* comes from Greek, not Latin, the Latinate variant *octopi* is inappropriate and is frowned upon by usage authorities.

but I found it wasn't all it was cracked up to be.

WHAT IDIOT PROGRAMMED MY SPELL-CHECKER?

Ever wonder whether your computer's spell-checker is trustworthy? Try running it on this passage:

> I have bin trying too improvise my spelling for sum thyme now cents my secretary all ways says that it isn't two grate. I try too right good butt eye half trouble with spelling and usages and I doughnut under stand why my computer don't seam to ketch my airs.

I ran my Microsoft Word spelling and grammar wizard on that mess many times on many different occasions, and it burped a grand total of three times. It suggested that I change *improvise* to *improvising*, change *two grate* to *two grates*, and change *right* to *righting*. Huh?

So pat your son on the head and tell your husband I say *nyah-na-nyah-na-nyah-na*. And thanks for not asking me to explain why octopuses have so many legs.

Who's Guarding the Gates?

Q. *Is* supercede *now an acceptable spelling variation of* supersede? *One of my staff members says it is and claimed Microsoft Word's spell-checker accepts both spellings. That surprised me, to say the least. Are Bill Gates and his minions now the chief arbiters of the English language?*

A. Heaven forfend! Cobbler, stick to thy last.*

When I ran the sentence "Is it *supercede* or *supersede*?" through my Microsoft Word spell-checker, it burped on *supercede* but did not offer to replace it with *supersede*. Instead it said, "Non-standard word (consider revising)," inserting a nonstandard hyphen in

*See the discussion of *ultracrepidarian* on page 108.

◄੨I I could have been a writer

nonstandard. When I ran the spell-checker on *supercede* alone, all it did was suggest that I capitalize the word.

I could go on a rant, but I'll forbear. Let's just say that spelling and grammar checkers are not dictionaries and usage manuals, and that they are about as close to dictionaries and usage manuals as pig slops are to haute cuisine. Anyone who relies solely on Microsoft Word's ability to identify errors or problems in a piece of writing is a blockhead. Tell your staff member, "Get thee to a dictionary!" The correct spelling, historically and etymologically, is *supersede,* not *supercede.* Even the complacently permissive *Merriam-Webster's Collegiate Dictionary,* which lists *supercede* as a variant, admits that it is "widely regarded as an error."

And while we're at it, it's *minuscule* (from Latin *minusculus,* somewhat small), not *miniscule.* Microsoft Word's blockheaded spell-checker accepts both spellings.

Don't Send Me Your Regards

Q. *What is your opinion of* in regards to *and* irregardless? *I have a supervisor who uses them constantly and it drives me bananas. Am I wrong to object to this?*

A. Not at all. Your supervisor is a grobian (a rude, clownish, blundering oaf). *In regards to* is a semiliterate blunder; it should be *in* or *with regard to* or, even better and more succinct, *regarding, concerning,* or *about.* And *irregardless* is an illiterate blunder, a useless word that means the opposite of what its clueless user intends: *not without regard.* Careful writers and speakers always use *regardless.*

The Plane Will Land Momentarily

Q. *When did* momentarily *stop meaning "for a moment" and start meaning "in a moment"? I hear it used in the latter sense all the time nowadays.*

A. The *Oxford English Dictionary* shows that *momentarily* has been used in print to mean "at any moment" or "in a moment"

but I found out it wasn't such a novel idea.

🦋 QUOTE UNQUOTE 🦋

*"I find TV very educational. The minute somebody turns it on,
I go to the library and read a book."—Groucho Marx*

since at least 1928. This sense is widespread in North America, where it originated, and rare in Britain.

Though some argue that context always makes the intended sense of the word clear—whether it's "for a moment" or "in a moment"—I disagree. If your supervisor says she can meet with you momentarily, how can you be certain what she means? If the tour guide says you'll be able to see the Gorgeous Mountains out the bus window momentarily, does it mean the mountains will be visible soon or you'll just be able to catch a glimpse of them? To avoid ambiguity and confusion (and perhaps ridicule), I recommend restricting *momentarily* to the original and much older sense "for a moment," which is still very much alive. And when you mean "in a moment" just say *in a moment*; your meaning will be clear and you'll save a syllable.

What Mails You?

Q. *At work I recently said, "They're using those lists to send solicitations through the mails." Some respected colleagues thought I should have said "through the* mail." *Is* mail *singular, plural, both, neither?*

A. Both *mail* and *mails* have been recorded for the sense in which you used it: "the postal system." The singular form is by far the dominant one, however. Current American dictionaries label the plural form with *also* to indicate that it is, as one dictionary puts it, "appreciably less common."

Mail formerly was also used of the bag in which mail was transported, and dictionaries still record the definition "a train, boat, or

🦋 *I could have been a photographer*

other vehicle in which mail is conveyed." It is probably because of these meanings that the plural form survives in such phrases as *in the mails* and *through the mails*. My sense, though, is that the plural form not only is far less common but now also old-fashioned, which no doubt is why your colleagues called you on it.

Not for Everybody

Q. *Which is correct or preferable:* safety is everyone's business *or* safety is everybody's business? *The first sounds better to me.*

A. *Everyone* is preferable only because it sounds better, not because *everybody* is incorrect in this context. The terms are interchangeable, and as one authority notes, "euphony governs the choice in any given context." *Everyone* must sound better to most people because it's used about twice as often in print. But in many other casual contexts *everybody* is preferred (*C'mon, everybody!*). As in so many cases, let your ear be your guide.

Asbestos We Can

Q. *The phrase* as best as we can *is, to my ear, like fingernails on a chalkboard. I have heard President Bush and many others use it. Am I right that it's wrong?*

A. You're right. The second *as* in *as best as* is superfluous. *As best we can* is the preferred form. Probably false analogy with locutions like *as far as, as long as,* and *as well as* has caused the confusion.

A Seedy Question

Q. *Why do words that derive from the Latin* cedere *have different spellings—for example,* proceed, succeed, concede, precede?

A. *Proceed, succeed,* and *exceed*—the only common words from the Latin *cedere* (to go, proceed, or to give ground, withdraw) that end in *-ceed*—are aberrations, the regular form being *-cede*. English spelling before 1800 was volatile, and various forms of these words (ending in *-cede, -ceede, -ceed,* and even *-ceid* and a couple of other

but I had a negative experience as a child. 🔄

variants) competed for ascendancy, sometimes for centuries. The *-ceed* variants for *proceed, succeed,* and *exceed,* which have obtained since the sixteenth century, won out.

On the Take

Q. *Why are people in diplomatic circles always "taking" a decision? Could it be that for a long time French was the language of diplomacy, and the French don't "make" (*faire*) decisions, they "take" (*prendre*) them?*

A. *Take a decision* may have come to English from French (your speculation is certainly plausible), but this idiom is incontestably British. Norman W. Schur's excellent and authoritative *British English, A to Zed* gives *take a decision* as the British version of the American *make a decision.* Another salient difference of this type is the American *run for office* versus the British *stand for office.*

Cantankerous

Can I get? Can I get?
No you can't, at least not yet.

Can I get? Can I get?
Your diction makes me quite upset.

Can I get? Can I get?
The question lacks all etiquette.

Can I get? Can I get?
Do I hate it? Yes, you bet!

I want to tell the *can-I-getter*
That *may I have* is far, far better.

Better still is when you say:
May I please have? Indeed, you may!

⇥ *I could have been a fortune-teller*

> ## ⚘ QUOTE UNQUOTE ⚘
>
> *An aspiring writer once asked Samuel Johnson, the great eighteenth-century lexicographer and literary sage, to evaluate his manuscript. Dr. Johnson obliged and dashed off this critique: "Your work is both original and good. Unfortunately, the parts that are good are not original, and the parts that are original are not good."*

Nonissue

Q. *Our company's marketing director writes the ad copy for us, which then comes to me for editing. We are squabbling over whether it should be* nontraditional *or* non-traditional. *The sources I checked say no hyphen (or at least not anymore). The marketing director insists it should be hyphenated. What's your opinion?*

A. The sources you checked are right. Words beginning with *non* should *not* be hyphenated, even when *non* is followed by a vowel or an *n*. Thus, modern style prefers *nontraditional, noninterference, nonflammable, nonbeliever, nonunion,* and so on. Though you often see *non-profit,* to take one common erroneous example, it "is always ill-advised," says *Garner's Modern American Usage.* The word is properly written *nonprofit* and is listed so in current dictionaries.

The stylebook of The Associated Press recommends using a hyphen "in awkward combinations, such as *non-nuclear,*" but fails to define what an awkward combination is or provide any other examples, thus leaving things up to individual editors and turning a nonissue into a potentially contentious non-issue. You are best off following the other style guides, which note that the only time a hyphen occurs after *non* is when the following element is a capitalized word: *non-Christian, non-Turkish, non-Darwinian.*

but I didn't see any future in it. ⟵

Going after *After*

Q. *The use of* after *as an adverb instead of a preposition with a proper object always rubs me the wrong way: "Soon after, we left the party." I would change it to* afterward. *Do you know of a rule for this?*

A. I guess you're going to have to change those fairy-tale endings to "and they lived happily ever afterward." The *Oxford English*

TEA-TOTALLY

This is truly a brain-*tea*-ser because it's about words with the sound of *tea* at the end. One day, while sipping some delicious Honest Tea, it occurred to me that there were a lot more words beside *honesty* that ended with *tea*. Thus was born this game.

These teas end in -ty:

1. This tea makes you nervous, raises your stress level:

   _ _ _ _ _ _

2. This tea is inexpensive; it's perfect for pennypinchers:

   _ _ _ _ _ _

3. This tea will set you free:

   _ _ _ _ _ _

4. This tea is preferred at twelve-step program meetings: _ _ _ _ _ _ _

5. This tea is exceptionally smooth (like satin):

   _ _ _ _ _ _

6. This tea is for when you're very, very bad: _ _ _ _ _ _

7. This tea is loaded with hormones: _ _ _ _ _ _

These teas end in -ity:

8. This tea is very strong:

   _ _ _ _ _ _ _ _

9. This is the chief tea, the first tea you want in the morning:

   _ _ _ _ _ _ _ _

10. This tea makes you rich:

    _ _ _ _ _ _ _ _ _

Dictionary traces the adverb *after* in its temporal sense to A.D. 950. It appeared in *Beowulf,* and Shakespeare, Donne, and Burke used it. It is especially common, says the *OED*, "in combination with another adverb of time," as in *soon after, long after,* and *before and after.* Would you object to "Long before, they had left the party"?

I could have been a jockey

To my ear, there's a whiff of windiness about *afterward* that probably has discouraged its use in favor of the idiomatic *after.*

Playing Ketchup

Q. *While chowing down at my favorite greasy spoon, I inspected the label of a well-known tomato condiment that I had just squeezed on*

11. This tea is for old folks:
    _ _ _ _ _ _ _ _

12. This is the tea that never ends: _ _ _ _ _ _ _

13. This tea has the power to prevent illness:

    _ _ _ _ _ _ _

14. This tea you must drink very quickly: _ _ _ _ _ _ _

15. These teas make you famous: _ _ _ _ _ _ _ _ and

    _ _ _ _ _ _ _

16. This tea's flavor is so-so:

    _ _ _ _ _ _ _ _ _

17. This tea's flavor is saucy and bold: _ _ _ _ _ _ _

18. This tea is pure as the driven snow: _ _ _ _ _ _ _

19. You drink these teas just for laughs: _ _ _ _ _ _ _ _ and

    _ _ _ _ _ _ _ _ _

20. This tea is for liars:

    _ _ _ _ _ _ _ _

21. This tea is for happy couples or happy families:

    _ _ _ _ _ _ _ _ _

22. These teas impart wisdom:

    _ _ _ _ _ _ _ _ and

    _ _ _ _ _ _ _ _ _ _

23. These teas are what your voluble author likes to drink:

    _ _ _ _ _ _ _ _ and

    _ _ _ _ _ _ _

Answers appear on page 264.

my food. The label said ketchup. *I always thought it was* catsup. *Has* catsup *been corrupted into* ketchup?

A. Nope, 'tis the other way around. *Ketchup* is by far the dominant spelling, in Britain as well as in America. It has the distinct advantage of best representing the dominant pronunciation and also

but I didn't feel like horsing around. 🖎

best approximating the probable origin of the word, the Malayan *kechap*, fish sauce. Although dictionaries list *catsup* and sometimes *catchup* as alternative spellings, about the only place you'll find *catsup* these days is on the condiment bottles themselves (although, as you noticed, it's becoming rare there too). *Catchup*, the least common spelling today, belongs to the semiliterates and to children under ten.

Go Fish

Q. *What's with* tuna fish? *Shouldn't it be* tuna? *Why not* sardine fish *or* salmon fish?

A. It's *tuna* in the water and *tuna* or *tuna fish* in the can. Why? Long-standing usage has established the acceptability of *tuna fish*, and I think it's a tad pedantic to insist today that "I'll have a tuna fish sandwich, please" is wrong. Of course we don't say *sardine fish* or *salmon fish* for the same reason: It's not customary. But we do often say, quite acceptably, *codfish* for *cod*. I can tell you that Bostonians eat codfish and baked beans, not cod and baked beans, although I have no idea *why* they eat them. It was once common to say *whalefish* as well. One of my favorite ballads, "Greenland Fisheries," contains the line, " 'It's a whale, it's a whale, it's a whalefish,' he cried."

A Run-In with *One In*

Q. *I'm the editor of a newsletter for a healthcare corporation and I'm having a knock-down, drag-out battle with one of my writers about this sentence: "One in four Americans have high blood pressure." I say it should be "One in four Americans has high blood pressure." Which is correct, a plural or a singular verb?*

A. Editor wins; writer loses. *One in* [*a number*] always takes a singular verb. Most usage guides are strangely silent on this point, but the two I found that comment on it both fully support you: *Garner's Modern American Usage* and *Bryson's Dictionary of Troublesome Words*, which suggests inverting the sentence to see the

⇥ I could have been a psychiatrist

proper noun-verb agreement. Thus: "Out of every four Americans, one has high blood pressure."

Unwise to Chastise

Q. *I have a confession to make. I embarrassed myself during a Toastmasters meeting by chastising several members for using dangling participles, when in fact they were ending their sentences with preposi-tions. What is a dangling participle? When, if ever, is it acceptable to end a sentence with a preposition?*

A. The belief that we should not end sentences with preposi-tions is, according to one of the most famous arbiters of usage in the last century, "a cherished superstition." There is nothing wrong with ending a sentence with a preposition if doing so sounds like natural English. Thus, we don't say that people who end sentences with prepositions don't have a leg on which to stand; we say they don't have a leg to stand on. When I write, I put on music to write by, not by which to write. We ask, "What are you looking at?" not "At what are you looking?" If it sounds stilted *not* to end with a preposition, then leave your sentence alone.

A *participle* is the verb form ending in *-ing* (called the present participle) or ending in *-d* or *-ed* (called the past participle). When a participial phrase (a participle combined with other words) is too far away from the word or words it modifies, the phrase is said to "dangle" because it is not clear what the participial phrase is modi-fying. Some examples:

When swimming across the lake, the boat always followed Judith. (The boat is not swimming, Judith is.)

After eating our lunch, the bus went on to Chicago. (The bus ate lunch!)

Loaded with plates, the waiter carried the tray. (It's the tray that's loaded with plates.)

The car was reported stolen by the police. (The police didn't steal the car; they reported that it had been stolen.)

but why do you think I could have been a psychiatrist? 🙂

Sic or Stet?

Q. *In my writing, when I want to indicate that I'm reproducing exactly what someone wrote or said without correcting an error (for example, of spelling or grammar), which word do I use, sic or stet? Do I put it in parentheses or brackets? And should it be italicized?*

BODACIOUS BRAINTEASER

ETC. = ET CETERA = AND SO ON

Below are various abbreviations of Latin terms. Some are common while others are used chiefly in scholarly writing. Do you know what they stand for in Latin and in English?

1. MS *or* ms. = Latin = English?
2. PS *or* P.S.
3. e.g.
4. i.e.
5. N.B. *or* n.b.
6. et al.
7. c. *or* ca.
8. ibid.
9. cf.
10. q.v.
11. sup.
12. et seq.
13. viz.
14. fl.
15. QED *or* Q.E.D.

Answers appear on page 264.

A. You should use *sic*, a Latin word meaning "so, thus, in this way." It is traditionally enclosed in brackets and italicized. A word of caution: *sic* is a scholarly device; using it sarcastically or scornfully is undignified. The fifteenth edition of *The Chicago Manual of Style* advises that *sic* should be used only where it is necessary to call attention to an error or discrepancy "or where paraphrase or silent correction is inappropriate." Also, don't get carried away. "Where material with many errors and variant spellings . . . is reproduced as written," says *CMS*, "a prefatory comment or a note to that effect will make a succession of *sics* unnecessary."

⇥I I could have been a baker

The Latin word *stet* means "let it stand." It is not normally used in prose. It is a copyediting notation, usually written in the margin of a page, indicating that something marked for revision or deletion should be left intact.

G Whiz

Q. *Do you eat your* vegies *or your* veggies?

A. Both *veggie* and *vegie* are listed in dictionaries (meaning they have been attested often in print), but *vegie* is much less common and, in my opinion, ill-formed, problematic to pronounce, and not likely to survive the linguistic version of natural selection. *Veggie,* the more robust and dominant form, is by far the better choice.

Are the Media on the Agenda?

Q. *Have the words* agenda *and* media *become singular forms? One often hears* the media is *and* agendas. *Maybe Latin is truly dead.*

A. *Agenda* has long been accepted as a singular noun meaning "a program" or "a list of things to be done." Decrying this use, says one current usage expert, is "bootless." As far back as 1965, in *The Careful Writer*, Theodore M. Bernstein—then managing editor of *The New York Times* and one of the most respected commentators on usage in the last century—pronounced the Latin singular *agendum* "extinct" and said that "no one refers to the next *agendum*, but rather to the next item on the *agenda*." Bernstein even embraced the plural *agendas,* which is commonplace now.

Some people still treat *media* as a plural (I do), but most now consider it singular, although in conservatively edited writing you are still likely to see *the media are. Data* has gone this way as well, with most people treating it as a singular collective noun, a synonym of *information*. Only a few nerds like me still say *these data are,* and even I am beginning to wonder if I should just drop it and go with the flow. But I will forever hold the line on *bacteria,* which

but I wanted more out of life than dough.

you may have noticed is constantly misused (even in reputable publications) for the singular *bacterium:* for example, *This bacteria is deadly.** Likewise with the plural *vertebrae,* which improperly appears for the singular *vertebra.*

Latin may be dead, but the battle for sensible English goes on.

To Whom It May Concern

Q. *Barnes and Noble once ran a full-page ad in* The Wall Street Journal. *The headline read, "Who's kidding who?" Shouldn't it have been "Who's kidding whom?"*

A. Barnes and Noble is wrong and you are right. But *whom* has been taking a beating for almost a century and many experts believe it is moribund. Most Americans (and I must confess I count myself among them) are mystified by the distinction between *who* and *whom.* Even the redoubtable William F. Buckley Jr. sometimes gets it wrong.

Then there's the matter of hypercorrectness—in other words, should we be grammatically unimpeachable at the risk of sounding like a snoot, or should we bend the rules and go with what seems more natural to the majority? *Newsweek* chose the latter course when it ran the headline "Black Like Who?" on its cover of March 17, 1997. And the makers of *Ghostbusters* surely must have known their film would flop if the lyrics of their theme song had been "Whom are you going to call?" instead of "Who ya gonna call?"

Like many of us, William Safire, the longtime language maven of *The New York Times Magazine,* is uncomfortable with *whom.* His advice? When you feel you need to use *whom,* recast the sentence. I won't argue with that; I've been doing that myself for years. But I think there are some simple constructions where *whom* is not unnatural and most would agree that using *who* instead is incorrect, especially in print and especially in printed ads for bookstores, the

*For my tirade on *bacteria,* see page 59.

I could have been a librarian

presumed havens of our literary culture. So, although I do not mourn the gradual demise of *whom*, I'm still with you in standing up for "Who's kidding whom?"

Mrs. Stress

Q. *Can you tell me how to spell the word for which* Mrs. *is the abbreviation?*

A. *Mrs.* is an abbreviation of *mistress*. Probably the most common spellings of the pronunciation of *Mrs.* are *missus* and *missis*.

A(n) Historical

Q. *I'm a freelance writer who sometimes writes with a partner. Recently we were composing some copy and we got into an argument about whether it was* an historical *or* a historical. *I said it was* an. *My writing partner said it was* a. *We checked various grammar books but couldn't find anything on* an *or* a *with* historical. *We have to settle this before we both go crazy. What's the rule?*

A. First, I think you need some good usage manuals rather than these "grammar books" you consulted. Just about every usage manual since the nineteenth century comments on this, and I'm afraid I have to tell you that the weight of authority is on your writing partner's side (*a historical*). Back in 1882 Mark Twain, referring to the words *humble, heroic,* and *historical,* remarked: "Correct writers of the American language do not put *an* before those words."

The general rule, say the usage guides, is that if the *h* is sounded, use *a.* If it is silent, use *an.* Thus, *a history, a happening,* but *an hour, an honor.* The problem of choice arises when the word is not stressed on the first syllable and the aspirated *h* is less audible, as in *hysterical, habitual,* and *historical.* If you go looking, you can find plenty of citations from educated and accomplished people—even from historians themselves—of *an* before *historical,* and you may conclude, if you wish, as one authority does, that "at the present time . . . the choice of form remains open," but that's too

but I shelved that idea.

LET'S SHOW SOME RESPECT FOR *DISRESPECT*

The transitive verb *disrespect*—as in *to disrespect someone*—is often maligned as a substandard usage of the young, and specifically as an unsavory product of the hip-hop subculture, which has further shortened the verb to *dis* ("Are you dissing me?").

I once heard a story about a lawyer who used the verb *disrespect* one day in court and the crusty old judge barked at her, claiming that "one can be disrespectful toward someone else" but that "*disrespect* as a verb isn't a word and it is not welcome in my courtroom." A soi-disant usage expert I found on the Web called the verb *disrespect* "street slang" and counseled that "an applicant for a job who complains about having been 'dis-respected' elsewhere is likely to incur further disrespect . . . and no job."

This kind of ignorant leaping to conclusions is unbecoming to judges and gives usage commentators a bad name. To *dis* may be "street slang," but the verb *disrespect* is in fact quite reputable and quite old. Although it fell into disuse for most of the twentieth century, it was listed in good standing in the *Century Dictionary* (1914), *Webster's New International* (1934), and the first (1966) and second (1987) unabridged editions of *The Random House Dictionary*. A peek into the second edition of the *Oxford English Dictionary* (1989) shows that *disrespect* has been used since the early seventeenth

wishy-washy for my taste. For me the choice is clear: Nearly all authorities favor this "rule of *h*"; it's sensible and speech-friendly; it's based on over a century of good usage; and if you follow it, no one can ever accuse you of affectation.

Bi- Gum

Q. *A coworker wanted to set up a meeting twice a month, and he called it a* bimonthly *meeting. I told him the meeting would be* biweekly,

⇥ *I could have been a prostitute*

century as the opposite of *respect:* "to have or show no respect, regard, or reverence for; to treat with irreverence." The *OED*'s citations include "If he love the one he must disrespect the other" (1633); "He was disrespected in Oxford by several men who now speak well of him" (1706); and "You will judge whether he disrespects me" (1885).

Although all the major current American dictionaries list the verb *disrespect* in good standing, I'll admit it still has some way to go before it becomes a respectable word again. But that's only because the resistance to it is founded on prejudice, not reason, which makes it harder to overcome. Would those who ob-

ject to *disrespect* have us use the pompous and awkward *disesteem* instead? Would the job applicant who said he'd been *disesteemed* be more likely to get that job?

I predict this word will overcome the prejudice against it, simply because there is an undeniable need for it. Not long ago, in *The New York Times Magazine,* I saw this ad copy about a bicycle messenger: "Potholes, Pshaw. Sewer Grates, Yawn. But never disrespect the door of a taxi." The words *insult, offend, mock, ridicule, scorn,* and *deride* would all be inappropriate, and even rather ludicrous, in that context.

---

which can mean either *every two weeks or twice a week, while* bimonthly *can only mean every two months. Much to my horror, my dictionary contradicted me. It said* bimonthly *can mean every other month or twice a month. What's going on? Can you set me straight on this?*

A. Most authorities say that, strictly speaking, *bimonthly* means every two months and *biweekly* means every two weeks. But your dictionary is right about this one; it cuts both ways and it's not clear-cut. The whole *bi-* business has become such a rathole of

but I refuse to lie down on the job. ☞

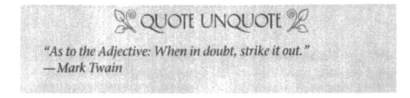

ambiguity that it's often impossible to know whether the intended meaning is twice or every other. So to be safe I usually eschew *bi-weekly* and *bimonthly* in favor of a more precise phrase such as *twice a week, twice a month, every two weeks,* or *every other month.* You can also use *semimonthly* without any confusion to mean twice a month, and that's what I would recommend as your solution here: *semimonthly meetings* or meetings *twice a month.*

L on Wheels

Q. *I have always used the spelling* traveling. *Recently I wrote a letter to an elected official, who wrote me back using the spelling* travelling. *Both spellings are in my dictionary, with my spelling listed first. Which one is preferred?*

A. Your spelling, *traveling* with one *l,* is preferred in American usage, while *travelling,* with two *l*'s, is preferred in British usage. The same is true for *barreled, canceled, counseled, dueled, funneled, imperiled, initialed, labeled, signaled, swiveled, totaled, unraveled,* and various other words; American style calls for one *l.* (This is true for the present participles too: e.g., *canceling, labeling, signaling,* etc.) But Americans are not always consistent stylists, and from time to time you will see a British doubled *l,* especially in the commoner words *canceled, counseled, labeled,* and *signaled.*

There is one word where the final *l* in the inflected form *is* customarily doubled both in American and British English: *tranquil* makes *tranquillity.*

I could have been a baseball player

Adverbiage

Q. *Lately I've been wondering how adverbs are formed. I've noticed that some are made from adjectives (*lately, roughly, keenly, smartly, silently*), some are made from the present participle of a verb (*lovingly, sparingly, haltingly*), and some are made from the past participle (*excitedly, guardedly, hurriedly*). I've also noticed that adverbs formed from the past participle can be clunky (*angeredly? gratifiedly? satisfiedly?*). Is there a method to this madness? Are there any rules governing the formation of adverbs?*

A. Adverbs constitute one of the hugest word classes, comprising not just words ending in *-ly* (a common misconception) but modifiers in many shapes and forms, from *else, quite,* and *soon* to *often, always, backward, downstairs,* and *so.* I wouldn't pretend to know all the rules and subtleties governing their use, but speaking as a stylist I can tell you one thing (or actually two)—they are often badly made and they are often overused.

Many experts have admonished us not to create ugly adverbs, but from time to time you will come upon an abomination like *uglily* in edited prose, or a form contrary to idiom, like *funnily.* My rule of thumb is if it's not in the dictionary, don't use it, and even if it is in the dictionary, if it doesn't roll easily off your tongue, don't use it. Thus, *anticipatorially* and *ghastlily* are not happy adverbs, and *agitatedly, constructionally,* and *opinionatedly,* though they are in the dictionary, are borderline at best. Adverbs formed from the past tense or past participle (*-ed*) are the most dangerous; some work but many (*thrilledly, friendlily, consideredly*) don't. Again, apply the rule of thumb: If it sounds awkward, it is awkward. (Hey, John Updike, did you hear that?)

Overuse of adverbs, which I call *adverbiage,* is rampant today, especially in business communication. It's a problem not only because it results in wordy, hackneyed writing but also because it smacks of insincerity and hyperbole. When everything is *critically*

but I couldn't get to first base. ✍

important and *completely* effective, when people must be *absolutely* right and make things *perfectly* clear, we are *definitely* in trouble. Now that's something to *seriously* consider.

Alumni Illumination

Q. *Isn't it incorrect to say, "I'm an alumni of such-and-such"? I was taught to call a male graduate an* alumnus *and a female graduate an* alumna. *And what's your opinion of the shortened form* alum?

A. Dictionaries list *alum* and I think it's okay in informal speech, but I wouldn't use it in writing that aspires to any sort of dignity. I would also eschew the plural *alums* both in speech and writing. Why? *Alum* may be a handy informal singular for the male *alumnus* and the female *alumna,* but *alums* for the established plural *alumni* is nonstandard and at best jocular, while using *alumni* as a singular—as in your example: "I'm an *alumni* of such-and-such"—is semiliterate. If college grads (notice the acceptable shortening) should know any Latin at all, they should at least know how to use the words *alumnus, alumna, alumnae,* and *alumni.* And here's how to do it:

Alumnus (in Latin a masculine noun) refers to a male graduate or former student; *alumni* is the plural. *Alumna* (in Latin a feminine noun) refers to a female graduate or former student; *alumnae* (pronounced uh-LUM-nee) is the plural. Traditionally, *alumni* refers to men or, more often, to a group composed of both sexes; this use is still widespread and respectable. Sometimes, to avoid any suggestion of sexism, both plurals are used for mixed groups (the *alumni* and *alumnae* of Indiana University), but some consider this wordy or redundant. (I do.) The noun *graduate* and the plural *graduates,*

⊣ *I could have been an opera singer*

though not quite equivalent in meaning to their Latin counterparts, offer a convenient, gender-neutral alternative.

Marksmanship

Q. *I'm wondering about where to place other marks of punctuation with quotation marks — periods, commas, semicolons, colons, and question marks. Sometimes I see them inside the quotation marks, sometimes outside. Do they all go one way or the other, or do some go inside and some outside?*

A. You are not alone in your confusion. Most people, whether they know it or not, are in punctuation denial.

Deciding where to place other punctuation with quotation marks causes as much misery and consternation as the federal income tax code. Although misuse is rampant and many people misunderstand the conventions, they are not as daunting as they seem and can be easily memorized. Here is all you have to remember:

In American usage periods and commas always go *inside* quotation marks and semicolons and colons always go *outside* quotation marks. (In British usage periods and commas go outside, but you don't have to worry about that.)

The question mark goes inside the quotation mark if it belongs to the material quoted: *"Is that right?" she asked. She looked at him and said, "Is that right?"* The question mark goes outside if the whole sentence is a question and the quotation is only a portion of the sentence: *Didn't Mark Twain say, "I never lie, except for practice"?*

Able Was I Ere I Saw *-ible*

Q. *An antiques store in my neighborhood has a sign in the window advertising "collectibles." Is it* collectible *or* collectable? *Also, is there some rule or saying that explains whether a word should end in -ible or -able?*

A. The store has it right: *collectible* has long been the preferred form, and, according to *Garner's Modern American Usage*, it's about ten

but I'd rather watch The Sopranos.

HOW TO SCRIBBLE -IBLE

Because we are all susceptible to error, and because our spelling is often fallible (and occasionally even contemptible), I offer you this legible, sensible, accessible, and easily digestible list of forty of the most commonly misspelled words ending in -ible.

accessible
admissible
collapsible
collectible

combustible
compatible
contemptible
convertible
corruptible
deductible
defensible
destructible
digestible
discernible
divisible
eligible

---

times more common today. Although -able is vastly more common than -ible, in this case the -able form is considered a "needless variant."

I'm not aware of any rule or mnemonic device for getting the -able and -ible words straight, and if there were one I'd be skeptical of its reliability for such a large and unruly class of words. Though the number of words ending in -ible is finite (because -ible is a defunct combining form and not a living suffix like -able), there are still enough differently -ibled words to cause problems. The best you can do is memorize as many of the -ible words as you can and consult a dictionary when you're unsure of the preferred form. That's what some of the antique dealers in my neighborhood failed to do when they painted "collectables" in their shop windows.

Ms. Use

Q. *My colleagues and I have been debating the origin and use of the abbreviation* Ms. *Some of us believe it was created as a substitute for* Miss *and* Mrs. *so that women could conceal their marital status, in the*

⇥ *I could have been a farmer*

exhaustible	perceptible
expressible	permissible
fallible	plausible
feasible	reprehensible
forcible	repressible
gullible	resistible
indelible	responsible
intelligible	reversible
invincible	sensible
legible	susceptible
negligible	transmissible
ostensible	visible

same way that Mr. *does not reveal a man's marital status. Others maintain that* Ms. *refers only to divorced women, while* Miss *still designates an unmarried woman and* Mrs. *a married one. Which side is right?*

A. You're right that *Ms.*— which is properly printed with a period, like *Mr.* and *Mrs.,* even though it's not a real abbreviation — was created as a counterpart to *Mr.,* but the point in creating it wasn't so that women could conceal their marital status. (That sounds like the notion of a misogynist — or a *Ms.*-ogynist?) The point was to simplify business communication by eliminating the need, as one source puts it, "to determine personal information usually irrelevant to the matter at hand."

A 1952 booklet published by the National Office Management Association recommended that we "use the abbreviation *Ms.* for all women addresses. This modern style solves an age-old problem." That may be true, but the publishers of that booklet quickly realized that many women still preferred the old-fashioned designations, so they soon revised their advice, recommending that we

but that idea never took root.

use *Ms.* "if not sure whether to use *Mrs.* or *Miss.*" Today *Ms.* is the predominant form when the marital status is unknown and irrelevant. The theory that *Ms.* designates a divorced woman is entirely unfounded.

BODACIOUS BRAINTEASER

FAMOUS FIRST LINES

Can you identify the DWMPs (Dead White Male Poets) who wrote these famous first lines, and the names of the poems they begin?

1. Whan that April with his showres soote
2. Of Man's First Disobedience, and the Fruit
3. A Gentle Knight was pricking on the plaine,
4. Shall I compare thee to a summer's day?
5. There was a time when meadow, grove, and stream,
6. It was many and many a year ago,
7. I celebrate myself, and sing myself,
8. Turning and turning in the widening gyre
9. Let us go then, you and I,
10. Something there is that doesn't love a wall,
11. Now as I was young and easy under the apple boughs
12. I saw the best minds of my generation destroyed by madness, starving hysterical naked,

Answers appear on page 265.

Bracket Up

Q. *When you see brackets around a word or phrase in an article or book, what does that mean?*

A. Brackets are used within a quotation to enclose material that is not part of the quotation. With brackets, you can insert relevant information in a quotation (*"The Canterbury Tales* [1387-1400]

I could have been a cattle rancher

by Geoffrey Chaucer [b. ca. 1342–43, d. 1400] is a frame story written in Middle English"), or you can clarify something ambiguous, such as a pronoun ("I support [Peter Q. Politician] for mayor"), without altering the quotation. Scholars also use brackets to supply something left out by mistake ("Hal[l]ey's comet") or to indicate a change in capitalization from the original ("The opening words of the Declaration of Independence are '[w]hen in the [c]ourse of human [e]vents'").

Yes You Cannot

Q. *I had an argument with a coworker about* can not, *which I insisted was two words and he said was one:* cannot. *Who's right?*

A. *Cannot* is properly one word. This form has been recorded since the fourteenth century and preferred since the mid-twentieth century; the *Oxford English Dictionary* says *cannot* is "the ordinary modern way of writing *can not.*" The only exception is a rare one: when *can* appears as part of another construction, such as "You can not only email and fax with this device but also access the Internet."

If you were taught to write *can not,* it's time to get with the program. Most commonly linked words merge into a single word over time: *horseshoe* and *henhouse* have been closed for centuries; *backyard* is a compound word despite the best efforts of The Associated Press to keep it open; and someday, I have no doubt, a *bow tie* will become a *bowtie,* if they don't get rid of the silly looking thing first.

Pompom Pilot

Q. *What is the past tense of* cheerlead? *That is, assuming* cheerlead *is a verb. I think it is, as a cheerleader is one who cheerleads. So, would it be* cheerled? *Or* cheerleaded?

A. *Cheerlead* is in fact a verb sanctioned by dictionaries; *cheerled* is the past tense.

but the challenge of it cowed me. 🖘

Discourse on Dialogue

Q. *There's a tendency lately to use* dialogue *for a discussion between more than two people: "She had a dialogue with her six coworkers." Is this use proper now?*

BODACIOUS BRAINTEASER

NURSERY RHYME NAMES

Do you know which nursery rhyme character(s) each clue refers to?

1. They went up the hill.
2. She went to the cupboard.
3. She lost her sheep.
4. He could eat no fat.
5. For all six of them it was high diddle diddle.
6. She sat on a tuffet.
7. He sat on a wall.
8. He had a wife and couldn't keep her.
9. He sat in a corner.
10. He jumped over the candlestick.
11. He sings for his supper.
12. She was asked how her garden grew.
13. He was under the haycock fast asleep.
14. He was a merry old soul.
15. He met a pieman.
16. He runs through the town.

Answers appear on page 265.

A. *Dialogue* never did refer strictly to conversation between two people. Since 1400 it's been used to mean "a conversation between two or more persons" (*OED*) or "conversation as opposed to monologue, to preaching, lecturing, speeches, narrative, or description" (H. W. Fowler, *Modern English Usage*, 1926). The prefix here is not the Greek *di-*, twice, but the Greek *dia*, through, across, and the Greek source of *dialogue* meant "conversation"—as in the *Dialogues* of Plato, which recounted conversation among learned men. The precise word for a conversation between two people is *duologue*.

◁ I could have been a farmer

And by the way, as you can see from the foregoing, the word is properly spelled *dialogue,* not *dialog;* despite the techno-geek's preference for *dialog boxes,* all the current dictionaries give priority to the longer spelling, which authorities on usage prefer. Avoid the verb to *dialogue,* so popular today in business and government jargon. This pompous substitute for *talk* or *discuss* was scorned by 98 percent of the usage panel of *The American Heritage Dictionary.*

Paying the Pipor

Q. *Everyone where I work (in hospital administration, dealing with insurance companies) seems to spell the word* payor, *but my spell-checker says it should be* payer. *Is one preferred, or are both correct?*

A. *Payor* is legalese. In legal jargon *-or* is the giver, *-ee* the receiver: *vendor, vendee, licensor, licensee, payor, payee. Payer* is standard English, *-er* being the far more common agent suffix. Legal dictionaries prefer *payor* but general dictionaries prefer *payer* and sometimes don't list *payor.* My ruling? You can get away with *payor* in legal contexts, but your spell-checker (for once) is right: *payer* is preferable and unobjectionable in any type of writing.

Also Can or Can Also?

Q. *I have a question about this sentence: "Cleaning up the environment also can provide material for art." Is the word* also *placed correctly, or should it be* can also provide?

A. *Also can provide* is not flat-out wrong, but it is, in the view of many stylists and usage authorities, unnecessarily fastidious. The traditional and normal placement of the adverb in such constructions is between the two elements of the verb phrase: *can also provide.* Thus the conscientious stylist will prefer *she will probably call today* over *she probably will call today,* and *representatives are currently elected every three years* over *representatives currently are elected every three years.*

Many people think this construction is the same as a split infinitive, and so avoid it. But it is not the same; it is natural English.

but the idea never grew on me. 🖘

An infinitive involves *to* plus the verb, and contrary to what many believe, there is nothing wrong with splitting infinitives; good writers have been doing so for emphasis for centuries ("to boldly go where no man has gone before"). The one exception I make is when the splitting adverb is superfluous—that is, when the emphasis it adds is merely hyperbole. For example, *we must seriously consider* conveys less serious intent than *we must consider,* and *I am absolutely certain* is histrionic compared with the simple and powerful *I am certain.*

Prickly Plurals

Q. *I'm stuck, so to speak. Or maybe I'm on pins and needles. Can you tell me the correct plural of* cactus?

A. I could poke fun at your puns, or stick it to you, or be a thorn in your side, but I won't because your wordplay was bloody good.

I'm not surprised that you're stuck because there's no definitive answer here. *Cacti* and *cactuses* are both correct. Some dictionaries list a third variant, *cactus* (same as the singular), which is best avoided. Most authorities (including The Associated Press) favor the anglicized form *cactuses,* which probably predominates in common usage, but all accept *cacti,* often noting that it is preferred in botanical contexts, and, for what it's worth, *cacti* is listed first in most dictionaries. I must confess I don't have a preference myself and I've used both forms. If pressed, I suppose I'd choose the anglicized *cactuses* because that's ordinary usage rather than scientific, and I'm more ordinary than scientific.

There's also a strong trend in the language to anglicize classical plurals; established examples include *forums* (not *fora*), *stadiums* (not *stadia*), *premiums* (not *premia*), *octopuses* (not *octopi,* a faux-Latin plural for a Greek word),* and *ignoramuses* (*ignorami* is illiterate Latin and English). *Formulas* and *focuses* are fast replacing the

*See the discussion of the plural of *octopus* on pages 118–20.

❧ *I could have been a surgeon*

formal *formulae* and *foci; indexes* is preferred over the pretentious *indices;* and "although most dictionaries list only the Greek plural *oxymora* . . . in fact, *oxymorons* is now about 60 times as common as *oxymora* in print sources, and it ought to be accepted as standard," says *Garner's Modern American Usage.* Though surgeons remove *appendixes* (uh-PEN-dik-siz), it is not true, as is often supposed, that books must have *appendices* (uh-PEN-di-seez). Both plurals are standard, but since the 1980s usage experts have noted that *appendixes* has become the dominant form.

Yet there are still many words that cleave to their classical roots. Cultivated writers and speakers know that the singular is *crisis* and the plural is *crises;* the singular Is *criterion* and the plural is *criteria;* the singular is *bacterium* and the plural is *bacteria.* But alas, how often have you heard or read the solecisms *several crisises, another criteria,* and *this bacteria?*

Apostrophe Catastrophes

Q. *I'm a member of the Friends of Valley Vista Library, and we're about to open a bookstore inside the library. The group wants to know whether the name should be* Friends' Book Shop, *with an apostrophe, or* Friends Book Shop, *without an apostrophe. Some members claim either is acceptable, while others are adamantly taking sides—especially in favor of the apostrophe. Can you help us solve this dispute?*

A. The only way to settle this one may be with a vote.

The traditional approach is to use an apostrophe because the use is clearly possessive. But in recent years there has been a strong trend to drop the apostrophe in the names of organizations, publications, et cetera, presumably for a "cleaner" look: *Authors Guild, Writers Digest, Publishers Weekly, San Diego Professional Editors Network.* So it's a matter of whether your group wants to stick with tradition or follow what is now the dominant trend.

That said, to me *Friends Book Shop* looks naked without an apostrophe. It also suggests a store that sells stuff pertaining to the

but I didn't have the guts. ✍

TV show *Friends,* not a store run by library lovers. And *Book Shop* is preferably spelled *Bookshop.* But to avoid protracting the controversy, allow me to suggest a compromise: *Friends of the Library Bookshop.*

Half It Your Way

Q. *Are the phrases* half an hour *and* a half hour *equally acceptable?*

A. Yes, they are. You may say "We have half an hour more to drive" or "We have a half hour more to drive." Your ear will be the judge of which to use depending on context—assuming you have half an ear for words. When *half hour* is a phrasal adjective it should be hyphenated, as in *it's a half-hour show.* Good style eschews the pleonastic form *a half an hour* (the initial *a* is unnecessary).

An Interesting Determination

Q. *I am writing a book with a partner, and we have a dispute about phrasing that we'd like you to settle. I want to write* we were interested to determine. *My partner prefers* we were interested in determining. *Which should we go with?*

A. I'm glad you're interested in knowing the answer—which I've just revealed.

It's unidiomatic to use *to* after *interested.* You aren't interested *to* find out if you won the lottery. You are interested *in* finding out if you won the lottery. And since *in* must follow *interested,* a participle (the *-ing* form of the verb) is required. Thus, you are interested in determining, finding, learning, and so on.

Lb. for Pound

Q. *As an executive chef, I pride myself on knowing as much food lore and cooking trivia as I can—if only to stay one step ahead of my*

⊸ I could have been a minister

staff. The other day one of them asked a question that stumped me: How did we get the abbreviation lb. *for* pound, *which has no* l *or* b*? This has been weighing on my mind, you could say. Do you know the answer?*

A. I think I can cook you up a satisfactory answer.

The abbreviation *lb.* stands for the Latin *libra*, meaning "pound." Technically, the plural should be *lbb.*, just as the plural of the Latin abbreviation *ms.* for *manuscript* is *mss.* But nobody was interested in spelling it that way, and *lbs.* is the accepted plural. You can also see the Latin *libra* represented in the symbol for pounds sterling, the British monetary unit: £. The constellation Libra, represented by a pair of scales, also comes from the Latin *libra*.

Who's on First(ly)?

Q. *Which is preferred:* first, second, *and* third, *or* firstly, secondly, *and* thirdly*? And what is your opinion of* first of all *and* second of all*?*

A. First of all, let me begin by saying that you should never begin by saying, "First of all, let me begin by saying." That said, here's my ruling:

Firstly, secondly, thirdly are now "considered inferior" to *first, second, third,* says *Garner's Modern American Usage,* and I agree. The shorter form is cleaner, crisper style.

First of all is acceptable in casual speech, but it's a wordy construction that should be avoided in writing. *Second of all* should be avoided entirely.

Food for Thought

Q. *An ad for a local restaurant says to "award your appetite" with their food.* Award *sounds clumsy there—whose appetite deserves a prize? Wouldn't* reward *be better?*

A. *Reward* is better here because it means to give something *to* somebody, whereas *award* means only to give something due or merited. To accommodate *award*, the phrase would have to be the peculiar "award [something] to your appetite" or the nonsensical "award your appetite to [something]." But *reward* also implies

but the spirit never moved me.

giving something in return for service, and it's hard to imagine how an appetite can render a service; on the contrary, an appetite demands to be served. The copywriter should have used a different verb, such as *treat* or *spoil*. But the business of copywriters is to bend the language in attention-grabbing ways; unfortunately, all too often they bend it so far that it almost breaks.

Son Tropes Dad

Q. *In a report for school, my son described a certain place as being "lonely." I told him that only people could be lonely, not places. Now I'm not so sure. Was I right or wrong?*

A. Sorry, Dad. Your son's a poet and you don't know it. In ascribing a human emotion to a place, your son was employing a time-honored figure of speech called the pathetic fallacy, which Samuel Cooper's *Dictionary of Literary Terms* defines as "the portrayal of inanimate nature as having human feelings and character (e.g., 'the cruel sea,' 'the evil night')."

An Opinion on *Humble Opinion*

Q. *Could you settle this, please? Is* humble opinion *an oxymoron?*

A. An oxymoron must juxtapose contradictory or incongruous words, as *cold fire, cruel kindness, laborious idleness,* and Milton's *darkness visible.* It is, to quote one authority, "a condensed paradox." There is nothing paradoxical or contradictory about the words *humble opinion,* just as there is nothing paradoxical or contradictory about *honest opinion* or *considered opinion.*

The appropriate rhetorical term for this expression as it is commonly used—where the speaker professes humbleness, pretending to belittle his opinion in the hope that you will forgive or at least tolerate his ensuing pontification—is *irony,* which in this case is usually unintentional because the phrase was cliché even long before it morphed into the popular online initialism IMHO. With irony, there is a contradiction or discrepancy between intent and meaning, between appearance and reality; something is

I could have been a drill sergeant

ironic when it says one thing and means or connotes another. IMHO is ironic because humble people aren't likely to offer opinions, and the opinion that invariably follows IMHO is not a humble one.

And that's my honest and considered opinion—not my humble one.

Wish Not, Want Not

Q. *I'm an impecunious attorney working on a pro bono case, and I need an authoritative explanation of the distinction between* wish *and* want. *I can't afford to pay you anything, but if you can help me I will sing your praises to other attorneys who can.*

A. "Impecunious attorney"? Pardon me while I look up the word *oxymoron* again. Ah yes, "a combination of contradictory or incongruous words," like *well-heeled writer.* Well, I don't want to be a heel, and I suppose one pro bono turn deserves another, so here's the answer to your question.

There's but a fine line of difference between *wish* and *want,* a nuance that is usually understood subconsciously by native speakers of English, which is probably why little has been written about it. The two words are close in meaning, but I would argue that they are not interchangeable. It is wrong, for example, to say "Do you wish another drink?" And it would be eccentric to say "Do you wish to have another drink?" because it sounds stilted and may even imply insufficient desire; idiomatic English prefers the simpler, straightforward "Do you want another drink?" Likewise, it would be wrong to make *want* stand in for *wish* in a sentence like "I want I could be there." Idiomatic English calls for the firmer "I want to be there."

So what's the difference? *Wish* applies chiefly to abstract things and suggests a longing, either weak or intense, to attain or possess something, and often something unattainable. (I *wish* you could come; she *wished* they would serve dinner; the prisoners *wished* for freedom.) *Want* may apply to physical or abstract things and

but I don't know my left from my right. 🖙

suggests a feeling of need or a craving that demands fulfillment, an imperative longing to obtain something or attain some end. (I *want* you to come; she *wanted* them to serve dinner; the prisoners *wanted* freedom.)

In short, to *wish* is to long for something without volition, by which I mean the will to accomplish or obtain it. To *want* is to long for something prompted by volition. For example: "I wish you were dead" does not imply an intent to commit murder, but "I want you dead" implies the will to kill.

You may now start singing my praises.

I Wish I May, I Wish I Might

Q. *My husband and I, who often get into deep discussions during dinner about the fine points of language, landed in a real quagmire the other night. We were talking about the words* may *and* might. *My husband said they were essentially interchangeable while I maintained they were not, though I couldn't quite put my finger on the distinction. Are* may *and* might *interchangeable? If not, what is the difference?*

A. That's a mighty good question, if I may say so myself.

May and *might* are not interchangeable. There are two differences between *may* and *might,* one of grammar and the other in meaning. The grammatical distinction—that *may* is the present tense and *might* the past tense—rarely causes a native speaker of English trouble. We say "I think I may go home" and "I thought I might go home" (never "I thought I may go home"). But we can say "I think I may go home" or "I think I might go home," and in this choice there is a subtle difference in the degree of probability the words express.

"*May* poses a possibility; *might* adds a greater degree of uncertainty to the possibility," writes Theodore M. Bernstein in *The Careful Writer.* "This shade of difference appears in the following sentence: 'Any broadcasting station that airs more commercials than the code allows may be fined, and in extreme cases its license might be taken away.'"

⇥ I could have been a drill sergeant

Toward(s)

Q. *"They walked —— each other."* Toward *or* towards? *Which is preferred?*

A. Standard American English prefers *toward,* and that is the dominant form in print in the United States, although *towards* is common in speech. British English favors *towards,* which is the dominant form in British speech. The British pronounce it tuh-WARDZ. In the United States the preferred pronunciation is TORD (rhymes with *bored*).

Crank It Up

Q. *What do you call a telephone call that's a practical joke? When I was a kid we called them* crank calls, *but my kids call them* prank calls *and I've heard this from some other adults. So which is it, a* prank *call or a* crank *call?*

A. The call is indeed a prank—a joke—but the established expression for it is *crank call.* There are also *crank letters.* The adjective *crank* here means "coming from a *crank*—a mischievous, eccentric, irrational, or hostile person."

Are You a People Person?

Q. *For a long time I've wondered about the words* people *and* persons. *Are they interchangeable, or is there some rule I ought to know that distinguishes them?*

A. *People* and *persons* both mean "a number of human beings," but over the years the question has been when to use one or the other for a given number of human beings. For example, should you say "a jury has twelve people" or "a jury has twelve persons"? "There were five people in the car" or "there were five persons in the car"? "Millions of people celebrated in the streets" or "millions of persons celebrated in the streets"?

The traditional distinction is that *people* is general (used for large groups) and *persons* is specific (used for small or exact numbers of

but it was the wrong discipline. ☞

individuals). Journalists were the main champions of this distinction, which they upheld arbitrarily. As Theodore M. Bernstein notes in *The Careful Writer,* "the use of *people* preceded by a numeral used to be verboten, especially in newspaper offices"; in other words, if a reporter wrote that *eight people were arrested* the copyeditor would change it to *eight persons were arrested.* This numerical prohibition led many to stigmatize *people* in all contexts and to substitute *persons* for it, contrary to idiom and common sense, as in *a comedian's job is to make persons laugh* and *the persons responsible for this will be prosecuted.*

Today, I think most people (not persons) would agree that there's something a bit stuffy, old-fashioned, and fastidious about the word *persons.* Recent commentators on usage have called it "a little unnatural or strained" and "stilted." They've observed that it is "especially popular with lawyers and journalists" and is typically found in legalese and self-consciously formal notices (e.g., *persons under seventeen not admitted unless accompanied by a parent or adult guardian*). Thus, while a police report might say "three persons armed with guns entered the bank," the witnesses to the crime would say "three people with guns robbed the bank."

Personally speaking, I'm a *people* person. I think the time has come to put *persons* in its place—the word museum. *People* is by far the more commonly used word, and it never sounds unnatural, strained, or stilted. So here's my ruling: With the exception of a few established idioms like *displaced persons* and *missing persons bureau,* use *people* as the plural of *person.*

And guess what? That's precisely what *The New York Times Manual of Style and Usage* recommends—proving that even journalists eventually can see the light.

Holy Caps

Q. *Should pronouns referring to God and Jesus be capitalized or put in lowercase?*

↦ *I could have been a surgeon*

A. You may see pronouns referring to God and Jesus capitalized in religious publications, but that practice is out of step with the conventions of modern style. *The Chicago Manual of Style*, fifteenth edition, issuing the equivalent of a divine pronouncement to the editorial world, proclaims that "pronouns referring to God or Jesus are not capitalized": for example, *God in his mercy, Jesus and his disciples*. This lowercase style, by the way, is what you will find in the King James Bible, also called the Authorized Version, published in 1611.

E-gads!

Q. *I'm a technical writer for a software company. My colleagues and I need to explain that something (a window, for example) can be maximized or minimized, and we're considering using* -able *to create the adjectives* maximizeable *(or* maximizable*) and* minimizeable *(or* minimizable*). What do you think? Also, I know that a lot of* -able *adjectives drop the final* e *of the verb (*movable, scalable, *etc.). Should we keep the* e *or drop it?*

A. In the word-making game one must always be wary of creating a monster out of disparate parts. Simply sewing one suffix onto another often generates a cumbersome and ugly word, and this result is even more likely with the suffix *-ize*, which does not combine comfortably with other suffixes. Yes, we have accepted *recognizable, memorizable,* and *realizable,* but would you honestly want to read or hear such miscreations as *finalizable, prioritizable, specializable, jeopardizable, sympathizable, homogenizable,* and *overemphasizable*? The words you propose are not listed in dictionaries, and for good reason: People have shunned them.

That caveat expressed, the answer to your question about spelling is simple. Formerly it was fashionable to retain the terminal *-e* of the stem, but today it is standard practice to drop it, except in words that have a soft *c* (e.g., *enforceable*) or a soft *g* (e.g., *changeable*). Thus, *size* becomes *sizable, move* becomes *movable,*

but I just couldn't cut it. 🔙

ignite becomes *ignitable, advise* becomes *advisable, blame* becomes *blamable,* and so on.

So if you choose to give life to your Frankenwords, they should be spelled *maximizable* and *minimizable*. But before you operate, Herr Word Doctor, you should know that dictionaries already contain at least two pairs of words for what you describe: *closable* and *openable* and *enlargeable* and *diminishable*.

Going Dotty

Q. *I'm noticing something in magazines that I haven't seen before. Sometimes when two vowels appear in succession, there are double dots over the second one. I've noticed that these double dots appear only in words where both vowels are separately sounded* (coöpt, preëminent). *At first I thought it was a gimmick, but now I've noticed it in the august pages of* The New Yorker *and I'm wondering, Have I missed something? What is this double dot called, and what are the rules for using it?*

A. It's called a dieresis (dy-ER-uh-sis) and it is placed over the second of two adjacent vowels to indicate that they are pronounced separately. The vowels need not be identical, but they often are. *Naive, preeminent,* and *cooperate* are perhaps the three most common words that used to be printed with a dieresis, but we do not use the dieresis anymore because no one mis-

I could have been an astronaut

pronounces these words. *The New Yorker* has made something of a fetish out of clinging to this old-fashioned mark; it is an affectation that you would not do well to emulate.

One exception. Because so many people mispronounce *zoology* as *zoo-ology*, I would support spelling it *zoölogy*, with a dieresis, to reinforce the proper pronunciation: zoh-AHL-uh-jee. Maybe I can persuade *The New Yorker* to print it that way.

Sign Language

Q. *My wife and I were discussing whether it is correct to ask for a* signature *or an* autograph *when endorsing a check or credit card slip. Some dictionary definitions imply that they're the same, but my sense is that one would pay for or treasure an autograph but merely sign a check or contract. Yet we are routinely asked to* autograph *our credit card slips, and it just seems wrong to us. Sometimes I feel like writing (under my signature? autograph?), "To our waitress, with fond memories." Any thoughts on this?*

A. I think your instincts are on target. The usage guides are largely silent on this matter, but a well-regarded one from 1957 (*A Dictionary of Contemporary American Usage* by Bergen and Cornelia Evans) says the distinction at first was between a *signature,* a name signed either by hand or by a stamp or machine, and an *autograph* (from the Greek *auto-,* self, and *-graph,* writing), a name signed by the person. With the rise of the cult of celebrity, *autograph* came to be used for the signature of some person of distinction for an admirer. The people who ask you for your autograph

---

FASCINATING FACT *continued*

weren't enough, the circumspect labeling of potentially offensive terms is nothing short of paranoid. Consider this entry:

hoot•ers *npl.*
OFFENSIVE TERM an offensive term for a woman's breasts, especially when large (*slang*)

Thankfully, this and the other blunders noted were corrected in the subsequent *Microsoft Encarta College Dictionary* (2001). ⓢ

---

but I was too spaced-out. 🖝

on a credit card slip are technically not wrong, but they are muddying this useful distinction. Or maybe they think you look like somebody famous.

Continuity

Q. *Is there a difference between* continual *and* continuous, *or are they interchangeable?*

A. Dictionaries often list the words *continuous* and *continual* as synonyms, and today many educated speakers use them interchangeably. They are not interchangeable, however, and the ability to distinguish *continual* and *continuous* precisely is one sign of a careful user of the language.

Continual means happening again and again at short intervals. We speak of continual reminders, continual attempts, or the continual ringing of the telephone. *Continuous* means uninterrupted or unbroken. We speak of continuous noise, continuous rain, a continuous effort, or the continuous rotation of the earth.

Invaluable Answer

Q. *I always thought that the prefix* in- *was privative, meaning it reverses or negates the meaning of what follows, as in* insignificant, indecent, *and* incredible. *So why does* in- *before* valuable *make* valuable *more valuable?*

A. Many prefixes have more than one meaning or function. For instance, *trans-* can mean "beyond" (as in *transcend*), "across" (as in *transfer* and *transport,* literally "to carry across"), or "through" (as in *transpire,* which traditionally means "to pass from secrecy into knowledge, to be revealed").

A number of prefixes can also serve as intensifiers, adding the sense of "extremely," "completely," or "thoroughly" to the word they're attached to. *Trans-* performs that function in *transform,* "to change completely." Likewise, *perfervid* means "extremely fervid" and *bespatter* means "to thoroughly spatter." This is the function of

☜ I could have been a vacuum cleaner salesman

the prefix *in-* in the word *invaluable.* Often, though, this intensify-
ing *in-* has little apparent force. It is somewhat apparent in *inflame,*
but hardly detectable in *insist, inscribe,* and *inspect.*

And by the way, although *in-* is often privative, as you note, it
also commonly means just what it says: *in* (as in *insert, inter, incar-
cerate*). It shares this duty with the prefix *en-.*

Burning Question

Q. *How is it that* flammable *and* inflammable *can mean the same
thing? They look like opposites. Do we have a single word that means
"not flammable"?*

A. Yes, *flammable* and *inflammable* are an odd pair. That's because in this case the *in-* is simply an intensifier, not a privative prefix negating the meaning of what follows. And as you point out,
they're synonymous. The traditional forms were *inflammable* and
noninflammable, which are kind of clunky. Nowadays we prefer the
more streamlined *flammable* and *nonflammable.*

Emotional Plea

Q. *I have trouble distinguishing the words* sympathy *and* empathy. *What's the difference?*

A. You are probably having trouble distinguishing these words
because in recent years *empathy* has become a trendy substitute for
sympathy. You often hear people say "I empathize with you" when
they mean "I sympathize with you." They do this, no doubt, to
show you how they do not need to rely on ordinary words.

Sympathy is compassion, a sharing of the feelings of another,
while *empathy* is much stronger, a thorough identification with
another, a sharing of experience and feelings either imaginatively
or actually. *Sympathy* is what you feel for someone who displays a
flashy word when an ordinary one is called for. *Empathy* is what
you feel when you realize you've been making the same stupid mistake yourself.

but that would've sucked. 🖘

Foot-in-Mouth Disease

Q. *What has happened to the distinction between a* podium *and a* lectern? *It used to be that you would stand on a* podium *(a small platform) and put your notes on the* lectern *(a reading stand for a public speaker). But nowadays you rarely encounter* lectern; *you hear about people speaking from a* podium *instead.*

And just the other day I was flipping through the fourth edition of The American Heritage Dictionary *when I saw a photograph of a speaker at a* lectern *with the word* podium *underneath. That dictionary's definitions of* podium *further confuse things; the first is "an elevated platform" while the second is "a stand for holding the notes of a public speaker; a lectern." No wonder people constantly confuse these words. Is there no hope for the traditional distinction?*

A. As long as people misuse words or use them imprecisely, misuse and imprecision will infiltrate the dictionaries. The only hope lies with those of us who care about precision and clarity and who make distinctions. We must spread our gospel and let others know that you can't always trust your dictionary in such matters. The dictionary is not an arbiter. It's a mirror. Wherever words have become wrinkled or flabby, you'll see wrinkles or flab.

Anyone who wants to write and speak well needs a lot more help than a dictionary can provide—help that can be found only in thoughtful usage guides, which do not sanction the substitution of *podium* for *lectern*. The substitution, "once widely condemned as a misuse, has become commonplace," says *Garner's Modern American Usage*. "But careful writers should avoid it."

◄ I could have been a trumpeter

Hare Ye, Hare Ye

Q. *My wife says I'm* harebrained. *I say I'm* hairbrained. *Which is it?*

A. There is no *hair* in *harebrained.*

"A wild, rash, heedless, foolish, volatile or giddy person is said to be harebrained because he has or shows no more brains or sense than a hare or rabbit," writes George Stimpson in *A Book About a Thousand Things.* "The word is sometimes incorrectly written *hairbrained,* even by reputable writers, and that spelling, which began to occur before 1600, has misled many into seeking a different origin of the term."

Tell Your Harebrained Husband . . .

Q. *I say it's* Welsh rabbit, *but my husband scoffs and insists that it's* Welsh rarebit. *He even showed me a cookbook that says* rarebit. *Am I wrong?*

A. In his *Devil's Dictionary,* Ambrose Bierce defined *rarebit* as "a Welsh rabbit, in the speech of the humorless, who point out that it is not a rabbit. To whom it may be solemnly explained that the comestible known as toad-in-the-hole is really not a toad, and that *riz-de-veau à la financière* is not the smile of a calf prepared after the recipe of a she banker."

The original and still proper form is *Welsh rabbit.* As Mark Morton explains in *Cupboard Love: A Dictionary of Culinary Curiosities,* "Welsh rabbit contains no rabbit and is not Welsh in origin; instead, it is a dish of melted cheese poured over toast, invented by the British and given its name to mock the Welsh, who were supposedly so gullible that they would accept such a dish as real rabbit." This eighteenth-century culinary jest was forgotten by the nineteenth century, but the dish survived, which left people wondering why they were calling cheese toast *rabbit.* Thus was born the sanitized and euphemized *rarebit,* as in a "rare bit" of food. "This

but I don't like blowing my own horn. 🙌

well-intentioned explanation caught on," writes Morton, "promoted, no doubt, by the Welsh themselves and by restaurateurs who feared that a customer might order Welsh rabbit and actually expect to receive a rabbit."

Stop That Wracket

Q. *Do you* wrack *your brains or* rack *your brains?*

A. Yikes! Stop *wracking* your brains because it's *rack,* which in this sense means "to strain or stretch." "*Wrack* is an archaic variant of *wreck,*" notes *Bryson's Dictionary of Troublesome Words,* "and now almost never appears except in the expression *wrack and ruin.*" Mnemonic device: Think of the instrument of torture with a brain on it, being stretched. (Don't you just love that image?)

Incidentally, it's also *nerve-racking,* not *nerve-wracking.*

Row of Celibacy

Q. *More and more these days I hear or read the word* celibate *used to mean "not having or refraining from having sexual relations." Maybe I'm old-fashioned, but I always thought the word for that was* chaste. *Can you please comment on this?*

A. You appear to be among the dwindling number of people who know something about the history of this word. *Celibate* comes from the Latin *caelebs,* unmarried, and unmarried is what it meant in English until the mid-twentieth century, when the sense of "not having or abstaining from sex" developed. I suspect this new sense came about because people mistook the ecclesiastical phrase *vow of celibacy* to mean a pledge to abstain from sexual relations, when in fact it meant a pledge not to marry. (Not being married, if you can believe it, once implied abstinence from sex for both the laity and the clergy.)

◄ I could have been a grocery clerk

The American Heritage Dictionary, which has an interesting note on *celibate,* says that "the new sense of the word seems to have displaced the old" and that 68 percent of its usage panel rejected the older use in the sentence *He remained celibate* [unmarried], *although he engaged in sexual intercourse.* These days, if you'd rather be understood than be a stickler, you'll go with the majority. But, pedant that I am, I avoid *celibate* and use *unmarried* instead.

By the way, *American Heritage* defines *chaste* as, among other things, "abstaining from sexual intercourse; celibate." Did I mention that dictionaries are not in the business of promoting clarity in language?

Horton Hears a *That, Which,* and *Who*

Q. *It has always been my understanding that* which *refers to things,* who *refers to people, and that* may refer to either people or things, although some prefer to use who *when referring to people and* that *when referring to things. Is it really that simple?*

A. It's that simple. You nailed it. My work here is done.

But—nobody gets off that easy with this word maven—let me emphasize two points: first, that it is perfectly acceptable, no matter what some may say, to use *that* with people (as in Mark Twain's *The Man That Corrupted Hadleyburg*). To quote just one of many authorities that sanction *that* for people as well as for things: "*That* for *who* is sometimes objected to, but the objection has no basis" (Roy H. Copperud, *American Usage and Style: The Consensus*). Second, it is a grave sin to use *who* of things, as in "the company *who.*"

This grave sin, regrettably, is becoming more and more common. I call it "the corporate *who,*" and in recent years I've been hearing and reading it all over the place. My citation file runneth over: "Rite Aid is the only drugstore who . . ."; "Analysis Research, who is looking for . . ."; "It's still being opposed by the farming industry, who say that . . ."; "California is one of only twelve states who don't regulate . . ." I have heard a Pulitzer prize-winning reporter say

but I bagged that idea. ❧

"companies who," and I have seen the corporate *who* in the pages of respected publications like *The New York Times Magazine.*

To me, a corporation is the furthest thing from a human being I can think of, so this trend to anthropomorphize industry and government with the relative pronoun *who* is mysterious. I suspect it may be self-delusional—a subtle way of putting a human face on a faceless, unfeeling thing—and that is even more reason to avoid it.

Obsolutely

Q. *What is the difference between* obsolete *and* obsolescent*?*

A. *Obsolete* means "no longer used," *obsolescent* means "passing out of use." The baseball announcer's hackneyed phrase for a home run in progress ("going, going, gone!") could be translated into highfalutin English as "obsolescent, more obsolescent, obsolete!" The suffix *-escent,* from the present participle of certain Latin verbs, means "growing or occurring gradually," as in *juvenescent,* growing younger, and *senescent,* growing older.

Get Serial

Q. *What's your opinion on the so-called serial comma? Should it be* every Tom, Dick, and Harry *or* every Tom, Dick and Harry*?*

A. I'm a serial commander and I frown on serial killers who eliminate the comma before *and.* But that's just a deeply ingrained personal preference. I realize that newspaper copy has been unserialized for years, and outside the world of book publishing the final comma is now usually omitted.

Nonetheless, I can guarantee that if you use the serial comma you will never get into trouble. You will never have to deal with an awkward or confusing construction like "I have many TVs in my house, including digital, high-definition, black and white and color." And you will never stumble into ambiguity, as in this ludicrous dedication: "To my parents, Ayn Rand and God."

I could have been a syndicated cartoonist

Quake or Quaker?

Q. *Why isn't there an* r *in* temblor*? Shouldn't it be* tremblor *or* trembler*?*

A. You may tremble when you feel a temblor, but there's nothing shaky about this word. *Temblor* is so spelled because it's a loanword from Spanish, which dropped the *r*.

Et Too, You Brute

Q. *I am a writer of fiction, and I have an ongoing argument with my publisher—otherwise known as the tyrants in New York—about using or not using a comma with the word* too*. They insist on inserting a comma before* too *in sentences like* I wanted to go, too *and setting it off with commas in sentences like* I, too, wanted to go. *I think the comma is often unnecessary and I want the option to use it or not according to my ear.*

A. Some stylists—including your "tyrants in New York"—favor always employing the comma to set off *too,* but that is an arbitrary preference unsupported by usage or authority. In fact, you are right: The comma is optional, depending on how much of a pause is required, and it is usually unnecessary.

So says Edward D. Johnson in his *Handbook of Good English* (1991). "In its *also* meaning, *too* is often set off with commas, as in *You, too, are an Aries,*" he writes. "Parenthetical constructions are generally set off with commas, and *too* is essentially parenthetical in the example. However, an overriding principle of modern punctuation is to use none when it performs no helpful function and cannot be heard when the sentence is spoken. I advise not setting off *too* unless setting it off is helpful in some way. *You too are an Aries* is smoother."

The citations in the *Oxford English Dictionary* show that writers in the first half of the twentieth century tended to use the comma (or commas): *He did, too!* (Booth Tarkington, 1914); *He was, too, in the army* (Margaret Mitchell, 1936); *She is, too* (P. G. Wodehouse,

but I didn't want to make peanuts.

1937). But prose style since then has favored omitting the punctuation: *She did too have appendicitis* (1939); *You have too* (1963); *I do too care* (1969); *You can too!* (1978). Today, I think, a comma before *too* constructions like these seems peculiar, old-fashioned, and bumpy, especially in dialogue.

I have found the comma-less *too* in countless nonfiction books and novels, and in respected periodicals like *The New York Times Book Review*. I have found it in the work of my esteemed colleagues in language mavenry, Jan Freeman of the *Boston Globe* and Barbara Wallraff of *The Atlantic Monthly*. I have found it in H. L. Mencken's *The American Language* (1937), in Bergen and Cornelia Evans's *Dictionary of Contemporary American Usage* (1957), and in several current dictionaries. And those are only a few of many examples I could give you. Tell that, my friend, to "the tyrants in New York."

❧ FIVE ❦

A CIVIL TONGUE

Wherein the Author Launders Your
Pronunciation and Presses You
To Speak with Propriety and Poise

Friends and fellow Americans, lend me your ears. From the halls of academe to the hills of Hollywood, from the White House to your house, we are wallowing in poor speech.

Listen to the politicians bicker about Social Security, which they call *Sosal* Security or *Sosa* Security, as if it were for the benefit of baseball player Sammy Sosa. Listen to the radio reporters who say *progrum* for *program* but who wouldn't dream of slurring the *-gram* in *diagram, telegram, milligram,* or *anagram.* Listen to the *meter*-ologists who tell you the *tem-puh-chur.* Listen to the sportscasters interviewing professional ath-*uh*-letes. Listen to the voiceover in the credit card commercials pronouncing *Visa* with an *s* as in *sell.* (The word comes from French and the *s* is properly soft, as in *rose.*) Listen to the precious *see* we so often hear in *negotiate* and *negotiation* instead of the traditional *she.* Listen to all the people (perhaps you are among them?) who say *nucular* instead of *nuclear.*

My fellow Americans—or *Amerkins,* as Lyndon Johnson used to say—it is high time we paid some attention to our pronunciation, which so many regrettably call pro-*noun*-ciation. As Shakespeare counseled, "Mend your speech a little, lest it mar your fortunes."

I'm not going to pontificate about the decline and fall of oral civilization. The logorrhea of modern life may be mindless and sometimes mind-numbing, but I don't believe it's destroying Discourse As We Know It. Also, unlike Shaw's Henry Higgins, I'm not out to transform guttersnipes into gentry. It's the millions of bumbling educated speakers—the ones with diplomas—whose unmended speech most needs help.

Years ago we may have been a nation of pronunciation slobs and pronunciation snobs, but that stark contrast no longer obtains. The problem is that we have become a nation of pronunciation *blobs.* We are literate but lazy, intelligent but uninformed, educated enough to worry a bit about our spelling and grammar but too complacent to take any pains to improve our speech.

Part of the problem is lack of instruction. Remember speech class? It's ancient history now. Today many teachers and parents are reluctant to tutor young people in pronunciation, often because they're unsure themselves of what's correct. No one ever taught *them.* We tell our kids that it's *spaghetti,* not *puhsketti,* and *synonym,* not *cinnamon,* but after those rudimentary admonishments they're on their own.

In the first half of the twentieth century many Americans apparently were concerned about mending their speech, because there was no shortage of books with titles like *Everyday Errors in Pronunciation* and *You Don't Say!* and no shortage of respected arbiters like W. Cabell Greet, a Columbia English professor and speech consultant to CBS. But with the ascent of descriptive linguistics, which proscribed value judgments about language, pronunciation manuals and consultants fell out of fashion, and since the 1960s it's been hard for hoi polloi to find reliable advice on the spoken word.

⇥I could have been an arborist

Instead, what little guidance you're likely to find on pronunciation today is in our dictionaries, and it's often confusing and disingenuous. For example, the recent editions of *Merriam-Webster's Collegiate Dictionary* note that the pronunciation *liberry* for *library* is heard "from educated speakers, including college presidents and professors, as well as with somewhat greater frequency from less educated speakers." If a few college presidents and professors say *liberry*, does that somehow make it less incorrect? Should we now emulate them and the "less educated speakers"? Such ambiguous pronouncements can only cause frustration or apathy. In fact, they seem designed to *create* pronunciation blobs.

Increasing informality at all levels of American culture has made our writing more colloquial, which is by no means a bad thing. Who doesn't prefer a casual style over a stilted, pretentious one? In our speech, however, many of us fail to distinguish between what is easy and natural and what is just plain sloppy. Others, aware of this pitfall and fearful of being thought careless, overcompensate by adopting fastidious and eccentric pronunciations. It's a lose-lose situation.

There is also the persistent myth that higher education and professional achievement will somehow eradicate faulty speech. If you believe that, listen again, for it is from the lips of some of the most successful and prominent people that you will hear not only all the usual beastly mispronunciations but also some of the most preposterous affectations.

For example, I have heard a high-level administrator at a prestigious California university pronounce *consortium* as *consor*-see-*um*. I have heard Dan Rather pronounce *respiratory* after the British fashion, with the stress on *spy*. And I have heard a former congressman pronounce *anal* to rhyme with *channel*. How can the perpetrators of such anomalies fail to realize that they stick out like a sore tongue?

Which Realtor would you trust — the one who says REE-luh-tur or the one who says REE-ul-tur? Which jeweler would you buy

but I didn't want to go out on a limb. ☞

from—the one who sells JOO-luh-ree or the one who sells JOO-wuul-ree? Which arborist would you hire—the one who trims FOH-lij or the one who trims FOH-lee-ij? Would you retain a lawyer who pronounces *grievous* in three syllables and puts a *he* in *heinous*? If all these questions seem *irrevelant* rather than *irrelevant,* you may skip this chapter (at your own risk).

Let's face it. We judge others by the way they speak, and they judge us. It is time to admit that how we choose to say our words can matter as much as the words we choose to say.

Many of us wonder, at times, if the way we speak is a liability. I can assert unequivocally—and not *unequivocably,* as it is often mispronounced and misspelled—that mispronunciation is a liability. I also believe that becoming a better speaker is a lot less daunting than losing thirty pounds or learning French. And there is no question that we sorely need more cultivated speakers, who have arrived at their pronunciation not simply by imitation and conjecture but by careful consideration and practice.

Cultivated speakers do not invent pronunciations for unfamiliar words or adopt novel pronunciations for familiar words. Cultivated speakers also do not model their speech after those "whose abilities and character entitle [their] opinions to respect," as Noah Webster wrote, "but whose pronunciation may be altogether accidental or capricious."

Finally, cultivated speakers are not opposed to linguistic change. They know such a position would be untenable. However, they are skeptical of ignorant, pompous, and faddish change. They are, as Alexander Pope wrote, "not the first by whom the new are tried, / Nor yet the last to lay the old aside."

Can a nation of pronunciation blobs become a nation of cultivated speakers? The answer is on the tip of your tongue.

Note: In this chapter I often refer to "the six major current American dictionaries." These are the fourth edition of *Webster's New World College Dictionary* (1999); the fourth edition of *The American*

◈ I could have been a runner

Heritage Dictionary (2000); *Random House Webster's College Dictionary* (2001); *The New Oxford American Dictionary* (2001); the *Microsoft Encarta College Dictionary* (2001); and the eleventh edition of *Merriam-Webster's Collegiate Dictionary* (2003).

Stressful Opinion

Q. *Where should the stress fall in the word* formidable*?*

A. On *for*, not on *mid*. Because so many people have taken to mispronouncing *formidable*, you will find second-syllable stress listed in current dictionaries. But the traditional pronunciation, with the stress on the first syllable, is listed first, and modern authorities prefer FOR-*midable*.

There Is No *O* in *Homage*

Q. *I hear a lot of people pronouncing* homage *as if it were French—with a silent* h, *a long* o *as in* home, *and the stress on the second syllable so it rhymes with* garage. *To me this sounds pretentious. Isn't* homage *an English word, and shouldn't it have an anglicized pronunciation?*

A. Yes it's English, and yes it should be pronounced in English: HAHM-ij.

The variant you describe, oh-MAHZH, is a vogue pronunciation perpetrated by those who think that by Frenchifying this word they gain some measure of prestige. They don't. *Homage* has been an English word since the thirteenth century, and the *h* has been pronounced in cultivated speech since the eighteenth century.

The *h*-less variant AHM-ij is recorded in dictionaries but frowned upon by modern authorities on pronunciation. "It is a silly (but quite common) pretension to omit the /h/ sound," says *Garner's Modern American Usage*. In other words, if you say AHM-ij you're pretentious, and if you say oh-MAHZH you're a twit.

Get Short *I*

Q. *I'm perplexed when I hear people pronounce the word* primer— *meaning a book that teaches children to read, not an undercoat of*

but I couldn't get a leg up.

paint—with a short i *as in* pin. *It seems to me it ought to be pronounced like the undercoat of paint, with a long* i *to rhyme with* timer, *because it's spelled with one* m *rather than two (as in* swimmer*) and it's a book that* primes *(prepares) children for reading. What is your opinion?*

A. Ah, the dangers of applying too much logic to matters of pronunciation. Analogy and etymology are useful guides in matters of speech, but when pitted against long-standing custom—no matter how illogical it may seem—it is custom that invariably prevails.

Such is the case with *primer,* the elementary book, which dates back to Chaucer and the fourteenth century. By contrast, *primer,* the undercoat of paint, dates only from the eighteenth century, and until the twentieth century it appears to have been used only for the undercoatings used in fine art. At any rate, for a long time the word was spelled in various ways (*prymmer, prymer, primmer,* etc.) and the British used both the pronunciation rhyming with *swimmer* and the one rhyming with *timer.* By the early twentieth century the rhyme with *timer* had become dominant in British speech, prompting H. W. Fowler to remark in his classic *Modern English Usage* (1926) that "the traditional pronunciation is [PRIM-ur], and the word was very commonly spelt with -*mm*- . . . but in the names of modern school manuals [PRY-mur] is now more usual."

In the United States, however, the traditional pronunciation PRIM-ur never faced much of a challenge from the "more logical" PRY-mur, and it prevails to this day. That situation may eventually change, though, for the word is not as common as it used to be and

I could have been a gambler

history shows that unfamiliar words are more vulnerable to spelling pronunciations. But for now, American authorities agree that the rhyme with *swimmer* is preferred and the rhyme with *timer* is British.

What Say *Ye*?

Q. *I always thought the Old English* ye *was pronounced to rhyme with* me *whether it meant* you *(O* ye *of little faith) or the (*Ye Olde Inne*). But a friend of mine says that when it means* the *it should be pronounced like* the. *Is that true?*

A. Your friend is correct. *Ye*, meaning "you," and *ye*, meaning "the," are different words with different pronunciations. The *ye* that means "you" is the archaic form of *you*; it comes through Middle English from the Anglo-Saxon *ge* and is pronounced to rhyme with *see*. The *ye* that means "the" is the old way of writing or printing the definite article *the*, with the *y* representing the Anglo-Saxon runic *th* character called "thorn." This *ye* is popularly but erroneously pronounced like the other *ye*. Thus, in *ye great ones in ye court* the first *ye* rhymes with *me* and the second should be pronounced *the*.

Ominous Words

Q. *It is very common to hear "I'm gonna" instead of "I'm going to," even from broadcasters. What is your opinion of that?*

A. *I'm gonna* and the slurvier *ominna* (or *omunna*) are common and venial in informal, everyday conversation but sloppy and inappropriate in situations calling for more careful speech. I would hardly expect everyone on the radio these days to speak formally, but announcers and hosts and newsreaders ought to enunciate precisely and avoid this kind of slurring.

Finding Your Niche

Q. *I often hear people pronounce the word* niche *as* neesh, *to rhyme with* leash. *I always thought the proper pronunciation rhymed with* ditch. *Have things changed? How should the word be pronounced?*

but the odds were against it. 🖘

❧ QUOTE UNQUOTE ❧

"The price of learning to use words is the development of an acute self-consciousness. Nor is it enough to pay attention to words only when facing the task of writing. That is like playing the violin only on the night of the concert. You must attend to words when you read, when you speak, when others speak. Words must become ever present in your waking life, an incessant concern, like color and design if the graphic arts matter to you, or pitch and rhythm if it is music, or speed and form if it is athletics."—*Jacques Barzun,* Simple and Direct: A Rhetoric for Writers

A. *Niche* should be pronounced your way: to rhyme with *ditch*.

The word entered English from French in the early 1600s and the anglicized pronunciation has been preferred since the mid-1700s. The pompously re-Frenchified variant *neesh* has been heard at least since the early twentieth century. There is evidence suggesting that *neesh* is originally British, which is probably why it appeals to certain pseudosophisticated American speakers. *Garner's Modern American Usage* says that "many consider [*neesh*] a pretentious de-anglicization of a word that has been anglicized since the 1700s." Three of the six major current American dictionaries sanction only the traditional anglicized pronunciation, and the other three list it first.

Savor That Foreign Flavor

Q. *I'm wondering about the pronunciation of the word* gyro. *I worked in a Greek restaurant one summer when I was in college, and the owner, who was Greek, hammered the Greek pronunciation, year-oh, into our heads. But I often hear people pronounce it with a* j *sound for the* g, *as in* gymnasium. *Maybe that's right in terms of consistency, but to me the* j *just sounds wrong. What do you think?*

❧ I could have been an editor

❧ SOUND BITE ❧

Brontë (sisters Charlotte, Emily, and Anne): BRAHN-tee (rhymes with *Monty*).

The surname of these talented sisters is commonly mispronounced BRAHN-tay (-tay rhyming with *day*), and sometimes brahn-TAY, as if it were French. But their father, Patrick Brontë, was Irish, and he placed the dots over the *e* to show that the letter is pronounced as a separate syllable, for many *e*'s at the ends of English names are silent: e.g., *Browne, Wilde, Crabbe, Trollope.*

A. It's not a matter of consistency. It's a matter of etymology. *Gyro* is a loanword; it comes directly from modern Greek. *Gymnasium* is English and belongs to a sizable family of English words formed from ancient Greek roots in which the initial *g* is pronounced like *j*.

Gyro is very new to English (circa 1970–75) and still very Greek behind the ears, so if you want to pronounce it in Greek, go right ahead. You have every right to do so and plenty of authority to back you up: Three of the six major current American dictionaries list *year-oh* first. Though an anglicized pronunciation with initial *j* will probably win out eventually, there's nothing wrong with saying it the way you were taught. Your pronunciation is both authentic and comfortable for you, and in my opinion that's enough authority to justify sticking with it. But if you should ever become uncomfortable saying it that way, you may want to consider adopting an anglicization. Current dictionaries list three of them: *jeer-oh*, which is half-anglicized and unobjectionable; *zheer-oh*, which is neither Greek nor English but pseudo-French and best avoided; and *jy-roh*, which takes all the foreign flavor out of the word and makes it sound like a prefix rather than a tasty repast.

but I didn't want to be a copycat. ❧

IT'S GREEK TO THEE

The English language has a myriad of words formed or borrowed from ancient Greek—like *myriad*, for instance. Read each clue below and guess which ancient Greek-influenced English word it describes.

1. This noun means literally "written or drawn with light."

   _ _ _ _ _ _ _ _ _ _

2. In rhetoric and Greek drama, this word refers to a speech to someone who is not present. It is also a mark of punctuation. _ _ _ _ _ _ _ _ _ _ _

3. This noun means literally "a down-turning" or "an overturning." It is also the formal term for the third and final part of a Greek drama.

   _ _ _ _ _ _ _ _ _ _

4. This word combines the Greek word for "the marketplace" with the suffix *-phobia* to mean "fear of public places or open spaces."

   _ _ _ _ _ _ _ _ _ _ _

5. This locution is actually two Greek words that in Greek meant "the many." It is used in English to mean "the masses, the common people." _ _ _ _ _ _ _ _ _

6. This noun comes from the name of a place in Greece near Athens. As the story goes, when the Athenians defeated the Persians there in 490 B.C., a messenger ran from there to Athens to announce the victory.

   _ _ _ _ _ _ _ _

7. This adjective comes from a Greek verb that meant "to tear flesh." Today we use it of biting, ironic humor.

   _ _ _ _ _ _ _ _ _

8. This noun comes from the Greek word for "dog" and originally referred to a group of ancient Greek philosophers who sneered at wealth and personal comfort.

   _ _ _ _ _

I could have been a personal trainer

9. This noun comes from a Greek verb that meant "to exercise or train naked." (In the original Olympic games the contestants competed in the buff.) Today we stage some sporting events in it.

_____

10. This noun comes from a Greek word meaning "a slave who took children to and from school and supervised them." Now it's a fancy synonym for a teacher.

_____

11. This verb originates in the ancient Athenian method of removing people considered dangerous or embarrassing to the state. Citizens would vote by writing the name of the person to be expelled on a potsherd or earthenware tablet. Banishment was for a period of ten years, after which time the person was considered vindicated and free to return. _____

12. This adjective originally referred to fourteen books of an early translation of the Old Testament into Greek called the Septuagint. The authenticity of these books was called into question, and they were subsequently rejected by Judaism and considered uncanonical, or not authoritative, by Protestants. However, eleven of these fourteen books are accepted by the Roman Catholic Church. Today, this word usually refers to any writings of doubtful authenticity or authorship, and means not genuine, counterfeit, spurious. _____

Answers appear on page 265.

but it didn't work out.

Here's my rule of thumb concerning native versus anglicized pronunciations. Assuming that a word is truly a loanword, and not just an English concoction from another language or languages, then you may use the native pronunciation with impunity if (a) you know it and are comfortable with it; (b) you aren't saying it that way to appear smarter or act superior; and (c) it won't sound completely weird to most people.

A Swore Point

Q. *Is* sword *the only word beginning with* sw- *in which the* w *is not pronounced? And why isn't it pronounced?*

A. You're right—*sword* and its compounds appear to be the only words beginning with *sw-* in which *w* is silent.

In the late 1700s some people pronounced *swoon* like *soon,* an elision not favored by the orthoepists of the time. The early American lexicographer Noah Webster—who championed a number of oddball pronunciations, like rhyming *ant* with *want* and saying *ax* for *ask*—advocated bringing *sword* in line with the other *sw-* words, and in the early editions of his dictionary, first published in 1828, he listed the pronunciation with an audible *w* first. But from the 1860s on, this eccentricity was dropped from the Webster line of dictionaries. In his dictionary of 1860, Joseph Emerson Worcester, Webster's archrival, notes Webster's preference for /sword/ alongside the preference for /sord/ of nine other authorities dating back to 1760. So we know this much: The pronunciation /sord/ was firmly in place by the mid-1700s. But how that *w* came to be lost—or if it always was silent—is still a mystery.

Don't Seize the Day

Q. *How do you pronounce the plural of* process?

A. *Processes* should end with the sound of *is,* not with the sound of *seize* (that's a British pronunciation). The mistaken notion that *processes* is akin to Greek plurals like *theses* (singular *thesis*) and

⇥ I could have been Santa Claus

crises (singular *crisis*) may account for the variant *process*-eez, which is an affectation. *Processes* is a regular English *-es* plural, like *faces* and *purposes*—you wouldn't say FAY-seez and PUR-puh-seez, would you?—and should be pronounced with a regular *is* at the end.

Stressing Out

Q. *I have a question about where to place the emphasis in three phrases:* Empire State building; Knott's Berry Farm; *and* God only knows. *The way people commonly stress them seems illogical to me. They say "Empire* State building" *instead of "*Empire State *building";*
"Knott's Berry Farm" *instead of "Knott's* Berry Farm"; "God only knows" *instead of "God* only knows." *Can you explain this?*

eyeliterate
given to pronouncing words as they are spelled, by guess-work, without both-ering to check the pronunciation in a dictionary: for ex-ample, saying "chick" for chic *or pronounc-ing* extraordinary *in six syllables instead of five. An eyeliterate person is a dumbel-letrist, someone in* diacritical condition.

A. We stress certain phrases in an apparently illogical manner because the laws of prosody take precedence over meaning and logic. By "the laws of prosody" (pronounced PRAH-suh-dee) I mean the conventions and tendencies governing rhythm and accent in language.

In each of your examples—*Empire State Building, Knott's Berry Farm,* and *God only knows*—the phrase begins with a dactyl, a long or stressed syllable followed by two short, unstressed syllables: EM-py-ur, NOTS-ber-ee, GOD-ohn-lee. Then the dactyl is followed either by a single, stressed syllable (*Farm, knows*) or by another dactyl (STATE-bill-ding). Thus, in simplified metrical terms the rhythms of *Knott's Berry Farm* and *God only knows* are DA-da-da DA, and the rhythm of *Empire State Building* is DA-da-da DA-da-da.

The dactyl and its opposite, the anapest (two short syllables followed by one long: da da DA) are powerful rhythms, hardwired into the language and into much music. They have a lilt that's

but I didn't have the presence. ☛

SOUND BITE

Boleyn, Anne Properly, BULL-in (like *bull in*).

Traditionally, the last name of this second wife of Henry VIII of England and mother of Elizabeth I is pronounced like *bull in* with the stress on *bull*. Shakespeare, for example, spelled the name *Bullen*, indicating this pronunciation. Second-syllable stress (buh-LIN) has been standard only since the 1960s. Four of the six major current American dictionaries list BULL-in first.

difficult to resist. Though it may make more sense to say *Knott's* BERRY *Farm* or *God* ONLY *knows*, it would go against our innate sense of rhythm; it just wouldn't feel right. So in these cases, and in many others, when sense is not obscured by sound, sound takes priority over sense.

Comptrol Freak

Q. *Why do we sometimes spell it* comptroller *but pronounce it* controller?

A. "*Comptroller* is an erroneous spelling of *controller*," explains Bergen Evans in *Comfortable Words*, "introduced about the year 1500 by some zealous pedant who had found out that the French word for *account* was *compte*. This absurd spelling became established in the titles of certain positions and in these titles it remains. Thus it is the Comptroller General of the United States, so fixed by law. But it is still pronounced *controller*—though one hears *comptroller* every now and then from some earnest soul who just can't believe that *mp* is ever pronounced *n*."

Vice Advice

Q. *Should the* vice *in* vice versa *be pronounced in one or two syllables?*

A. The *vice* in *vice versa* isn't the same *vice* that's in *vice squad*,

I could have been a beautician

which has one syllable. It's from the Latin *vicis,* change, turn, alternation, and properly has two syllables. Older authorities preferred a precise rendering of the two long Latin vowels: VY-see (rhymes with *high see*). Over the years that got softened into VY-suh, the pronunciation now preferred by most cultivated speakers. No authority I know of prefers the monosyllabic *vice* (rhyming with *mice*), which first achieved dictionary recognition in 1961, in the infamously permissive *Webster's Third New International Dictionary,* where it was listed last. Four of the six major current American dictionaries list VY-suh VUR-suh first.

Go Bysshe

Q. *How do you pronounce the middle name of the poet* Percy Bysshe Shelley?

A. The only recognized pronunciation for *Bysshe* is BISH, rhyming with *fish.*

Check Your *Cache*

Q. *I'm curious about the pronunciation of* cache, *as in a cache of* weapons. *I've heard it pronounced by reporters on radio and television sometimes in one syllable, like* cash, *and sometimes in two syllables, like* cash hay. *Are both ways of saying it acceptable?*

A. *Cache,* meaning "secretly stored items or a secret storage place," is pronounced just like *cash;* the *e* at the end is silent. Unfortunately, people sometimes confuse *cache* with a different word, *cachet,* meaning "prestige," which is pronounced in two syllables to rhyme with *parfait:* ka-SHAY.

but I couldn't make up for lost time. ✍

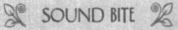

SOUND BITE

Chavez (César) CHAH-vez (*ch* as in *chop*).
The *ch* in *Chavez* should sound like the *ch* in *chop*, not like *sh* in *shop*. There is no authority whatsoever for the beastly SHAH-vez, or for the even beastlier shuh-VEZ. For the man's first name, you may say SES-sahr, like the Spanish, or anglicize it to SEE-zur, like the salad.

Out of Syncope

Q. *I've often noticed how some speakers clip their pronunciation of certain words. For example,* president *comes out as* prezdent, *government as* govment, *and* Social Security *as* soshsecurity. *Is there a term for this kind of abbreviated pronunciation? Why do people do it, and are there any other prominent examples of it?*

A. The technical term for what you describe is *syncope* (like *sink a pea*), the contraction of a word by eliminating a sound or syllable from its middle. *Prezdent* and *govment* are but two of many syncopated pronunciations in the language, and while these two examples are not representative of the best speech (three syllables for these words is more cultivated), syncopated pronunciations are not always objectionable. Long-established examples of syncope include *kernel* for *colonel,* *Wenzday* for *Wednesday,* and *bizness* for *business.* More recently, educated speakers have embraced VEJ-tuh-bull for *vegetable,* LAB-ruh-tor-ee for *laboratory,* AHP-ruh for *opera,* FAM-lee for *family,* and CHAWK-lit for *chocolate,* to cite just a few examples. However, AK-rit for *accurate,* YOO-zhul for *usual,* puh-TIK-lur for *particular,* and VUR-bij for *verbiage* are still considered objectionable by many.

Syncopated pronunciations tend to improve the fluidity of speech, which is why they're so common. It's easier to say VAK-

I could have been a jailer

🦋 SOUND BITE 🦋

Coleridge (Samuel Taylor) KOHL-rij.

This name is perennially mispronounced—even by English teachers—in three syllables, either like *cola ridge* or like *collar ridge*. But it should be pronounced in two syllables, like *coal ridge*, which is in accord with the poet's own usage.

yoom than VAK-yoo-um. But easier is not always clearer. When the syncopated pronunciation garbles the word (or sometimes the phrase), it is usually considered slovenly. Your *soshsecurity* for *Social Security* falls into this category. It is an example of Slurvian, a facetious term apparently coined by John Davenport in a 1949 *New Yorker* piece to denote an American dialect characterized by highly syncopated, semiliterate pronunciation.

Here are some examples of Slurvian: *Yerp* (Europe); *forn* (foreign); *surp* (syrup); *human bean* (human being); *claps* (collapse); *myrrh* or *mere* (mirror); *fiscal* (physical); *sport* (support); and *hits, runs, and airs* (errors). "Slurvian words that, when spelled exactly as pronounced, also make good English words," are considered "pure Slurvian," says Davenport. Thus, *lore* means lower, *plight* means polite, *gnome* stands for "no, ma'am," and a *paramour* is a power mower.

Devious *Mischievous*

Q. *I grew up saying mis-CHEE-vee-us for* mischievous. *Is this just wrong or is it a "legitimate regional variant"?*

A. Your four-syllable pronunciation of *mischievous*—as if it were spelled *mischievious*—is not standard English and not a "legitimate regional variant." *Mischievous* "is a three-syllable word," says *The New Oxford American Dictionary*. "Take care not to use this

but I was missing a key element. 🦋

incorrect four-syllable pronunciation: 'mis-CHEE-vee-uhs.'" Also nonstandard is a three-syllable pronunciation with the stress on the second syllable: mis-CHEE-vus.

No modern authority sanctions these variants, and many educated people consider them semiliterate. In short, you will not be judged favorably for stressing the word on the second syllable. The proper pronunciation has three syllables, with stress on the first: MIS-chi-vus.

Also take care with the words *heinous, grievous,* and *intravenous,* which are often mispronounced (and sometimes misspelled) as if they had an *i* before the *-ous.* Properly, they are HAY-nus, GREE-vus, and in-truh-VEE-nus.

One Short-Lived to Live

Q. *Which is the correct way to pronounce* short-lived, *with* -lived *as in the verb to* live *or as in* alive?

A. "Two of the most common mispronunciations heard on the air and in the speech of average and otherwise literate Americans are *long-lived* and *short-lived* pronounced with the short 'i' of the verb 'live,'" says the *Harper Dictionary of Contemporary Usage.* "Both words should be pronounced with a long 'i,' as heard in the noun 'life.' Why? Simply because the adjectives are formed from the noun 'life,' not from the verb 'live.'"

The pronunciation with a short *i,* as in the verb to *live,* is a British import. Although authorities continue to prefer the traditional pronunciation with long *i* and three of the six major current American dictionaries list it first, the etymologically unsound British import has become the dominant American pronunciation.

Who Goes *They're*?

Q. *My fourth-grade daughter has an assignment where she must divide words into syllables. She's wondering whether* they're *is one or two syllables. Can you help?*

⏴ *I could have been an insurance salesperson*

🦋 SOUND BITE 🦋

Dreiser (Theodore) DRY-zur, not DRY-sur.

The *s* is properly soft, as in *rose* and *raise*.

Dreiser should be pronounced with the same German *z* sound for the *s* that one hears in the last name of Theodore Geisel (GUY-zul), the real name of Dr. Seuss. DRY-zur is the pronunciation of the writer's family.

A. *They're* is a monosyllabic contraction of *they are*. Although it may sometimes sound like two syllables, especially coming from New England Yankees and Southerners, *they're* is generally pronounced with a diphthong (a one-syllable, two-sound glide, as in *oil* and *fear*) and is treated by dictionaries as monosyllabic.

On the Dot

Q. *I have always heard the name of the opera* Turandot *pronounced with a silent* t *at the end, and I seem to recall reading an article in a publication for opera buffs that said that was the proper pronunciation. But recently, on the radio, I heard the director of our city's opera company pronounce the final* t. *Whose pronunciation is correct?*

A. I would award the day to the opera director. The *NBC Handbook of Pronunciation* and John K. Bollard's *Pronouncing Dictionary of Proper Names* give TUR-un-daht (with *dot* at the end), and that is the pronunciation I always heard from my father, who for thirty-eight years was the principal harpist of the Metropolitan Opera Orchestra.

Smear Campaign

Q. *Can you please settle an argument that my artiste brother and I are having about the pronunciation of* patina? *He and his artsy friends all place the accent on the middle syllable (pa-*teen*-a) while my scientific*

but it was against my policies. 🦋

buddies and I place the accent on the first syllable (pa-tina). Whose pronunciation is correct?

A. Yours, without question. The stress should be on the *first* syllable (PAT'n-uh), not the second. Second-syllable stress runs contrary to etymology and analogy, which is a fancy way of saying that it's trendy, bogus, and sham-refined.

The erroneous variant puh-TEE-nuh is a vogue pronunciation apparently encouraged by association with such words as *farina, sestina,* and *ballerina.* It may also be an ignorant attempt to evoke the word's continental past. *Patina* comes through Italian, where the accent falls on the first syllable, from Latin, where the accent also fell on the first syllable. Properly, *patina* follows the pattern of *retina, stamina,* and *lamina,* also trisyllabic words from Latin with antepenultimate stress.

Patina entered English in 1748; second-syllable stress was first recorded in 1961 by *Webster's Third New International Dictionary* (a work noted for its diligence in sanctioning questionable variant pronunciations) but was not recorded in other publishers' dictionaries for another twenty years. In the 1980s puh-TEE-nuh became a vogue pronunciation, and now you hear it all over the place, including from the "experts" on PBS television's *Antiques Roadshow.*

The weight of authority, however, is still squarely on the side of first-syllable stress. Four of the six major current American dictionaries list PAT'n-uh first, and five modern sources—from Lass and Lass's *Dictionary of Pronunciation* (1976) to *Garner's Modern American Usage* (2003)—prefer it.

A Treatise on *Transient*

Q. *I hear the word* transient *pronounced in a variety of ways. Sometimes it's* tran-see-int. *Sometimes it's* tran-zee-int. *Sometimes it's* tran-she-int. *And sometimes it's* tran-jint *or* tran-shint. *I'm not sure which pronunciation is best. Can you help?*

I could have been a traveling salesperson

✥ SOUND BITE ✥

Halley's (comet) HAL-eez, not HAY-leez.

Halley's comet, which appears about every seventy-six years, was named after the English astronomer Edmund Halley (1656–1742). The variants HAY-leez and the less frequent (and anachronistic) HAW-leez may have come from the various spellings of the astronomer's name (*Hailey, Haley, Hawley*), which were used interchangeably during his time. By the nineteenth century, the spelling *Halley* and the pronunciation HAL-ee had become fixed. Today, HAL-ee for the astronomer and HAL-eez for the comet are the prevailing pronunciations, and the ones modern astronomers usually recommend.

A. The last is best: TRAN-shint. That is the traditional standard American pronunciation.

The British are responsible for the three-syllable variants TRAN-zee-int and TRAN-see-int, which were recorded by the *Oxford English Dictionary* and other British authorities of the 1920s and 1930s. They first appeared in an American dictionary in 1961, where they were labeled infrequent. But since then—thanks to the inferiority complex many Americans suffer from when faced with a choice between an American and a British pronunciation—droves of speakers have adopted the British variants, while others hoped to improve on them by inventing the variants TRAN-she-int or TRAN-jint.

My fellow Americans, do not be misled by the unwitting Anglophile in your midst or the talking head on your TV. Heed the word of your country's authorities. TRAN-shint is the preference of an overwhelming number of sources since the 1960s, and it is the first pronunciation listed in five of the six major current American dictionaries.

but I've been down that route before. ✥

The noun *transience* is also properly pronounced in two syllables: TRAN-shints.

A Flaccidental Tourist Who Is Holding the Forte

Q. *I often tell people that the word* flaccid *is pronounced FLAK-sid rather than FLAS-id because double c should be pronounced like k-s, as in* accident *and* success. *I also often tell people who pronounce the word* forte *as FOR-tay or for-TAY that it should be pronounced like* fort *because it's from French; it's not the Italian musical direction meaning "play loudly." And usually people find it hard to believe that I'm right. Are my strict pronunciations, which I consider cultivated English, too old-fashioned?*

A. You are correct on all counts. If you are still comfortable using the traditional pronunciations FORT and FLAK-sid, then they are not yet old-fashioned — in the way that, say, the traditional gri-MACE for *grimace* is old-fashioned. The turning point occurs when you become uncomfortable with what you know is right and you just can't quite spit it out anymore.

For example, I don't use the word *lingerie* anymore (I say "ladies' underwear" instead) because no one would understand me if I pronounced this French loanword properly, as lan-zhuh-REE; for too long it has been manglicized to lon-zhuh-RAY. Yet I don't hesitate to pronounce *minuscule* with the stress on the second syllable, mi-*nus*-cule, even though I know everyone says *mini*-scule these days (and they often misspell it *miniscule,* too). I can't resist basking in my own pedantry.

The editors of our dictionaries have decided that FLAS-id is now respectable, and so they duly list it as standard along with FLAK-sid. But the usage experts are another matter. *Garner's Modern American Usage* calls FLAS-id a "limp, flabby pronunciation" and says "*flaccid* is preferably pronounced /**flak**-sid/, not /**flas**-id/. All the traditional pronunciation guides have said so — and they're right."

Although FORT is still an unimpeachable pronunciation of

⊰ I could have been Jesus

forte, meaning one's strong point, be prepared to get some odd looks and not a few queries about it. For better or for worse, FOR-tay is now the dominant pronunciation, preferred by a whopping 74 percent of the usage panel of *The American Heritage Dictionary.* The variant for-TAY, with second-syllable stress, remains (as it should) a pathetic and risible affectation.

Insertin' Terms

Q. *I'm wondering if there's a word for when a sound that shouldn't be there gets inserted in the middle of a word—for example, when somebody says* ath-*uh-*lete *for* athlete.

A. The word that linguists use for this is *epenthesis,* pronounced ep-EN-thuh-sis. By derivation it means "a placing in addition," and it denotes the insertion of a sound anywhere in a word, though it usually occurs somewhere in the body. The nonstandard *ath-*uh-*lete* is a prominent example; others include *bunk* for *bump,* *flustrated* for *frustrated* (an unwittingly humorous blend of *flustered* and *frustrated*), *rememberance* for *remembrance,* and the two-syllable pronunciations of *height* and *drowned* as *height-th* and *drown-dead.*

In these examples the epenthesis is nonstandard or dialectal, but various pronunciations that began as epenthetic are now embedded in the language. Historical examples include the *b* in *nimble,* which comes from Middle English *nimel;* the *d* in *daffodil,* which was once *affodil* (and related to *asphodel*); and *empty,* which in Old English had no *p.*

By the way, there's also a word for when you insert a whole word in the body of a word, as in *what-place-soever* and *abso-bloody-lutely* (and a few other obscene insertions that I'm sure you've encountered). It's called *tmesis* (T'MEE-sis), which by derivation means "a cutting."

Pardon My French

Q. *How do you pronounce* denouement?

but it wasn't my cross to bear. ↩

A. Only through a handkerchief? At great risk to your standing in the community? (All right, I'm sorry. Anglophone handwringing over how to pronounce French loanwords always brings out the worst in me.)

Perhaps because *denouement* is a highbrow literary word, confined chiefly to college classes, book reviews, and stuffy cocktail parties, it retains its French flavor in pronunciation. The British like to stress the second syllable, but that's a no-no (or as the French would say, a *no-no-no-no*) in American English, where the preferred pronunciation is more French: day-noo-MAH(N). The accent is on the final syllable, *-ment,* in which the *t* is silent, the *n* is nasalized (as in the French *vin* or *mon*), and the whole element has a sound somewhere between the *ma-* in *mama* and the *maw-* in *mawkish.*

Sibilant Rivalry

Q. *Please settle a disagreement my sister and I are having concerning the word* lisp. *She says it refers only to the inability to pronounce the letter* s. *I say it can apply to difficulty pronouncing other letters as well. Who's right? And if you have trouble pronouncing the letter* r, *is it called a* lirp?

A. Your sister is right. *Lisp* refers to the misarticulation of sibilants, chiefly *s* and *z*. Those affected with this speech problem pronounce *s* like the unvoiced *th* of *thin* and *z* like the voiced *th* of *this.*

Lirp is a cute suggestion, but it's already a word (though not one anybody uses anymore) meaning to snap the fingers. Excessive use of *r* or its misarticulation (as in *Bahbwa* for *Barbara*) is called *rhotacism,* a horrendous word to pronounce for those who have this impediment. Mispronunciation of *r* as *l* is called *lallation.*

◄│ *I could have been a beggar*

🦋 SOUND BITE 🦋

Hammett, Dashiell HAM-it, duh-SHEEL (rhymes with *reveal*).

That's right: duh-SHEEL for the writer's first name, not DASH-ul, as it's so often mispronounced. One authority notes, "The name was originally French; generations earlier it had been spelled 'de Chiel.'"

So Tsoo- Me

Q. *How should we pronounce the first syllable of* tsunami? *My American Heritage Dictionary (fourth edition) and the NBC Handbook of Pronunciation disagree. The former says* tsoo-, *the latter* soo-. *After the terrible Asian tsunami of 2004 you first heard broadcasters saying* tsoo-, *but soon most of them dropped the* t. *What say you?*

A. The Japanese loanword *tsunami* is formed from *tsu*, harbor, and *nami*, wave. The word was introduced in the 1890s, and the earliest dictionaries in which it appears give only tsoo-NAH-mee. The *t* is pronounced in Japanese, and it is perfectly pronounceable in English, so I have to conclude that dropping it is simply laziness.

I think the *NBC Handbook* is guilty not only of misjudgment but also inconsistency, for it says *t* should be pronounced in *Tsushima* (a Japanese island), which begins with the same *tsu*, harbor, of *tsunami*. The handbook is also not in step with other current authorities, which favor pronouncing the *t*.

Spilling the Beans

Q. *I've seen the word* zydeco *but never heard it pronounced. I want to say* zy-DEK-oh *but a musician friend told me the accent is on* zy-. *Where should the stress fall?*

A. Your musician friend knows whereof he speaks. *Zydeco* is

but I had nothing to offer. 🖙

properly stressed on the first syllable, *zy-*, and rhymes with *try to go*. The word entered English about 1955, coming from a corruption of the Louisiana French *les haricots* (lez-ah-ree-koh), which means "the beans." The phrase was part of the title of a popular dance tune that inspired the musical genre. Occasionally you'll hear someone mispronounce it with the stress on the second syllable, perhaps because of a mistaken association with *art deco*.

Pronounced Genius

Q. *My biggest pet peeve these days is hearing all these educated speakers pronounce* homogenous *(huh-MAH-juh-nus) with a genius in it, as if it were* homogeneous. *Doesn't this bother you?*

A. Nope. I'm afraid you need to cool that collar, pal. *Homogeneous,* "composed of like elements, not diverse," is the usual and etymologically preferable form, and it is properly pronounced hoh-moh-JEE-nee-us. *Homogenous,* pronounced huh-MAH-juh-nus, is a biological term meaning "having a common descent or alike in structure because of a common origin." Probably a confusion with *homogenized* has led people to say *homogenous* when they mean *homogeneous.*

Expert Witness

Q. *At the marine life theme park where I work, the experts all pronounce the word* baleen, *as in a* baleen *whale, with a long* a *so the first syllable rhymes with* hay. *One time a friend questioned that pronunciation and looked up the word in a dictionary, which gave a schwa sound for the* a: *buh-LEEN. Since then I've checked various dictionaries and found this pronunciation. Am I justified in contradicting the experts, or is the dictionary pronunciation becoming obsolete?*

A. Are the experts right because they're experts, or are the dictionaries right because they're dictionaries? A fascinating question, indeed.

I checked numerous dictionaries, and all but one give only

⇥ I could have been a beggar

🦋 SOUND BITE 🦋

Presley (Elvis) PRES-lee (first syllable like *press*).
Ed Sullivan, Steve Allen, and Milton Berle, on their respec-
tive TV shows, all introduced the King as Elvis PREZ-lee,
with the *s* pronounced as in *present*. But hey, baby, guess
what? Elvis himself pronounced his last name PRES-lee.

buh-LEEN, with the schwa in the first syllable. The one, *Merriam-
Webster's Collegiate* (tenth and eleventh editions), gives buh-LEEN
and the alternative ba-LEEN, with a short *a* in the first syllable. No
dictionary recognizes the long *a* rhyming with *hay*.

One way of dealing with the problem is to say it the way the
experts do when you're around them, and say it according to the
dictionaries everywhere else. That's the path of least resistance, but
it may make you feel two-faced or wishy-washy. If you want to take
a stand, then I say go with the dictionaries and to hell with the
experts.

Here's why. In my experience experts are often wrong, sometimes wildly so, when it comes to pronouncing terms in their field
of expertise. Just because they have expert knowledge of a subject
doesn't mean they know diddly about pronunciation—especially
if it involves any Latin. Sometimes, as may be the case here, experts
will employ a certain pronunciation (usually a pompous one)
merely as a way of showing they are experts. And who are you—
an intellectual peon without the requisite sheepskin—to say that
they, the great-minded ones, are wrong?

Those are the general sociolinguistic reasons. Now, here are my
more technical reasons. It's unusual for a vowel that ends an unstressed syllable to have its long alphabetic sound. Most vowels in
such a position are a schwa or they sometimes have their short
sounds. In particular, the vowel *a* ending an unstressed syllable is

but it was too much to ask. 🦋

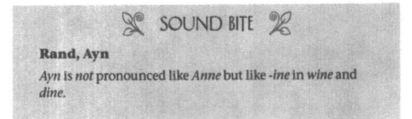

Rand, Ayn

Ayn is *not* pronounced like *Anne* but like *-ine* in *wine* and *dine.*

nearly always a schwa. To say bay-LEEN, therefore, goes against the grain, against English analogy. In short, it is an overpronunciation (which doesn't surprise me since it's coming from experts).

Finally, when *all* the dictionaries agree in giving only one pronunciation for a word, that's mighty strong evidence that it's both correct and current. No doubt the lexicographers consulted an expert or two themselves before listing that pronunciation. Perhaps the experts you hang out with are the anomalous ones, who have invented their own eccentric pronunciation or adopted a vogue pronunciation within the field that the majority of experts do not embrace. At any rate, it's not often that dictionaries concur so nicely and all the weight of their authority falls behind only one pronunciation. When that happens, you're wise to follow them regardless of what you may hear to the contrary. Because if you're ever challenged on it, especially by an expert, you can just smile and say, "If you don't believe me, look it up."

Colonel of Truth

Q. *How did* colonel *come to be pronounced like* kernel*?*

A. The answer to this one is a case study in confusion, in which I'm more than happy to be your guide.

Let us begin at the beginning with the Latin *columna,* a pillar, column, then proceed to the later Latin *colonna,* a column, which became the source of the Italian *colonello,* the commander of a small column of soldiers at the head of a regiment. Then Spanish borrowed *colonello* and changed the spelling to *coronel.* From the

⊰》 *I could have been a weapons expert*

🎐 SOUND BITE 🎐

Roosevelt (Theodore, Franklin D., and Eleanor) ROH-zuh-velt or -vult.

There is indeed a *rose* in *Roosevelt.* The oft-heard ROOZ-uh-velt is a spelling pronunciation. At least two sources note that for the final syllable, -vult (like -*ult* in *tumult*) was the Roosevelt family's usual pronunciation.

Spanish pronunciation of *coronel* we inherit our modern English pronunciation.

For a long time the spelling *coronel* was common in English, "supported by the erroneous belief," says Bergen Evans in *Comfortable Words,* "that the officer was so called because he served the crown (as the *coroner* did)." Our modern English spelling *colonel,* which is more like the Italian, came from the Middle French *colonel,* which was "a variant spelling of the commoner *coronel,*" says *The Barnhart Dictionary of Etymology.* "This variant spelling became established primarily through familiar literary use and in translations of Italian military treatises in the late 16th century."

But while the French-Italian spelling *colonel* was becoming the norm, many people continued to pronounce the word kor-uh-NEL after the Spanish *coronel.* This eventually got anglicized to KUR-uh-nul, which was inevitably shortened to KUR-nul, and since the early nineteenth century we have spelled the word *colonel* and pronounced it *kernel.*

Why Be in Debt?

Q. *Where did the* b *in* debt *come from, and why don't we pronounce it?*

A. *Debt* did not originally have a *b.* The word was borrowed from Old French *dete* and spelled *det* or *dette* in early English; it was

but I would have gone ballistic. 🙾

spoken as we say it today or with two syllables, DET-uh, for the spelling *dette*. All was well until, in the early 1400s, some pesky pedants obsessed with making English words conform to classical roots determined (correctly) that *dette* hailed from the Latin *debitum*, something owed, and decided (arbitrarily) that the word

---

BODACIOUS BRAINTEASER

THINK KING

You have to put on your thinking cap for this quiz. Most of the answers have *king* in them, but some don't.

Who or what is . . .

1. The King of Beasts
2. The King of Rock 'n' Roll
3. The King of Beers
4. The Dream King
5. The King of the Round Table
6. The King of the Blues
7. The King of Radio
8. The King of the Bestsellers
9. The King of Tennis
10. The King of Boxing
11. The King of Swing
12. The King of English Bibles
13. The King of Crooners
14. The King of Twentieth-century British Novelists
15. The Sun King
16. The King of the Empire State Building
17. The King of the Copy Shops

Answers appear on page 266.

---

therefore ought to be spelled *debt* to reflect its origin. The *debt* spelling stuck, probably because in those days the scholars did all the writing, but the pronunciation remained the same, no doubt because articulating *bt* without an intervening vowel sound is damned awkward.

Will You Marry Merry Mary?

Q. *Somebody once told me that pronouncing the three words* marry, merry, *and* Mary *was a test of whether you could speak the English language correctly. Have you ever heard about that?*

I could have been a poet

A. The *marry, merry, Mary* test is an old one. It is not used to separate the correct speakers from the incorrect ones but rather to determine whether you hail from east or west of the Mississippi River, roughly speaking.

The easterner (and I am originally one) gives the vowel in each word a different sound: the *a* in *Mary* as in *mare;* the *a* in *marry* as in *mat;* and the *e* in *merry* as in *met.* The midwesterner and westerner will pronounce all three words with the same vowel sound the easterner uses in *Mary,* so that everything comes out rhyming with *fairy.*

Of course there's some geographical and phonetic variation, but overall I've found that the east-west generalization is a reliable one. Of course, I won't hide the fact that I take a certain pride in being able to distinguish these words phonetically. For it's always struck me as peculiar that people would pronounce the name *Harry* like the word *hairy* and make no phonetic distinction between *ferry* and *fairy.* But somehow we all manage to understand each other, so who am I to complain? (Yeah, right.)

but iamb what iamb.

SIX

BORN IN THE USA

Some Quintessentially American
Words and Expressions,
from Okay *to* Humongous,
with Some Other American Stuff
Thrown in Just for Fun

"As an independent nation," wrote Noah Webster in his *Dissertations on the English Language* (1789), "our honor requires us to have a system of our own, in language as well as government. Great Britain, whose children we are, and whose language we speak, should no longer be *our* standard; for the taste of her writers is already corrupted, and her language on the decline."

Webster's call to verbal arms was admirably patriotic, but it was hardly necessary. The ambitious, romantic, and hypercreative people of the new United States of America needed little prodding to get to work establishing their own standard and inventing their own vocabulary. While John Bull sniffed and scoffed and denounced the American language as "barbarous" and "debased," decrying its "improprieties and vulgarisms," Americans calmly went about the business of concocting indispensable nouns like *bedspread, chowder, landslide, lumber, ruckus,* and *sucker* (the kind born every minute); adjectives like *lengthy, highfalutin, ornery* (a contraction of *ordinary*), *scrumptious,* and *rambunctious;* and verbs like *to engineer, to splurge, to scoot, to locate, to endorse* (approve), *to loaf, to lick* (defeat), and of course *to Americanize.*

They enraged the hidebound British by extending the definition of *mad* to mean angry (as opposed to insane), and they fixed up the centuries-old verb *to fix* by using it to mean "mend, repair." Showing their irrepressible optimism and humor even when it came to misfortune, Americans took the word *fizzle,* which originally meant "to break wind without making noise," and used it to mean "to fail or flop." Even the founding fathers got in on the act: Thomas Jefferson coined the useful word *belittle,* for which (surprise!) he was loudly belittled by the Brits.

For well over two centuries now, Americans have been busy fashioning a flexible, vivid, candid, clever, playful, practical, and sometimes pompous language that perfectly expresses the American character. They have been busy making new words, but they have also been busy borrowing and adapting them from practically every other language on earth, making American English today a paragon of breadth and diversity.

In the following pages I will take you on a whirlwind tour of the American idiom, from *okay* and *23 Skidoo* to *bitchin'* and *humongous.* I'll treat you to a soupçon of New Yawk Tawk, Yinglish, Black English, medical slang, and all-American eponyms. You'll get the skinny on *skinny, eighty-six, the real McCoy,* and *sitting in the catbird seat.* And you'll get it all in just a little more than a *New York minute.*

Won't you come along for the ride? I promise you'll be *happy as a clam.*

O.K. Corralled

Q. *What is the origin of the word* okay*? Or should that be* O.K.*? Or* OK*? Please help, okay? (O.K.? OK?)*

◁ *I could have been a miner forty-niner*

A. OK, okay, relax, no problem. Everything's going to be all right, O.K.?

This little word, says *Garner's Modern American Usage,* is "the most successful Americanism ever—perhaps the best-known word on the planet." How should we spell it? All three forms are permissible, says Garner, "but *okay* is slightly more dressed up than *OK.*" *OK* is the dominant form in informal prose, and The Associated Press prefers it, but *okay* appears in most other edited writing, where according to Garner it has an advantage: "It more easily lends itself to cognate forms such as *okays, okayer, okaying,* and *okayed.*" *The New Yorker* and a few other publications still prefer the original *O.K.,* but this form is becoming old-fashioned.

In the 1960s a linguist at Columbia University named Allan Walker Read uncovered the earliest known use of *O.K.,* in an item appearing in the *Boston Morning Post* from March 23, 1839, where it was a facetious abbreviation for *Oll Korrect.* In those days it was all the rage to use goofy abbreviations like *O.K., K.Y.* ("Know Use"),

---

OKAY EVERY WHICH WAY

There has been no end to speculation about the origin of *okay.* Here are some of the theories: that it was from *Aux Cayes,* a port in Haiti famous for a premium brand of rum; that it came from a brand of crackers called *Orrin Kendall;* that it was short for *only kissing;* that it came from the Choctaw *okeh,* used as an affirmative; that it was from *Old Keokuk,* an Indian chief; that it was an abbreviation of the Greek *olla kalla* ("all good"); that it came from Martin Van Buren's nickname, *Old Kinderhook;* and that Andrew Jackson marked legal documents with it as an abbreviation for the illiterate *oll korrect.* In fact, it does stand for *oll korrect,* but Jackson was semiliterate, not illiterate, and he was by no means its inventor.

---

but it would have been a flash in the pan. ☚

and *K.G.* ("Know Go"), much as it's fashionable today to use abbreviations like *LOL* for "Laugh Out Loud," *BYOB* for "Bring Your Own Bottle," and *TGIF* for "Thank God It's Friday." *O.K.* gained national exposure in 1840 when the Democratic O.K. Club was formed to support Martin Van Buren's bid for the presidency. Americans found the abbreviation so concise and useful that it quickly became the property of all parties.

The Scoop on *Oops*

Q. *The last time I made a mistake, I caught myself saying* oops *and I wondered, Now where does that silly little word come from, and what does it have to do with mistakes?*

A. This thoroughly American exclamation, uttered upon making a mistake or doing something awkward or stupid, has been documented in print since the 1930s. By the 1980s it had also come to be used as a noun meaning a blunder and as a verb meaning to vomit. *Oops* is echoic, meaning it is formed in imitation of a natural sound, in this case, says Robert L. Chapman's *Dictionary of American Slang,* from "the involuntary lip-rounding and expulsion of breath that accompanies a regrettable mistake, and from an approximation of the sound of vomiting."

Now, won't it be pleasant to think about that the next time you make a mistake?

Right on Cue

Q. *Can you tell me the origin of the expression* dirty pool?

A. The *Random House Historical Dictionary of American Slang* dates the word from the 1940s, the same decade when *dirty tricks* appeared on the scene. The first citation is from the 1942 film *Pride of the Yankees.* The second is also from film, the 1947 *Gentleman's Agreement.* That was the time, it appears, when pool acquired the reputation of being a hustler's game.

↠I could have been a race car driver

The Skinny on *Skinny*

Q. *How did we come to use the word* skinny *to mean the facts, the lowdown, the truth?*

A. Although the exact origin is unknown, slanguists do know this much: It appears to have originated in the armed forces during World War II, and it is probably a variation on "the bare facts" and "the naked truth."

The Skinny on 23 *Skidoo*

Q. *I've always been fascinated by the curious expression 23 Skidoo, and I've always wondered where it comes from and what it really means. Why 23? Can you tell me?*

A. We tend to associate *23 Skidoo* (or *Skiddoo*) with the Roaring Twenties, but this expression actually enjoyed its greatest popularity between 1900 and 1910. "The great beauty of *23 Skidoo!* was its versatility," says Tom Dalzell in *Flappers 2 Rappers.* "It could be and was used to mean almost anything, ranging from enthusiastic approval to dismissive rejection."

The origin of the expression and the significance of the number 23 have not been definitively determined, and as is the case with many colorful slang terms whose provenance is uncertain, there are several competing explanations. The most likely one traces it to an 1899 play called *The Only Way,* which was based on Charles Dickens's *A Tale of Two Cities.* In the final scene a character calls out the number 23 as the hero, Sydney Carlton, is taken to the guillotine to be executed. Theater people began using *23* to mean "it's over, time to leave," eventually adding *Skidoo* (which is perhaps a variation on the earlier *skedaddle*) for emphasis.

Another story has it that the expression "dates back to the 1890s, when the Flatiron Building at Twenty-third Street and Broadway in New York was the town's first skyscraper and its most glamorous building," says the *Morris Dictionary of Word and Phrase*

but I wasn't up to speed. ☞

Origins. "The corner was also considered the city's windiest, so gallant blades of the day used to hang out on Twenty-third Street waiting for the breezes to lift the skirts of passing ladies. But policemen, then as always, disapproved of such unseemly loitering. Hence their order: *'Twenty-three skiddoo.'*"

On the Basket Case

Q. *Where did we get the expression* basket case, *and why does it mean a person who is emotionally messed up?*

A. *Basket case* has three senses, according to the *Random House Historical Dictionary of American Slang*. It may mean "a person who has been made helpless by stress or emotional illness"; this sense dates from the early 1950s. It may mean "anything, such as a country, whose functioning is impaired," as in *Much of the region is an economic basket case;* this sense dates from the early 1970s. And it may mean "a quadruple amputee," someone who has lost all four limbs and cannot be carried on a stretcher; this is the original sense, which arose during World War I.

"There were countless unofficial reports of such cases—and many soldiers were of the opinion that there were many of them—but their existence was denied by the government," writes Paul Dickson in *War Slang*. The earliest known citation is from a bulletin issued by the War Department (later the Defense Department) in

1919, which stated that "The Surgeon General of the Army, Maj. Gen. Merritte W. Ireland, denies categorically that there is any foundation for the stories that have been circulated in all parts of the country of the existence of 'basket cases' in our hospitals."

Faster Than a Speeding New Yorker

Q. *What is a* New York minute, *and how long is it, anyway?*

A. A *New York minute* is equivalent to *the blink of an eye.* The idiom has been around for fifty years or so, but it didn't see much print until the 1980s. It may have originated as a derogatory southernism that was adopted and ameliorated by New Yorkers. Here's a great definition from a Texan: "In a hot New York minute. Immediately. Equates to a nanosecond, or that infinitesimal blink of time in New York after the traffic light turns green and before the ol' boy behind you honks his horn." Or you could define it like this: "the imperceptibly brief moment between when you open your mouth to speak and a New Yorker interrupts you."

Cat on a Hot Tin Wampus

Q. *Can you tell me the meaning and spelling of the word* cata- wampus*? I can't find it in my dictionary. My partner used it to mean disorderly. And where does it come from?*

A. *Catawampus,* also sometimes spelled *caliwampus, canky-wampus, cattywampus, kittywampus,* and so on, is a vintage Americanism. It may mean "askew, awry, wrong, out of proper shape or order," or "in a diagonal position, catercorner." According to the *Dictionary of American Regional English,* it has been documented in all regions of the country except the northeast.

Catawampus "has long been fiercely debated as a word of various origins," writes Jeffrey McQuain in *Never Enough Words,* a celebration of American verbal inventiveness. "It is recorded as early as 1833 as the term for a remarkable or odd creature, jocularly applied

but it was only the stuff of dreams. ⬅

NEW YAWK TAWK

Some time ago I received an email from William Safire's research assistant. "For a special issue on New York (a survival guide for newcomers and immigrants)," she wrote, "can you give Mr. Safire a rundown on New York–specific pronunciation and what might be the most difficult for new arrivals?"

When the longtime language maven of *The New York Times Magazine* asks for your help, you don't tell him where to get off the subway. You hop to it and do your best.

In a New York minute, I composed this reply:

> You say you want to know what New Yawk Tawk might be most difficult for new arrivals, and I'm assuming you mean most difficult to understand rather than to master. Well, because New York speech is some of the speediest English on the planet, I'd say the first challenge for a New York newcomer would be simply distinguishing where one word ends and the next begins.

> Particularly difficult to decipher are the many slurred exclamations—the various grunts, growls, and barks—for which New Yorkers are infamous. Here are some of the printable ones: *whaddayanutz, whaddayatawkinabow, yagoddaprollumwiddat*, the much-imitated *fuggeddaboudid*, and *geddaddaheeuh*. These are *what are you, nuts?*; *what are you talking about* (typically pronounced without an interrogative inflection); *you got a problem with that?*; *forget about it*; and *get out of here* (which usually means "I don't believe it" rather than "please leave").

> Some of my other favorite high-RPM New York Slurvianisms include *smatter* for "What's the matter?"; *omina* or *ongana* for "I'm going to"; *jeet* for "Did you eat?"; and *alluhyuz* for "all of you," in which *yuz* (or *yooz* in a stressed position) is the New York equivalent of the Southern *y'all*.

⇥ *I could have been a doctor*

The New Yorker's propensity for slurvy pronunciation can sometimes be nothing short of miraculous. When I lived in New York, I remember how conductors on the Long Island Rail Road managed to slur the name of a certain station, Woodside, into the unintelligible *wuss-eye* (the eye of a wuss?).

New Yawk Tawk also features a diphthongal /aw/ sound that in heavy Nooyawkese sounds almost disyllabic. It's impossible for me to transliterate this elongated /aw/ here, but ask a dyed-in-the-wool New Yorker to pronounce *talk, lawn, dog, coffee,* or *because* and you will hear it. In fact, *because* could well serve as a shibboleth for identifying a New Yawk Tawker. In the purest Nooyawkese, it comes out almost like bee-KOO-uhz. Think of the /aw/ sound of *fall,* put a heavier /w/ in it, and you'll come close. (This sound typically does not occur in *frog* and *golf,* as some non–New Yorkers believe. They are pronounced with the dentist's /ah/.)

Another notable characteristic of the New York accent that may confuse newcomers is the distinct way of pronouncing the consonant blend /th/. *Father* and *mother* often come out *fahdda* and *mudda,* with becomes *wid* or *wit,* and *this and that* becomes *dis'n dat.*

New Yorkers are also renowned *r*-droppers. *Day eat wid a fawk* (they eat with a fork), *day wawk onna flaw* (they walk on a floor), *an day drink adda bah* (and they drink at a bar). The superintendent of their apartment building is *da soopuh,* and *The New York Times* is *da paypuh.* When newcomers attend a Mets or Yankees game, they will need to know that *bee-uh-hee-uh!* means "[I'm selling] beer here."

but I didn't have the patience. ☚

to a person. Also suggested as a mythical creature of the Southwest, this noun may have come from 'catamount,' another term for 'wildcat.' At the same time, however, 'catawampus' has been used in other parts of the country for 'askew, out of alignment.'

"That sense may have been influenced by the 1838 modifier 'catercorner,' heard in dialect as 'catty-corner' or 'kitty-corner,' to indicate a position diagonally opposed to the user. As *National Geographic* reported in a 1931 issue, 'A new fence post, set out of line, is "catawampus."'" Another word for this, notes McQuain, is *slantendicular,* a blend of *slant* and *perpendicular.*

Working on *Mojo*

Q. *I'm wondering about the word* mojo. *When the movie character Austin Powers—the goofy 1960s secret agent played by Mike Myers— says he's lost his mojo, the not-at-all-subtle implication is that he's a candidate for Viagra. Does* mojo *refer specifically to the male organ of reproduction? And what do you need to* get your mojo workin', *as they say?*

A. I don't know what *you* need to get your mojo workin', but I know what *I* need and it's not Viagra. It's a couple of stiff dictionaries.

Austin Powers (Myers) puts a salacious spin on the word *mojo,* using it sometimes to mean his sexual virility and sometimes to mean his sexual organ. And, because he has a fully developed twelve-year-old brain, there are copious unveiled references to the male member, especially when erect. This technique may arouse certain members of the audience and even make them cachinnate, but the long and the short of it is his use of *mojo* is a stretch. The core meaning of the word, as Geneva Smitherman defines it in *Black Talk,* is "a source of personal magic that one can tap into, enabling you to work magic on something or to put somebody under your spell."

Mojo probably comes through the Gullah word *moco,* witchcraft, magic, from the word *moco'o,* which in the Fula language of

◁ I could have been a wrestler

West Africa means "a shaman, medicine man." The word has been traced in print to the 1920s, but it is almost surely much older than that. Originally it meant "magical power, voodoo," or "a charm, amulet, or spell." Later it came to mean "power or influence in general, the ability to control things or enforce one's wishes," as in the old expression *the mojo and the say-so.* The expression *get your mojo workin'* (attested since the 1950s, though again probably older) means "get your act together, tap into your own special power and use it." Austin Powers (note the choice of last name) is not the first, nor yet the last, to interpret this power as explicitly sexual.

A Schmuck in the Face

Q. *The other day I called somebody a* schmuck, *and suddenly I realized that for years I'd been calling people* schmucks *and I had no idea where the word came from. Do you know the origin of this word?*

A. Do I know the origin? Better I should know where all those lousy schmucks came from instead! I'd tell them all, *"Gey kakn afn yam!"* ("Get lost!" Literally, "go crap on the sea.")

The word *schmuck* (or *shmuck*) entered English about 1890 — a whole lot of schmucks ago. Though its spelling comes from a German word for an ornament or jewel, its source is the Yiddish word *shmok,* meaning "penis," which the venerable lexicographer and Yiddish expert Sol Steinmetz informs me hails from the archaic Polish word *smok,* meaning "grass snake."

The Yiddish "*shmok* was always considered obscene," says Steinmetz, "just as its synonym *shlang* (spelled in Yinglish *shlong*), meaning literally 'snake,' was. The only acceptable Yiddish word for penis was the euphemism *eyver,* meaning literally 'limb.'"

In American English *schmuck* is not considered obscene or taboo; it's a mildly vulgar slang synonym of *jerk, dope, son of a bitch, asshole, bastard,* et cetera. But just as we wouldn't bellow those words, or even the word *penis,* in a public place, civility dictates that we eschew such a public display of the word *schmuck* — except,

but I couldn't get ahold of the right people. ☞

YINGLISH 101

"They're mainly here to schmooze with people in the administration, aren't they?" asked the broadcaster reportIng on the festivities surrounding the second inauguration of President George W. Bush. It was a British reporter on a BBC radio program (they never call it a *show*, and they wastefully spell it *programme*), and I thought, When you hear a Brit on the BBC use the word *schmooze*, you know that Yiddish English—often called *Yinglish*—has arrived.

"The speed with which Yiddish words, phrases and phrasings have become a part of demotic English . . . is a little short of astonishing," writes Leo Rosten in *The Joys of Yinglish*. "No one can spend twenty-four hours in any major city in America or Great Britain without encountering a surprising number of words and phrases and inflectional stresses that have been plucked directly from the language called Yiddish."

If you doubt that claim, then I'm not a language *maven*— which *Meshuggenary: Celebrating the World of Yiddish* defines as an "expert; pundit; smart aleck." (From me you don't just get a word to the wise, you get a word

from a wiseacre.) In that book, the authors—Payson R. Stevens, Charles M. Levine, and Sol Steinmetz—report that "the *Oxford English Dictionary* lists more than one hundred Yiddish words that are now considered part of the English language . . . Searching Google.com gives a good indication of which Yinglish words are most frequently used today." *Glitch* (didn't know that was Yiddish, did you?) and *kosher* "top the charts," says *Meshuggenary*, and some of the other most common Yinglish words include *bagel, maven, mensch, tush, schlock* (or *shlock*), *klutz, chutzpah,* and *schmooze* (or *shmooze*).

Here are some of my favorite Yinglish words and expressions:

bupkes practically nothing, the tiniest bit, beans ("They're not offering us *bupkes*!").
dreck crap, worthless trash (from the German for dung, excrement).
farmisht confused, mixed up or messed up.
goy a gentile, non-Jew. "A male gentile is a *shaygets*; the female, a *shiksa*," says Rosten.
kibbitz 1. to comment on a game someone else is playing. 2. to talk annoyingly while some-

---

I could have been an equestrian

one else is trying to work or concentrate on something else.

kvell to beam with pride ("Melvin called to *kvell* about his kids again").

kvetch to complain, whine ("Stop *kvetching* already and get moving").

mensch or *mensh* someone who is honorable and admirable, a person of character.

mishpoche or *mishpokhe* an entire family, including remote kin; one's clan ("Is she *mishpoche?*" means "Is she one of us?").

nebbish a wimp, namby-pamby; a loser, sad sack; a nobody, nonentity.

nosh to snack, or a snack ("He's as big as a barn because he *noshes* all day").

oy a highly versatile exclamation. "*Oy* is not a word; it is a vocabulary," says Rosten. "It is uttered in as many ways as the utterer's histrionic ability permits. It is a lament, a protest, a cry of dismay, a reflex of delight."

schlep to lug, carry, transport ("Oy, all day I *schlepped* the kids around town").

schmear or *schmeer* to spread, smear; a spread, paste; also, everything, the kit and caboodle: *the whole schmeer.*

schnorrer or *shnorrer* (rhymes with *snorer*) a clever, pushy, smooth-talking panhandler or chiseler. *Schnorrers* are the embodiment of chutzpah, says Rosten. They believe they have "a license from the Lord Himself; after all, they were *helping* Jews discharge solemn obligations to the poor and the unfortunate."

shtick or *schtick* a performance, routine, bit of business or clowning around.

tchotchke a knickknack, bauble, trinket, inexpensive item or toy. Rosten notes that among the cognoscenti *tchotchke* may also mean "a cute female," "a sexy but brainless broad," or "a kept woman."

toches (rhyme it with *duck hiss* or *caucus*, and make the *ch* guttural) the buttocks, rear end—can you guess what *kish mir in toches* means?

yenta a gossip, blabbermouth ("Don't tell her anything; she's such a *yenta*").

zaftig (of a female) pleasantly plump, well-rounded, buxom.

but I wasn't stable enough. 🖙

of course, if you're dealing with a *real* schmuck and you've had it up to here. As Mark Twain (certainly no schmuck) once observed, "In certain trying circumstances, urgent circumstances, desperate circumstances, profanity furnishes a relief denied even to prayer."

Going Bonkers

Q. *I have seen the word* bonk *used in running and mountain biking magazines and it seems to have something to do with tiring out. Can you clarify what it means?*

A. The *Random House Historical Dictionary of American Slang* shows that *bonk* has been used among cycling enthusiasts since at least the 1970s. As a verb it means "to reach a state of exhaustion, to run out of gas." It appeared in a 1979 dictionary of sports and games as a noun, *bonking*, defined as "a state of extreme fatigue caused by overexertion and lack of blood sugar." Here's a citation from 1991: "If you feel yourself, as we [cyclists] say, 'bonking' or 'hitting that wall,' a drink of water is a very good idea."

As a professional courtesy, I should point out to cycling enthusiasts enamored of this term that since the late 1970s the Brits have used *bonk* to mean "have sex." In his *Dictionary of Contemporary Slang,* Tony Thorne speculates that this use of *bonk* may have arisen from an earlier vogue word for copulate among teenagers, *knob,* which turned around is *bonk.*

Comma Robbery

Q. *Have you ever heard the term* three-comma people, *meaning*

🐟 *I could have been a firefighter*

"billionaires"? For example, you could say, "Bill Gates is a three-comma kind of guy."

A. That's a new one on me, and I like it. In the same vein, you could dub the billionaire club *serial commas* or *major zeroes.*

Hoopla

Q. *Do you know where the expression* my bad *comes from? In the last few years I've been hearing and even reading it all over the place.*

A. Although *my bad*—used to mean "I'm sorry, my fault"—has been much in vogue in recent years (cloyingly so, some would say), the evidence shows that this expression is older than you might expect. It arose in the 1970s in Black English, specifically in the urban playground slang of pickup basketball. It went mainstream in the 1990s.

Gone Miss Thing

Q. *My mom and I are trying to figure out the origin of* Miss Thing, *which is usually pronounced* Miss Thang. *I've heard people use this expression in a teasing way to mean someone who is stuck up. Then last night we were watching* A Raisin in the Sun *and we heard one character refer to another as* Miss Thang. *Can you help us figure this out?*

A. You're on the right track. This epithet is Black English, and has been attested in print since the 1950s. (*A Raisin in the Sun* was published and produced in 1959.) In *Black Talk*, Geneva Smitherman defines *Miss Thang* as "an arrogant woman, one who acts high and mighty." But another use, attested since the early 1970s, comes from gay and lesbian vernacular, where *Miss Thing* may mean "an effeminate homosexual man" (*Random House Historical Dictionary of American Slang*) or be "a greeting to a fellow homosexual man" (*Cassell Dictionary of Slang*).

In a Fix about an Infix

Q. *What in God's name does the* H *stand for in* Jesus H. Christ?

A. It doesn't stand for anything, but it once did. To modern

but I didn't want to climb my way to the top. ☜

A WALES OF A TALE

In his autobiography, Mark Twain tells an amusing story about the H in *Jesus H. Christ*. During his days as a journeyman printer, Twain worked with a fellow named Wales McCormick, who was possessed of "the most limitless and adorable irreverence." When a popular itinerant preacher comes to town to deliver a sermon, the townsfolk raise money to have the sermon printed. "It was a sixteen-page duodecimo pamphlet, and it was a great event in our office," writes Twain. "As we regarded it, it was a book, and it promoted us to the dignity of book printers."

But when Twain and Wales set up the "book," racing against a deadline to go swimming and fishing, they strike "a snag." They realize they have left out a couple of words and there is no way they can insert them without completely resetting several pages. "Then Wales had one of his brilliant ideas," writes Twain. "In the line in which the 'out' had been made occurred the name Jesus Christ. Wales reduced it in the French way to J. C. It made room for the missing words, but it took 99 per cent of the solemnity out of a particularly solemn sentence."

They send the proof to the preacher and presently the great man appears, his countenance

swearers the *H* is merely an "infix for oral emphasis," as one source puts it, meaning we stick it in there to give this common oath more zip (as in "That was un-*freakin'*-believable!"). Slanguists generally agree that it probably comes from an ancient monogram for Jesus, *IHC* or *IHS*, in which *H* is the Greek capital letter *eta*, a long *e*. Though the origin of the *H* is ancient, the profane use of the epithet is pure American and is attested since the mid-nineteenth century.

To Be or Not to Be

Q. *On several occasions I have heard members of my girlfriend's East Coast family drop the words* to be *and say something like* my car

I could have been a herpetologist

casting "a gloom over the whole place." In a stentorian voice he sternly rebukes Wales. " 'So long as you live, don't you ever diminish the Saviour's name again. Put it *all* in.' "

And that's precisely what Wales does. "In that day," Twain writes, "the common swearers of the region had a way of their own of *emphasizing* the Saviour's name when they were using it profanely, and this fact intruded itself into Wales's incorrigible mind.

"It offered him an opportunity for a momentary entertainment which seemed to him to be more precious and more valuable than even fishing and swimming could afford. So he imposed upon himself the long and weary and dreary task of overrunning all those three pages in order to improve upon his former work and incidentally and thoughtfully improve upon the great preacher's admonition. He enlarged the offending J. C. into Jesus H. Christ. Wales knew that that would make prodigious trouble, and it did. But it was not in him to resist it. He had to succumb to the law of his make. I don't remember what his punishment was, but he was not the person to care for that. He had already collected his dividend."

needs washed *or* my luggage needs carried. *They are not uneducated people, yet this usage sounds uneducated to me. Can you tell me where it comes from and why they say it that way?*

A. I'm glad you asked because this curious usage needs explained.

You're right that it is not standard English—meaning acceptable in all parts of the country in educated discourse—but it is not illiterate. It is regional, by which I mean that it is normal and acceptable in certain parts of the country, even among educated people who know that it isn't standard elsewhere.

That great treasure trove called the *Dictionary of American*

but I didn't like the pay scale. 🙞

HAPPY AS A CLAM

Most folks don't know that the familiar simile *happy as a clam* is an abbreviation of a longer expression. The full, original form is *happy as a clam at high tide.* Why? Because you can't dig for clams when the tide is high, so the clams are safe and happy.

Americans love similes, and here are some of the American language's most creative and colorful ones, culled mostly from *Happy As a Clam and 9,999 Other Similes* (1994) by Larry Wright:

Happy as a possum up a persimmon tree.
Happy as a pig eating pancakes.
Happy as a gnat in a dog's rear end.
Busy as ants at a picnic.
Busy as a long-tailed cat in a roomful of rocking chairs.
Busy as a tick in a tar barrel.
Busy as a one-legged man in a kicking contest.
Crazy as a mouse in a milk can.
Crazy as a dog in a hubcap factory.

Regional English (*DARE*) tells us that the use of the verb *need* followed by a past participle without *to be* probably comes from Scotland and Northern Ireland, and that in the United States it occurs chiefly in the Midland and especially in Pennsylvania. *DARE's* first citation is from 1954, but my editor friends there tell me it is undoubtedly much older than that. Here is an illuminating citation from 1959 that appeared in *American Speech:*

> Many western Pennsylvanians—educated as well as uneducated—often declare that the house *needs painted* or the television set *needs fixed* or the children *need spanked.* Certain radio and television announcers from Indiana, Johnstown, and Pittsburgh employ this construction, as do some newspaper writers and ministers. Numerous students at Indiana State Teachers College—and several indigenous professors—find it

⇥ *I could have been a proctologist*

Crazy as a woodpecker drumming on a tin chimney.
Silly as socks on a rooster.
Slicker than deer guts on a doorknob.
Cold as a Siberian toilet seat.
Cold as a cast-iron commode on the shady side of an iceberg.
Hard as following a mosquito through a mile of fog.
Hard as shoveling snow with a pitchfork.
Hard as stacking toothpicks in the wind.

Hard as putting panty hose on a porcupine.
Hard as packing barbed wire in a paper bag.
Hard as teaching a pig to play the piano.
Hard as tap-dancing in a swamp.
Hard as trying to get through a revolving door on skis.
Funny as a fart in a space suit.
Rare as lawyers in heaven.

easy and appropriate to say that American education *needs improved* and that teachers' salaries *need raised.*

DARE's evidence also shows that this construction is a prominent feature of Appalachian English, and that it has been recorded as far east as New Jersey, as far north as Wisconsin, and as far west as Colorado, Montana, and Idaho. It even occurs in parts of Canada where Scottish influence is strong. Perhaps your girlfriend's eastern relatives are of Scottish descent and grew up in Pennsylvania or the Midland?

Awesome Word

Q. *Does the use of* bitchin' *to describe something really good come from surfing slang?*

A. Indeed it does. In *Flappers 2 Rappers,* slanguist Tom Dalzell

but I pooped out. ☞

writes that Trevor Cralle, in his *Surfin'ary: A Dictionary of Surfing Terms and Surfspeak,* "recounts the claim by surfer Dale Velzy that he coined *bitchin'* as a classic bad-as-good slang word while surfing with the Manhattan Beach Surf Club in 1949." Although Valley Girls appropriated it in the 1980s and the hip-hop subculture adopted it in the 1990s, *bitchin'* has been part of mainstream youth slang since the 1960s.

Huckleberry Find

Q. *My dictionary says the word* huckleberry *denotes a kind of shrub, yet I've heard it used to mean something else. In the movie* Tombstone, *for example, one character says to another, "I'll be your huckleberry." I also vaguely recall the words "your huckleberry friend" in the lyrics to the song "Moon River." Can you tell me what this* huckleberry *means?*

A. You have a good ear. *Huckleberry* was used in the early and mid-nineteenth century to mean "a fellow, character, boy," or "the very person for a particular job." In the late nineteenth century it came to mean also "a foolish, inept fellow" or "country bumpkin." The "Moon River" lyric could be a rare attributive use of either of these senses.

The Heebee Bee Gees

Q. *I've heard that* bejesus *means "By Jesus" and goes back to Old English. Is that true?*

A. Yes, *bejesus* (also spelled *bejeezus*) is a slang variation of *By Jesus* but it doesn't go back to Old English, which is before the Norman Conquest in A.D. 1066. The oldest print citation in the *Random House Historical Dictionary of American Slang* is from 1861. It has been used emphatically ("Bejesus, will you come on already!"), as a synonym of *hell* ("Who the bejesus are you?"), and, most commonly, as a synonym of *daylights:* "That scared the bejesus out of me"; "They beat the bejesus out of him." *Bejabbers* is a variant form. *Bejesus, bejabbers, daylights, tar, stuffing, kishkes,* and *crap* are apparently all euphemisms for *shit.*

◈ *I could have been a homesteader*

Cowering Inferno

Q. *How did we come to associate the color yellow with cowardice? Why do we call a cowardly person* yellow*?*

A. Chapman's *Dictionary of American Slang* says that the adjective *yellow* meaning "cowardly, faint-hearted, chicken" was in use in America by 1856 and the noun *yellow* meaning "cowardice" was in use by 1896, most often in the expressions *yellow streak* or *streak of yellow*. Chapman notes that "the origin of the coward sense is unknown; perhaps it is derived from the traditional symbolic meanings of *yellow*, among which were 'deceitfulness, treachery, degradation, the light of hell.'"

Nothing to Crow About

Q. *Where did the term* Jim Crow *come from?*

A. In about 1828, an early blackface minstrel named Thomas D. Rice began performing a song-and-dance number called "Jim Crow" that had the refrain "Wheel about, turn about, do just so; every time I wheel about, I jump Jim Crow." Rice claimed his number was based on "the song and dance of an old field hand named Jim Crow he had observed in Kentucky," says the *QPB Encyclopedia of Word and Phrase Origins*. Though this was probably just a fabrication Rice used to spice up his act, there is no doubt that the source of his routine was, as the *Oxford English Dictionary* confirms, "a Negro plantation song of the early nineteenth century."

Rice's act was a huge hit in England as well as the United States, and because of it, from the 1830s the name *Jim Crow* was used to mean a black man or black person, as in the title of the British antislavery book *A History of Jim Crow*, and attributively (as an adjective) to mean black, as in a *Jim Crow dance* or the *Jim Crow car*. It is from this disparaging use that "the discriminatory laws and practices take their name," says the *QPB Encyclopedia*, "though the first Jim Crow laws weren't enacted until 1875 in Tennessee." By the 1940s *Jim Crow* was widely used to mean the institutionalized racial segregation and discrimination against African Americans in the South.

but I just couldn't settle down. 🦶

GORKING OUT

Does the inscrutable lingo of the medical profession leave you at a loss for words? Well, have no fear because the Word Doctor is here, and I'm going to help you penetrate a few of the mysteries of medical slang.

The men and women in white (or light blue, or pale green, or whatever) have several interesting locutions for people who present, as they say, with puzzling conditions. If they say you have a *fascinoma*, that means you have an illness that's unusual or difficult to diagnose. If they call it a *horrendoma* or *horrendioma*, it's an especially dangerous condition, usually cancer. If a doctor writes *FLK* in your medical record or on your hospital chart it means you're a "funny-looking

Great Green Gobs

Q. *Some old salt once told me that the word* gob, *meaning "a sailor," comes from the sealants that sailors use to waterproof a ship. Is that true?*

A. It's not sealant, it's spit. The comprehensive *Random House Historical Dictionary of American Slang* shows that in the second half of the nineteenth century *gob* was used in both British and American English to mean to expectorate. It appears to have first been used navally of British coastguardsmen who were in the habit of sitting around together smoking pipes and spitting copiously. The earliest citation in that sense is from 1890, and since the early twentieth century *gob* and *gobby* have been used of U.S. sailors.

Barberism

Q. *I've always been fond of the colorful expression* sitting in the catbird seat. *Can you tell me where it comes from?*

A. I'd be glad to. It's a southern idiom that probably originated in the late nineteenth century. Red Barber, the revered radio an-

I could have been a roofer

kid," someone with an unspe-
cified illness. Another term
for a patient with unknown
ailments is *GORK*, an acronym
that stands for "God only really
knows."

If someone in a lab coat or
scrubs calls you an *O* or a *Q*,
you're in big trouble. In doctor
code, these two letters refer to
the appearance of a bedridden
patient's mouth. If you're an *O*,
your mouth is hanging open and
you're laboring for breath. If
you're a *Q*, your mouth is hanging open, your tongue is hanging
out, and you are *circling the
drain*. First recorded in print in
1982, *circling the drain* means
dying, about to depart this
world.

nouncer for the Brooklyn Dodgers, is credited with popularizing it
in his broadcasts of the 1930s and 1940s. He would use it of a batter
who had three balls and no strikes on him, meaning he was in an
advantageous position, or of a team with a comfortable lead in a
game or in the standings. Outside of sports it has been widely used
to mean occupying an advantageous, prominent, or especially favorable position; being in control.

In a biography of Barber, *Rhubarb in the Catbird Seat* (1968), the
announcer tells the story of how, one night in Cincinnati, he
"bought" the expression. He had been playing poker for hours, losing steadily. "Finally," Barber says, "during a round of seven-card
stud, I decided I was going to force the issue. I raised on the first
bet, and I raised again on every card. At the end, when the show-
down came, it was between a fellow named Frank Cope and me.
Frank turned over his hole cards, showed a pair of aces, and won
the pot. He said, 'Thank you, Red. I had those aces from the start. I
was sitting in the catbird seat.' I didn't have to be told the meaning.
And I had paid for it. It was mine."

but I didn't feel like hanging out a shingle. ☞

"One question that has never been satisfactorily answered," observes *The New Dickson Baseball Dictionary*, "is why the catbird? James Rogers (*The Dictionary of Clichés*, 1985) commented: 'The catbird commands a good view from its lofty perch, but then, so do many birds. Why the catbird's vantage point was signaled out [*sic*] is beyond explaining.'" Beyond explaining? Perhaps. But I'm going to hazard a guess.

I think it's the bird's peculiar, evocative name. Cats prey on birds, and so a bird that occupies a lofty perch with a commanding view is safe from harm. Unlike the names of other birds that warble from on high, *catbird* conjures the image of the prey sitting pretty and lording it over the predator. Another factor that may have contributed to the choice of *catbird* is its anthropomorphic overtones: In the late nineteenth and early twentieth centuries *cat* was variously used as a slang term for an itinerant laborer, a hobo, or (in Black English) a man, fellow.

You Know Jack

Q. *Why is it a* jack *rabbit? Why not a* tom, dick, *or* harry *rabbit?*

A. Because presumably Tom, Dick, and Harry do not resemble a jackass, for it was the resemblance of the rabbit's long ears to those of a jackass that inspired settlers of the Old West to call it a *jack* rabbit. (Technically it's a hare of the genus *Lepus*.) At first it was also called a *mule rabbit* and a *Texas hare*. But the zestier *jackass* won out and was eventually shortened to *jack*. In the mind of Elmer Fudd, however, Bugs Bunny is still (and will forever be) a *jackass wabbit*.

Johnny on the Spot

Q. *All my life I've been offended that my name, John, is used as a slang term for a toilet or a bathroom. How did my good name come to be used for that?*

A. My heartfelt sympathies, sir. But things could be worse, you

I could have been a knight

know. Have you ever thought what life would be like had your parents named you Dick?

The powder room *john* is probably a variation on the British dialectal *jack* or *Jack's house* to mean a privy, which goes back at least to the early nineteenth century. It has been used this way in American English since the early twentieth century. The name *John* (for which *Jack* is a nickname) has or has had many other slang meanings, some of them just as uncomplimentary. Among them: a male servant; a Chinese man; a police officer (a play on *gendarme*); a merchant seaman; an army recruit; an experienced tramp; a man who fraternizes with actresses, showgirls, or lesbians; a gullible man, a sucker; a male victim of a swindle; the male client of a prostitute; and the penis.

Captain Hooker

Q. *Wasn't the word* hooker *once used of a sailing ship, especially one that was old and in bad repair? If that's true, then how in the world did* hooker *go from meaning "an old, beat-up boat" to meaning "a prostitute"?*

A. You're right that the word was used of a sailing ship, but the Dutch word (*hoecker-schip*) meant simply "a fishing vessel" and did not imply age or slovenliness, and it is clear from the citations in the *Random House Historical Dictionary of American Slang* that the English-language use of *hooker* to mean "ship" was not disparaging from the earliest citation in 1821 through much of the nineteenth century. By 1918, however, it had acquired the connotation you note.

Also, the evidence shows that there is probably no direct connection between this nautical *hooker,* which is British in origin, and the prostitute *hooker,* which dates in print from 1845 and is of American vintage. An 1859 citation in Random House suggests that the prostitute sense may have come from the brothels frequented by sailors in Corlear's Hook in New York, but more likely it is simply an extension of the "snare, entice" sense of the verb *to hook.*

but I didn't want my days to drag on.

Dare to Ask

Q. *I am eighty-five years old. When my brothers and I were children, my grandmother (who had roots in Mississippi) would say to us such things as "Don't open that drawer—there are* layoes *there to catch meddlers." All these years later I'm still wondering what* layoes *are. Can you tell me what the word means and where it came from?*

BODACIOUS BRAINTEASER

WHAT IS *WASPLEG*?

The word *waspleg* is a mnemonic device for seven words, all nouns. What are these words, and together what do they constitute?

w _ _ _ _

a _ _ _ _ _ _

s _ _ _ _

p _ _ _ _

l _ _ _

e _ _ _

g _ _ _ _ _ _ _

Answers appear on page 266.

A. In the amazing *Dictionary of American Regional English* (*DARE*), I found not only the word *layos* (so spelled) but also the precise phrase your grandmother used, *layos to catch meddlers*, which turns out to be a variant of *layovers to catch meddlers*, which in turn is the most common of dozens of variations on the phrase. "The wide variety of forms suggests that its sense was lost long ago," says *DARE*, but the use of the expression is clear. It is an all-purpose evasive answer to a question such as "Why?" or "What's that?" It can mean various things from "I don't know" to "None of your business." It's chiefly used as a nonsense response to a child's impertinent questions or, as in your case, to warn younguns not to open, look at, or otherwise fiddle with something.

"The saying, 'Lay rows to catch meddlers,' is still used in Mississippi, Alabama and Louisiana to nonplus inquisitive childhood's

⇥ I could have been a watchmaker

annoying questions," said an article in *American Mercury* in 1926. "It is simply a way of evading an answer." Although the map in *DARE* shows that the expression was chiefly used in the South, in his *Dictionary of Americanisms* (1848) John Russell Bartlett says, "I have never heard it except in New York." Evidence suggests that it probably goes back to eighteenth-century England.

Piece on War

Q. *I've been wondering who came up with the slogan "What if they had a war and nobody came." Do you know the source?*

A. The likely source is poet Carl Sandburg's line "Sometime they'll give a war and nobody will come" in *The People, Yes* (1936). It probably got turned into a question in the 1960s during the Vietnam War. A clever friend of mine once devilishly parodied it: "What if they had an orgy and nobody came?"

Fountain of Knowledge

Q. *My father was a great storyteller, and he liked to tell us kids tales about his adventures as a young man during the Depression and World War II. One story was about when he was in the navy and he and his pals "got eighty-sixed" from a bar in San Francisco. Ever since then I've wondered about the term* eighty-six *and where it came from. The meaning is clear, but can you tell me why the number* eighty-six?

A. I can. It's quite an interesting story, so have a seat and I'll tell it to you.

Eighty-six began life in the 1920s and 1930s behind the lunch counter, where the cooks and especially the soda jerks concocted their own colorful and often inscrutable language. In *Flappers 2 Rappers*, Tom Dalzell explains that "the soda jerk of the 1930s was as charming and clever as any 20th century slinger of slang. The language of the young men who worked behind soda fountains—venerable social institutions that were important gathering places for the young—more closely resembled a jargon than

but I didn't have the time. ✍

FASCINATING FACT 25

Have you ever wondered if there's a male counterpart to the word *feminist?* Well, there is, although it's extremely rare. A *hominist* is a person who advocates equal rights for men. George Bernard Shaw coined the word in 1903 in the preface to his play *Man and Superman.*

If we revive *hominist* (and we should), can *hominazi* be far behind?

slang, but it was a quick, warm, and funny vernacular that had a vibrant wise-guy ring to it . . . The speech of the jerk established him as a singular individual who was in the know; it gave him the opportunity to show off."

In this lunch-counter lingo a hot dog was a *Coney Island chicken;* ketchup was called *hemorrhage;* an order of hash was *the gentleman will take a chance* or *clean up the kitchen;* and two fried eggs over easy on toast was *Adam and Eve on a raft—wreck 'em!* An ordinary glass of water became the expressive *Adam's ale, dog soup,* or *one on the city; hold the hail* meant "no ice"; coffee was *java; burn it and let it swim* was a float; and *twist it, choke it, and make it cackle* was a chocolate malt with egg.

One characteristic of the soda jerk's slang was its use as a code so employees could communicate without the customers' knowing what was being said. For example, when a pretty woman walked in, the jerk might call out *vanilla* to his coworkers. And if that *vanilla* had what young people today call *serious hooters* (large breasts), then the jerk would cry *fix the pumps!*

This code also employed various numbers that would quickly send an important or urgent message. *Thirteen* and *ninety-eight* meant the boss or manager just came in; *eighty-seven and a half* was a synonym of *vanilla;* and your father's locution, *eighty-six—* perhaps the only example of lunch-counter lingo that survives today—originally meant *we're out of it, we don't have any.* (Slanguists speculate that *eighty-six* was chosen because of the rhyme with *nix,* meaning "nothing" or "none.") So if the soda jerk ordered

I could have been a Trekkie

ice the rice with maiden's delight and the cook replied *eighty-six (on) the maiden's delight,* that meant they could serve rice pudding with ice cream but they were out of cherries.

Bartenders soon picked up *eighty-six* and used it to mean "a customer who is not to be served more liquor," and restaurateurs began using it of customers who have made a nuisance of themselves and are to be denied service. By the 1950s *eighty-six* had also become a verb meaning either "to refuse to serve someone" or "to kick someone out," and this ejecting sense is how your father used it when he said he and his pals were eighty-sixed from that bar. The evidence of my ears says that "to send someone packing" is how *eighty-six* is usually used today, but the *Random House Historical Dictionary of American Slang* shows that it does have two other senses that occur from time to time: Since the 1950s it has been used as a synonym of *deep-six* to mean "to discard, get rid of," as in *eighty-six that idea;* and since the 1970s it has been used to mean "to kill, murder," as in *somebody tried to eighty-six me last night.*

Never Say Ever

Q. *The last time I was at the ballpark everyone sang "Take Me Out to the Ballgame" during the seventh-inning stretch, and they displayed the words to the song on the scoreboard. When we got to the part about "peanuts and Cracker Jack," the next words on the scoreboard were "I don't care if I never get back." I always thought it was* ever, *not* never. *Are both grammatically correct?*

A. You have a good ear for good grammar. Grammatically speaking, *ever* must go with negative statements ("Don't ever do that again") while *never* goes with affirmative statements ("It's now or never"). But when a fellow named Jack Norworth set down the words to this famous song in 1908, he indeed wrote *never* and not *ever.* If you think about it, perhaps it's more appropriate that it's wrong because baseball has never been synonymous with good grammar.

but I lacked the enterprise. ↞

Not the Real McCoy

Q. *Can you tell me if this story I got off a black history website is true? An African American mechanical engineer and inventor named Elijah McCoy patented a lubricating device for steam engines in 1872 that was of such high quality that it spawned a number of inferior imitations. Thus, the expression* the real McCoy *came to be used first of Elijah McCoy's device and then of anything that is superior or genuine. Is this true?*

BODACIOUS BRAINTEASER

ALL-AMERICAN EPONYMS

The clues below are for well-known words and phrases that come from the names of Americans, some famous and some not. Try to guess the eponymous word or phrase, then check the answers to learn more about the person who inspired it.

1. You could look it up in here; it's used (in the United States) to mean "the dictionary."

2. It's your signature, an autograph.

3. It's a popular stuffed animal, named after a U.S. president.

4. Their name comes from an unlucky Union general in the Civil War, who wore them on his face.

5. It's probably the best-known ongoing survey of public opinion.

6. It's a popular ride at many amusement parks.

7. It has bright-red flowers, and you see it a lot at Christmastime.

A. I wish I could endorse that story but alas, *the real McCoy* is still of unknown origin. Theories abound, of course, but "no reliable evidence exists" to prove them, says the *Random House Historical Dictionary of American Slang,* and other experts agree. "Nor does documentation support the more recent claim [dating from the late 1980s] . . . that general usage stems fr. the high quality of hy-

⇥ I could have been an electrician

drostatic lubricators for machine applications patented 1872 and after by U.S. inventor Elijah McCoy."

Among the theories advanced about *the real McCoy* is that it comes from a famous nineteenth-century boxer called Kid McCoy, from a nineteenth-century Irish ballad about a Mrs. McCoy who beat her husband to show him who was "the real McCoy," from a rivalry between two branches of the Scottish clan Mackay, or from

8. It comes from the name of a lawyer and cattle rancher, and it's used today to mean a nonconformist, a loner, someone who stands apart from the herd.

9. It's used in politics of an attempt to manipulate the boundaries of voting districts.

10. It refers to an unnecessarily complicated contraption or scheme for doing something simple. (It's a man's entire name used attributively.)

11. It's a genus of bacteria associated with food poisoning.

12. It's a rags-to-riches story, a [blank] [blank] story.

13. It's a cocktail, a martini garnished with a pearl onion.

14. It's a trademark that has long been used as a generic term for men's underwear.

Answers appear on page 266.

a prized Scotch whisky by that name. No doubt the expression was used of Elijah McCoy's invention but that was not its origin, for it is documented as early as 1856. All of these "explanations," says Hugh Rawson in *Devious Derivations*, "demonstrate the lengths to which people will go in order to avoid admitting that they do not know the answer to something."

but I found it revolting. 🖎

Wrote Learning

Q. *How did the expression* that's all she wrote *come to mean "that's all there is"?*

A. *That's all she wrote* dates in print from the 1940s. It may have become popularized as a stock response to the "Dear John" letters that World War II soldiers sometimes received from their sweethearts back home. From there it was an easy step to the meaning "that's it; there is no more."

The Line on *Punch Line*

Q. *As a comedian, I feel I ought to know something about the language of my trade—especially if it can be fodder for my act. So, can you tell me the origin of* punch line?

A. *Punch line* is not your fodder, it's your mudder. (Did I just hear a snare drum? Hey, who threw that tomato!)

But seriously, as you guys say, *punch line* is pure American. The earliest known citation for it is 1921 in *Variety* magazine. The *Oxford English Dictionary* has a 1934 citation from *All About Jazz* that mentions how lyricists would write songs with "punch lines," so there may be some connection to jazz or popular music. But that was probably just a specific application of the word to songs with funny endings, for *punch line* appears to have always had the general meaning of "the concluding part of a joke, which makes it funny." If I may be permitted to speculate, perhaps the *punch* came from the friendly poke in the shoulder that we often give someone who has just delivered a zinger.

Close Call

Q. *Where did we get the expression* close but no cigar?

A. Step right up, ladies and gentlemen, to the Wheel of Words, where in just one spin you can win a tantalizing taste of the finest stogie this side of the Ozarks!

I could have been a plumber

As you can gather from that bit of barkery, *close but no cigar* comes from the world of traveling carnivals and sideshows. A cigar was often the prize for some game of chance or skill, and when contestants lost (as they invariably did) the carnival barker would say, "Close—but no cigar."

Rock Hard

Q. *I'm between a rock and a hard place and I need your help. Where does the expression* between a rock and a hard place *come from?*

A. There's not a lot of agreement on the origin other than that it is American. One of my sources says it "was probably born in Arizona during a financial panic" early in the twentieth century, while another says it originated among cowboys and entered the general vocabulary by the 1940s. It is recorded as *between a rock and a hard place* and also *between the rock and the hard place*. Two other reputable sources note that it is a variation on the older expression *between the devil and the deep blue sea*. Both expressions mean "on the horns of a dilemma, faced with a difficult decision."

Ravin' Maven

Q. *Why is it that when I'm hopping mad I'm* fit to be tied?

A. Various sources confirm that *fit to be tied* is of American vintage. The earliest print citation is 1894 but it probably is considerably older. It soon spread to Canada and Great Britain, and James Joyce used it in *Ulysses* (1922). The origin is obscure. My guess is that it stems from the nineteenth-century practice of tying or restraining people who are "hopping mad" in the sense of violently insane. In other words, when you're having a fit you are *fit to be tied*.

Squaw King

Q. *A friend of mine who teaches Native American Studies at the local university tells me that the word* squaw *is derived from an Algonquian*

but somebody threw a wrench in the works. ☞

FASCINATING FACT 25

The hackneyed expressions *every dog has his day*, *to gild the lily*, and *all that glitters is not gold* come from Shakespeare. But Shakespeare did not write them that way. He wrote *dog will have his day*, *to paint the lily*, and *all that glisters is not gold*. ✺

term for female genitalia. *Because of this derivation, she says,* squaw *is offensive to Native Americans and should be avoided. Yet you see it all over the place, especially as a geographic name* (Squaw Valley, *etc.), for certain types of food* (squaw corn), *and even in the names of girls' athletic teams. Does my friend have a legitimate gripe or do you think she's off her nut?*

A. Yes she's got a legitimate gripe because *squaw* is now considered offensive, and yes she's off her nut because there is absolutely nothing pudendal in the derivation of the word; all sources agree that it comes either from the Algonquian Massachusett word *squa* or the Algonquian Narragansett word *squaws*, both of which mean "a woman or young woman." *Random House Webster's College Dictionary* adds, "The word is sometimes mistakenly thought to refer literally to the female genitals." To that I would have added *especially by people who ought to know better and have no excuse for spreading yarns.*

So there you have it. *Squaw* is offensive not because it refers to the female genitals but because people have come to see it as a disparaging term for a Native American woman or for any woman, girl, or wife. All the major current dictionaries label *squaw* offensive. The usage note in *The New Oxford American Dictionary* explains why:

> Until relatively recently, the word **squaw** . . . was used neutrally in anthropological and other contexts to mean 'an American Indian woman or wife.' With changes in the political climate in the second half of the twentieth century, however, the derogatory attitudes of the past toward American Indian women have meant that, in modern American English, the word cannot be used in any sense without being offensive.

➤ *I could have been a tightrope walker*

You could say that settles that, and the language is so much the better for this proscription, except we are left with one nagging question: What are we going to do about all those names (for places, food, etc.) that employ this unsavory word? The *Microsoft Encarta College Dictionary* takes a shot at an answer in this "correct usage" note:

> Because the term **squaw** is now generally avoided, traditional names of plants and animals that contain it are also being shunned in favor of more scientific alternatives. For example: the preferred term for *squawfish* is now *Colorado pikeminnow.*

That seems fair enough. Besides, what young woman would want to play on a team called the *Fighting Squaws* or the *Squarriors,* anyway? Yet I wonder what the residents of Squaw Valley, California, on the eastern slopes of Squaw Peak, will have to say if your friend the politically correct professor ever happens to roll into town.

Outtakes

Q. *I remember my grandfather using the expression* out *like Lottie's eye to mean in a deep sleep, and the other night I caught myself using it when I went to check on my slumbering four-year-old daughter. I told my wife, "She's out like Lottie's eye," and my wife laughed and said, "Where in the heck does that come from?" Do you know who this Lottie was and why a deep sleeper is out like her eye?*

A. Thanks to the help of my friends at the *Dictionary of American Regional English (DARE),* I can provide you with a passable explanation of the provenance of this obscure and interesting expression, which may—I'm speculating wildly here—be a predecessor of the common *out like a light.*

Out like Lottie's eye appears to be chiefly Southern; *DARE*'s citations come from Georgia, Louisiana, and Texas. It has been used of a person in a deep slumber, as you note, but it has also been used to mean knocked out, soundly defeated, and thoroughly inebriated;

but I was too high-strung for that.

in his *Word Treasury,* Paul Dickson includes it in his world-record collection of 2,660 synonyms for *drunk.* My guess is that these other uses are extensions of your sleeping sense.

Leonard Zwilling, the general editor of *DARE,* informs me that "there was a popular song published in 1874 by the title of 'Blue-Eyed Lottie May' by Mssrs. Arthur W. French and Walter Hewitt. The song is a tearjerking lament for the narrator's young inamorata untimely called to her heavenly reward. However, the refrain contains the lines: 'Lottie's sleeping, sweetly sleeping / Blue-eyed little Lottie May.' It is possible that this was seized upon by some vaude-villian who popularized the elements of Lottie, her eye, and sleep into a catch phrase." Zwilling admits to speculation on this, but I think it's a pretty doggone good explanation.

Humongous among Us

Q. *I'm a baby boomer who came of age in the 1970s. Back then we used to use the word* humongous *all the time to mean really, really big (for example,* What a humongous butt! *or* I scarfed a humongous amount of pizza and beer*). Now that this word is part of our everyday vocabulary I've been wondering where it came from. Did my generation make it up or is it older than that?*

A. Though it sounds as if it's nineteenth-century American tall talk—and a cousin of such highfalutin words as *highfalutin, absquatulate, obflisticated, ripsniptious, rantankerous,* and *sockdolager*—the word *humongous* (probably a blend of *huge* and *monstrous,* with an echo of *tremendous*) comes from mid-twentieth-century college slang.

In 1968 three linguistics students at Brown University published a glossary of undergraduate slang they had recorded at eighteen colleges, and that study is the first known appearance of *humongous* in print. The word was the exclusive property of young boomers in the 1970s, but by the 1980s—when it entered dictionaries labeled as slang—it had gone mainstream. *Mongo,* a clipped

◁Ⅱ I could have been a golfer

form of *humongous* that arose in the 1970s (no doubt influenced by the 1960s cult films *Mondo Cane* and *Mondo Bizarro*), has remained marginal slang.

Incidentally, there's another youthful word for "really, really big" on the horizon that I hope will take its rightful place beside *humongous*. A couple of years ago my two daughters, inspired by *gigantic* and *enormous,* came up with the fetching blend word *ginormous,* as in *That ugly yellow Hummer is ginormous!* or *Ew! Look at that ginormous zit!* Speaking as a disinterested language maven, of course, and not as a kvelling father, I hope their creation is a ginormous success.

but I just couldn't swing it. ☞

SEVEN

THE WONDER OF WORDS

A Fascinating Farrago of Word Lore
and Wordplay That Just Didn't
Fit Anywhere Else

"I've heard that more people speak English than any other language," writes yet another wordstruck wayfarer in the land of lex. "Is that true? How many people speak English worldwide?"

A lot, my friend. And I mean *a lot.*

In 1582, Richard Mulcaster, the most famous educator of his day in England, lamented that "the English tongue is of small reach, stretching no further than this island of ours, nay not there over all." Little did he know that English was already on its way to becoming the world's common tongue.

Today the English language is booming. We are witnessing the most rapid period of growth—in the number of speakers as well as in new words and meanings—since the great flowering of English during the Elizabethan era.

In the twentieth century, English displaced French as the language of diplomacy. English is the language used in international aviation. It has become the lingua franca of the global marketplace, partly because of its insatiable appetite for foreign words and phrases like *lingua franca*. English is the preferred language at academic conferences and in scientific publishing, and it is the dominant language of sports, advertising, and popular culture worldwide.

Thirty years ago, 10 percent of the world's population spoke English. Today, it's 20 percent—about 1.5 billion people. Of these, approximately 375 million are native speakers, 375 million speak it as their second language, and the rest speak it with some degree of fluency. Believe it or not, there are more people in China who speak English as a second language than there are native English speakers in the United States.

English is heard and read on every continent. In most major cities around the globe you can find an English-language daily newspaper. English is the language employed in more than 60 percent of the world's radio programs and more than 70 percent of the world's mail. And that percentage increases when you go online.

According to Kathy Rooney, editor in chief of the *Encarta World English Dictionary,* "it is estimated that English is the language of over 80 percent of the information stored in the world's computers and 85 percent of Internet home pages, and that English is the first language of 68 percent of Web users."

That, *amigo,* is one heck of a lot of English, *oui?*

In this chapter you will find a serendipitous salmagundi of word lore, wordplay, and other fascinating stuff that didn't quite fit anywhere else. It's a wordlover's tour of the peculiar curiosities and curious peculiarities of that gargantuan, gluttonous, and gloriously polyglot beast we call the English language.

In So Many Words

Q. *I am an English teacher, and I have always been curious about the number of words in the English language. I realize that the number is*

◀ I could have been a cattle rancher

increasing rapidly due to modern technology. However, could you please give me a ballpark estimate?

A. You're certainly right that the vocabulary of English is growing rapidly—some say by as much as 5,000 words a year, though that number seems high to me. At any rate, most new words are specialized or technical words, and the number of words entering the general vocabulary each year is probably at most a few hundred.

Estimates of how many words there are in the English language vary considerably and depend on whether you include such things as jargon, slang, obsolete words, scientific terminology, subcultural lingo, regional and dialectal words, foreign words and expressions, and so on. Every general dictionary contains some of each of these linguistic categories, but by no means all.

Some experts estimate that English may have as many as three to five million words, if you include all those categories. More experts believe the total is probably somewhere between one and two million. Even our most comprehensive dictionaries don't come close to comprising all those words. The first edition of the *Oxford English Dictionary* (1928) contained 414,000 words and covered little technical vocabulary and no slang. The second edition (1989), which generally follows the same policy, contains more than 616,000 words.

Positively Lost for Words

Q. *When you're insane, you're not sane. But when you're inane, are you not ane?*

A. I *ane* to please, but I *ain'* got the answer to this one. (Just kidding, actually. Of course I have the answer or I wouldn't have included this inane question in the book.)

If you're *inept*, does that mean you're not *ept*? If you're *disgruntled*, are you not *gruntled*? Is *sheveled* the opposite of *disheveled*? Recreational linguists call these words *lost positives.*

but I didn't have the head for it. 🙔

"They are simply common words stripped of their usual prefixes," explain William and Mary Morris in the *Harper Dictionary of Contemporary Usage.*

> Uncovering *lost positives* is harmless and amusing word play, an exercise we commend to one and all, old and young. There is nothing new about it, however. In the middle of [the 20th] century, columnist John Crosby represented a group labeled "The Society for the Restoration of Lost Positives.". . . It was the late James Thurber who first devised "gruntled.". . . Clive Barnes, the drama critic for the *New York Post,* once commented on a performer who failed to impress him: "Few have left so colorless and delible a memory in this role."

Lost positives fall into three categories: *pure* lost positives, words that have been truly lost (i.e., labeled archaic or obsolete by a dictionary or two) and remain lost; *jocular* lost positives, words that were never lost because they never existed in the first place; and *recovered* or *unlost* positives, words that have been brought back to life or that, though rare, were never dormant. The pure category includes *ert (inert), descript (nondescript), nocuous (innocuous), consolate (disconsolate),* and *defatigable (indefatigable).* The jocular category—which is potentially much larger—includes *digent (indigent), sidious (insidious), dignant (indignant), ertia (inertia), traught (distraught), vidious (invidious),* and *putable (indisputable).* And in the recovered or unlost category we have *couth* and *kempt.*

Couth was once a pure lost positive, but this archaic word, which formerly meant

FASCINATING FACT 🐚

Approximate number of words in Spanish, French, and Russian: 100,000 to 150,000

Approximate number of words in German: 185,000

Number of words in the second edition of the *Oxford English Dictionary* (1989): 616,500

Estimated total number of words in English: over 1,000,000 🐚

I could have been a bungee jumper

✂ WHAT THE DICKENS! ✂

When Charles Dickens wrote the following passage in his novel *Martin Chuzzlewit*, describing how Tom, the church organist, is infatuated with a member of the choir, he obviously had no idea how it would be interpreted by a modern reader:

> When she spoke, Tom held his breath, so eagerly he listened; when she sang, he sat like one entranced. She touched his organ and from that bright epoch, even it, the old companion of his happiest hours, incapable as he had thought of elevation, began a new and deified existence.

"known, familiar," was revived in the twentieth century in the sense of "smooth, sophisticated, polished" to serve as the opposite of *uncouth*. And though *kempt* may seem to be a quaint lost positive of *unkempt*, it is not; as the citations in the *Oxford English Dictionary* show, *kempt* has been used since the eleventh century to mean "combed, neatly kept." The same goes for *wieldy*, the opposite of *unwieldy*, *scrutable*, the opposite of *inscrutable*, and *pecunious*, the unusual positive form of *impecunious*, strapped for cash; dictionaries list all three of these "lost" positives in good standing.

Here are some other interesting lost positives: *(in)effable, (in)exorable, (in)finity, (dis)mantle, (in)alienable, (un)witting, (un)earth, (un)scathed, (de)molition, (over)whelm*.

Iggry! Get Your Aggry out of My Puggry

Q. *A question that's been circulating on the Web has been bothering me. "There are three words in the English language that end in -gry," it says. "Angry and hungry are two. What's the third?" I'm going nuts trying to figure out the answer. Do you know it?*

but I was already at the end of my rope. ✐

A. There are actually about fifty words that end in -*gry*. They are all obscure words or obsolete and obscure variant spellings of words. Here are some of them:

anhungry—a variant of *hungry* used by Shakespeare

mawgry, magry, maugry—all variant spellings of *mauger* or *maugre*

iggry—an exclamation (adapted from Egyptian Arabic) meaning "hurry up"

puggry—a light scarf worn wrapped around a sun helmet (from Hindi)

aggry (bead)—a variegated glass bead

gry—something very small or of little value; "the veriest trifle," says the *OED*

The question, of course, is a hoax—perhaps the biggest language hoax around, and this one's been around for several decades. It has wasted a lot of people's time for no good purpose. As Evan Morris writes in *The Word Detective,* "Trying to untangle the *gry* riddle today is right up there on the Pointlessness Scale with deconstructing the *Sergeant Pepper* album cover or assessing the structural dynamics of Donald Trump's hairdo."

Fallen Tents of Porpoises

Q. *What do you call it when you hear something and it comes out in different words in your head? You know, like when you hear "for all intents and purposes" but you think (as I did for many years until I finally saw the phrase in print) that it's "for all intensive purposes." Is there a word for this?*

A. There is. The phenomenon you describe is called a hearing disorder, and I advise you to see a specialist immediately.

As my kids say: *psych!* Actually it's called a *mondegreen,* a word that now re-

FASCINATING FACT 🐦

Q. In any given dictionary, words beginning with what letter will take up the greatest number of pages?

A. The letter *s.* 🐦

🐦 *I could have been a sailor*

sides in two current dictionaries, *Random House Webster's* and *American Heritage.*

Mondegreen is itself a mondegreen. It was coined in 1954 by Sylvia Wright, who used it in an article for *Harper's* magazine called "The Death of Lady Mondegreen," in which she recounted how she remembered the lyrics of an old Scottish ballad, "The Bonnie Earl of Morey" (pronounced like *Murray*):

> *Ye Highlands and ye Lowlands,*
> *Oh, where hae ye been?*
> *They hae slain the Earl o' Morey,*
> *And Lady Mondegreen.*

The problem was, as Ms. Wright later discovered to her chagrin, there was never any Lady Mondegreen. The actual words of the last line are "And laid him on the green."

Recreational linguists and lovers of wordplay soon seized upon this word *mondegreen* to denote the many soundalike slipups they'd come across over the years or had suffered from themselves since childhood: for example, the famous *pullet surprise* (Pulitzer prize); the Christmas song about Rudolph featuring *Olive, the other reindeer* (All of the other reindeer); the hymn *Gladly, the cross-eyed bear* (Gladly the cross I'd bear); Jimi Hendrix's lyric *excuse me while I kiss this guy* (excuse me while I kiss the sky); the Beatles' lyric *the girl with colitis goes by* (the girl with kaleidoscope eyes); the Lord's Prayer, *And lead us not into Penn Station* (And lead us not into temptation); and the Twenty-third Psalm, *Surely good Mrs. Murphy shall follow me* (Surely goodness and mercy shall follow me).

As William Safire, the language maven of *The New York Times,* hastens to point out, such mishearings should not be *taken for granite.*

The Pledge of Allegiance, in Pure Mondegreen
I bludgeon legion
screw the flab of DUI
test dates of omega,
and tuba the public
for Richard Stanz,
one Haitian, and her
cod, with liver, tea,
and just a sprawl.

but I missed the boat. ☞

WHAT IF WORDS MEANT WHAT THEY SOUND LIKE?

subsidies inferior cities

rebuff to polish again

sporadic fungus growing in your attic

commodious like a toilet

proscribe supportive of writers

mollify to transform a lady into a gangster gal

tirade an expedition to purloin men's neckwear

lucid a Freudian term for wild self-indulgence

dissident to insult a dentist

saturated evaluated by Louis Armstrong

adamant to flavor with an aromatic herb of the genus *Mentha*

gullible accessible to seagulls

In his book *On Language,* Safire identifies four distinct types of mondegreen. First there is "the Guylum Bardo syndrome," or misdivision of words, known technically as *metanalysis* ("wrong cuttings"). Here *a patchy fog* becomes *Apache fog* and *The Londonderry Air* becomes *The London Derrière.* "Many of the words we use correctly today are mistaken divisions of the past," Safire notes: *an apron* was once *a napron* and *a nickname* was once *an ekename.*

The second type, says Safire, is "the 'José, can you see?' syndrome," or "transmutation of words when they pass through different cultures or languages," as when *O Tannenbaum* becomes *Oh, atom bomb.* The third form of mondegreen is a kind of malapropism, an unintentional and humorous distortion of a word or phrase, as when people misread or mispronounce *misled* as *mizzled* or say *the house is in escarole* instead of *escrow.* And finally there is folk etymology, meaning "the creation of new words by mistake or misunderstanding or mispronunciation," like *the whole kitten caboodle* instead of *kit and caboodle* and your *for all intensive purposes* instead of *intents and purposes.*

⇥ I could have been a politician

cursory a room where people swear

defray to tie up loose ends

curtail the tail of a dog

surfeit a command to ride the waves or browse the Internet

protract in favor of wanton development

transitory a staunch supporter of public transportation

corroborate to consort with thieves

presumptuous almost sumptuous

malinger the word for when your mother-in-law overstays her welcome

morass what they're putting on television lately

Rhyme Time

Q. *Can you please explain rhyming slang and where it came from?*

A. Rhyming slang, which emerged in the early eighteenth century and still flourishes today, is the creation of the lower classes in England. It is believed to have originated in the criminal element in London, used as a secret language to deceive the "flats" (police), and then spread into the working classes, where it became most closely associated with the Cockney dialect.

The basic principle of rhyming slang, says Jonathon Green in *Cassell's Rhyming Slang,* is that "one takes a word one wishes to describe and in its place provides a brief phrase, usually of two but sometimes of three words, of which the last rhymes with the word for which it is a synonym. Thus *round me houses* means trousers; *Alan Whickers* knickers, *Artful Dodger* lodger . . . While the 'rule' of rhyming slang demands no more than the basic rhyme of the slang phrase and the word it defines, the best forms offer a greater depth. The 'perfect' example manages to use a rhyming phrase that has some amusing or satirical bearing on the word for which it operates.

but the thought of it left me speechless. ⟨⊷

CAN YOU DECIPHER THIS COCKNEY RHYMING SLANG?

One brave and bold day I was sittin' in my favorite Trafalgar Square readin' the nursery rhymes when some bag of coke comes knockin' at my Bobby Moore. It was my old finger and thumb Johnny and his china Jim. I introduced them to my new cheese and kisses and said, "Now then, don't go feasting your kidney pies on my ivory pearl, dry land?" We had some judy and punch and then we all went down to the rubadub for some horses and carts and Britney Spears.

Thus *trouble and strife* for wife or *God-forbids* for kids suggest the miseries of domesticity; *Mae West* for the female breast recalls the voluptuous Hollywood star . . ."

The secret element of rhyming slang is often achieved by clipping the word that rhymes with the intended word so that you have to know what the rhyming word is to understand what is meant. Thus, in rhyming slang *barnet* meaning "hair" is short for *barnet fair* and *hammer* meaning "to follow" is short for *hammer and nail* (to tail, follow).

Vowel Movement

Q. *I have heard that English has many words that do not contain any vowels—no a, e, i, o, u, or even y. Is this really true? Except for certain representations of sounds as words—like shhh, brrr, and tsk-tsk—I can't think of any word without a vowel.*

A. There are over a hundred vowelless words in the *Oxford English Dictionary*, nearly all of them obsolete variant spellings of modern words. For example, *hws* for *house, rvn* for *run, stw* for *stew*, and *wss* for *use*. Most of the rest are onomatopoetic words (words representing sounds). In addition to the ones you cite, there are the

I could have been a comedian

COCKNEY RHYMING SLANG TRANSLATION:

One brave and bold (cold) day I was sittin' in my favorite Trafalgar Square (chair) readin' the nursery rhymes (the *Times* of London) when some bag of coke (bloke) comes knockin' at my Bobby Moore (door). It was my old finger and thumb (chum) Johnny and his china (mate, short for *china plate*) Jim. I introduced them to my new cheese and kisses (missus) and said, "Now then, don't go feasting your kidney pies (eyes) on my ivory pearl (girl), dry land (understand)?" We had some judy and punch (lunch) and then we all went down to the rubadub (pub) for some horses and carts (darts) and Britney Spears (beers).

common *grrr, psst, hm* or *hmm,* and *nth* (as in *to the nth degree*). These are considered legitimate vowelless words.

Qu-less

Q. *Are there any words in the language where* q *is not followed by* u?

A. That's an interesting *qy.* (an abbreviation of *query*), which I'll answer on the *q.t.*

There are at least sixty-five English words (real words, not abbreviations) in which an initial *q* is not followed by a *u*. Most of them hail from Arabic and Hebrew and are so obscure that they are not listed in unabridged dictionaries. Among the somewhat less obscure ones are *qibla(h),* the point toward which Muslims turn to pray, in the direction of Mecca; *cinqfoil,* a variant of *cinquefoil,* an architectural ornament with five lobes or cusps; *qabbala,* yet another variant of the mystical word variously spelled *kabbalah, kabbala, kabala, cabala, cabbala,* and *cabbalah;* and *qwerty* (or *QWERTY*), a name sometimes used for the modern typewriter and computer keyboard, the reference being to the first six of the top row of alphabetic characters, beginning at the left.

but it would have been just for laughs. ❧

Latin Lover

Q. *On the United States dollar bill there are three Latin phrases:* e pluribus unum, novus ordo seclorum, *and* annuit coeptis. *I know that* e pluribus unum *means "one out of many"—meaning one country out of the many states—but what do the others mean?*

A. All three Latin phrases appear on the Great Seal of the United States, which is pictured on the back of the one-dollar bill. You're right about *e pluribus unum*; too bad the South at one time had other ideas. *Novus ordo seclorum* means "a new order of the ages is created"; this means that Americans can never have too high an opinion of themselves. *Annuit coeptis,* which comes from Virgil's *Aeneid,* means "He has favored our undertaking"; in other words, God has given his blessing to American democracy. This is what allows our leaders to tell us that God has endorsed whatever it is they want to do.

Stun Nuts

Q. *Could you help me and my coworkers solve something that is driving us nuts? What is the word for when you can spell a word backward the same as it is spelled forward?*

A. Something spelled the same forward and backward is called a *palindrome* (rhymes with *gal in Rome*), and it isn't limited to a single word. A palindrome can be a sentence, a paragraph, or even an entire novel—although no one has ever managed to compose one that long, the longest being about 10,000 words (of mostly gibberish). Perhaps the most famous palindrome is *A man, a plan, a canal, Panama.* An exceptionally lucid one is *Eva, can I stab live evil bats in a cave?* And here are two funny ones: *Go hang a salami, I'm a lasagna hog. Was it Eliot's toilet I saw?*

⇥ I could have been a miner

DO THE TWIST

Here are some famous and not-so-famous tongue twisters. Can you say them sweetly, swiftly, and precisely several times without a slipup or a stumble?

Mixed biscuits.
Lemon liniment.
The Leith police dismisseth us.
Old oily Ollie oils oily autos.
The sixth sheik's sixth sheep's sick.
She sells seashells by the seashore.
Six silly sisters sell silk to six sickly seniors.
This thistle seems like that thistle.
She was a thistle sifter and sifted thistles through a thistle sieve.
Which switch, Miss, is the right switch for Ipswich, Miss?
The rat ran by the rolling river with a lump of raw and livid liver.
What noise annoys a noisy oyster? A noisy noise annoys a noisy oyster.
Can you imagine an imaginary menagerie manager imagining managing an imaginary menagerie?

Allusion Conclusion

Q. *At what point does a literary allusion become a cliché? If a speaker says, "I have a dream," is that an allusion or a cliché?*

A. As long as most people are familiar with the source of the allusion, it is an allusion (although some allusions are more hackneyed than others). When people no longer know the source of the allusion, it becomes a stock phrase or a cliché. For example, if you say "that's his Achilles heel" or "this could be the beginning of a beautiful friendship," most educated people will recognize the allusion to Greek mythology and the movie *Casablanca*. But few who use the expressions *strange bedfellows, salad days, pomp and circumstance,* and *the ides of March* realize that all come from the plays of Shakespeare. These literary allusions have become cliché.

but I didn't want to dig a hole for myself. 🔙

Going to the Dogs

Q. *It struck me one day, in a moment of idle contemplation while walking my dog, that there are a lot of idioms in the language that incorporate the word* dog: *it's a dog's life, lie (or die) like a dog, going to the dogs, and so on. Just how many* dog *idioms are there, anyway?*

BODACIOUS BRAINTEASER

DON'T BE A SCAREDY CAT

The English language contains lots of expressions, or idioms, that incorporate animals, many of them clichés. For example, you can have a frog in your throat, you can cry wolf, or things can go to the dogs. Can you figure out the well-known animal idiom from the clues below?

1. We advise people not to count this animal.
2. This animal is known for being happy.
3. These two animals sometimes fall from the sky.
4. This animal likes to get together with its own kind.
5. You can live in luxury with this animal.
6. This animal is what you get when you lose your temper.
7. When you're done for or all washed up, you cook this animal.
8. This animal is known for its pride.
9. This animal—a bunch of them, actually—is always stuck in a large container and is always less fun.

A. Well, you said it—a lot. Here are some more: *dog-tired; dog tag; attack dog; watchdog; dogwatch; dog and pony show; dog-eared; dog towns; aching dogs* (probably from Cockney rhyming slang *dog's meat* for feet); *dog days; love me, love my dog; hair of the dog; dogs of war* ("Cry havoc, and let slip the dogs of war."—*Julius Caesar*); *hot (diggity) dog; dog in the manger* (someone who refuses to give to oth-

I could have been an actor

ers things he has no use for); *dogface* (a soldier); *doggie bag*; *it's a dog-eat-dog world*; *top dog*; *underdog*; *dogfight*; *to dog it* (to loaf, shirk duty, or not give 100 percent); *you ain't nothin' but a hound dog*; *dirty dog*; *lazy dog*; and *lucky dog,* one of the surprisingly few complimentary *dog* idioms, considering that *a dog is a man's best friend.*

10. This animal describes a very small community.
11. This animal is highly profitable.
12. This animal—an insect, to be precise—denotes a favored or preeminent woman.
13. When you shake a part of this animal twice, it means "quickly, immediately."
14. These two animals are part of a contest of pursuit and evasion.
15. This animal is a muscle cramp.

16. This animal is connected with church towers and lunacy.
17. This animal has a superlative memory.

Answers appear on page 267.

Venery Interesting

Q. *It's a gaggle of geese, a school of fish, and a pride of lions. But what about tigers?*

A. Before we get to what to call a bunch of tigers, let's begin with some history.

These terms for groups of animals have variously been called

but the lines were too long. 🐾

"nouns of multitude," "company terms," "nouns of assemblage," "group names," and, most commonly, "collective nouns." Connoisseurs of these words also know them by an older phrase, "terms of venery," *venery* here denoting not sexual intercourse but hunting or animals that are hunted (from Latin *venari,* to hunt).

"The venereal game," as the connoisseurs call it, is the art of inventing these playful and often poetic terms, and it has been going on for centuries. One of the earliest and most exhaustive records of them is *The Book of St. Albans* by Dame Juliana Berners (or Barnes), published in 1486. Dame Juliana's book contained a list of 164 collective nouns, including *a rafter of turkeys, a murder of crows, a murmuration of starlings, a shrewdness of apes, a leap of leopards, a skulk of foxes, a knot of toads,* and *a cowardice of curs.* It also included some terms—like *a pontificality of priests, a superfluity of nuns,* and *an abominable sight of monks*—that venture beyond the animal kingdom and into the human realm.

An Exaltation of Larks by James Lipton is one of the best-known books on the subject of collective nouns. It discusses the evolution of the venereal game from ancient terms for animals like *a clowder of cats, a sloth of bears, a siege of herons,* and *an ostentation of peacocks* to modern terms for all types of people like *a sneer of butlers, a rash of dermatologists, a flourish of strumpets,* and *an ingratitude of children.* (See the sidebar for more modern inventions.)

I could have been a football player

A CHUCKLE OF COLLECTIVE NOUNS

a blur of Impressionists
a lie of golfers
a void of urologists
a host of epidemiologists
a wheeze of joggers
a discord of experts
an entrenchment of full
    professors
a glaze of tourists
a shriek of contestants
a gush of sycophants
a stampede of philatelists
a strip of ecdysiasts
a slew of exterminators
a lot of used car dealers
a pan of reviewers

a galaxy of astronomers
a persistence of parents
an indifference of waiters
a sprinkling of gardeners
a shush of librarians
an escheat of lawyers
an acne of adolescents
a dash of commuters
a blarney of bartenders
an unction of undertakers
a wince of dentists
a pile of proctologists
a shrivel of critics
a score of bachelors

Now, what about those tigers? A *streak* of tigers is the term Lipton gives, and an *ambush* of tigers has also been proposed. But my friend Cory J Meacham, the author of *How the Tiger Lost Its Stripes: An Exploration into the Endangerment of a Species,* is unhappy with both of these descriptors. "As adult tigers are never found in groups in the wild, the collective noun *ambush,* while whimsically delightful, presents an image that will never exist," he writes. "And *streak* never struck me as appropriate, or even clever, in any sense . . . Since the only situations in which people are going to encounter groups of adult tigers are captive settings, and since those situations are artificial to the animal's nature by definition, *and* since the most famous example of tigers appearing in groups is the recently defunct-but-world-famous magic act in Vegas, I propose that a group of these cats

but I couldn't tackle the job.

UH-OH WORDS

When dictionaries began including slang, swear words, offensive terms, and other taboo words and expressions, the editors knew they were taking a risk and inviting possible criticism. But one thing they didn't count on, and that they may not have foreseen, was that some of these highly charged words—along with other indelicacies—would, simply by the luck of the draw, wind up being "guidewords," the boldfaced words printed at the top of each page of a dictionary, indicating the first and last entries on that page. When an offensive, indelicate, or suggestive word winds up being a guideword, it becomes an *uh-oh word*.

In *Webster's New World College Dictionary*, fourth edition (1999), you'll find *blow job*, *brothel*, *shitkicker*, and *shit list*. In *The New Oxford American Dictionary* (2001) you'll find *ass-kissing, bunghole, bushtit, fruitcake, fucker, fuckhead, puta,*

---

be referred to as an *illusion* of tigers." *Illusion*, Meacham adds, also suggests "the endangered/disappearing state of the species."

Other collective nouns I have come across that I thought were particularly funny or inspired include *a wad of gum-chewers, a stoppit of parents, a whatever of teenagers, a dissemblage of politicians, a lack of principals*, and *a wunch of bankers* (a spoonerism of a *bunch of wankers*—*wanker* being a popular British vulgarism for a complete jerk, especially one with a cushy job).

You Must Remember -*Dous*

Q. *I once saw something on the* Car Talk *website—one of their "Puzzlers," I think—about words that end in -dous. They said there were four of them in the English language, and the first three are* tremendous, stupendous, *and* horrendous. *What's the fourth?*

⇥ *I could have been a pilot*

wetback, and white trash. In The American Heritage Dictionary, fourth edition (2000), you'll find clitoridectomy, diddle, premature ejaculation, scuzzbucket, undersexed, whore, and whoredom. And in The Random House Dictionary of the English Language, second edition (1987), you'll find buttinsky, cock, frottage, frotteur, and toilet seat.

Merriam-Webster's Collegiate Dictionary, eleventh edition (2003), and the Microsoft Encarta College Dictionary (2001) can be classified as "family dictionaries." An informal survey—a couple of thumb-flipping trips through the pages—turned up only bastardise (the British spelling), cathouse, and phallus in Merriam-Webster and in Encarta no uh-oh words at all. (The most risqué guideword I could find in Encarta was cockamamie. What a disappointment!)

Was that just luck, or was it intentional?

A. The fourth common word ending in -dous is hazardous. But if you include the uncommon words as well, there are (some sources claim) over thirty words in the language ending in -dous.

Here are some of them: mucidous (moldy, musty); multifidous (having many divisions, said especially of animals' feet); nefandous (unspeakable); frondous (leafy, bearing or resembling fronds); steganopodous (web-footed); ligniperdous (wood-destroying); vanadous (containing vanadium); molybdous (containing molybdenum); decapodous and isopodous (pertaining to the Decapoda and the Isopoda, both orders of crustaceans); lagopodous (pertaining to the genus Lagopus, which comprises various types of grouse); heteropodous and gastropodous (pertaining to the Heteropoda and the Gastropeda, which comprise certain mollusks); and tylopodous (pertaining to the Tylopoda, which has something to do with the

but I couldn't land a job. ☞

FASCINATING FACT 🐚

The longest word in the *Oxford English Dictionary* is *floccinaucinihilipilification* (29 letters). It means "the action or habit of estimating as worthless."

The longest word in *Webster's Third New International Dictionary* is *pneumonoultramicroscopicsilicovolcanoconiosis* (45 letters). It is the medical term for miner's black-lung disease. 🐚

Camelidae, which has something to do with camels and llamas, which is as much as I want to know because it's time to answer the next question).

Let a Lexie Be Your Guide

Q. *Is there a technical term for the bold-faced words printed at the top of each page of a dictionary, indicating the first and last entries on that page? What do lexicographers call them?*

A. They call them *guidewords*, says the fourth edition of *The American Heritage Dictionary*, or *guide words*, say other dictionaries. (I'm with *American Heritage*.) Some dictionaries also note that they're called *headwords* or *catchwords*, but a high-placed lexicographer of my acquaintance assures me that everywhere she's worked they've called them *guidewords*.

Welcome to the Language Zoo

Q. *My favorite word in the world is* hippopotomonstrosesquipedaliaphobia, *which means "the fear of extremely long words." I know it's a real word, but I've never been able to find it in a dictionary. Why?*

A. You haven't been able to find this word in any dictionary because dictionaries deal in words that people actually use, not ones that wordlovers like us keep in language zoos and put on display for other wordlovers' viewing pleasure. To find words like that you have to go to what dictionary makers call "tertiary sources," namely, books for wordlovers about unusual words.

Two of my favorite *sesquipedalia verba* (Latin for "foot-and-

⇥ I could have been a chauffeur

a-half-long words") are the twenty-nine-letter *floccinaucinihili-pilification*, the estimation of something as worthless trivia; and the forty-five-letter *pneumonoultramicroscopicsilicovolcanoconiosis*, miner's black-lung disease.

"An old joke says that the longest word [in the English language] is *smiles* because there is a mile between the first and last letter," writes Tony Augarde in *The Oxford Guide to Word Games*. "The longest words that most people know are *antidisestablishmentarianism* (twenty-eight letters—allegedly coined by Gladstone, with the sense 'opposition to the idea that the Church should cease to be formally recognized by the State') and *supercalifragilisticexpialidocious* (thirty-four letters—popularized by a song in the 1964 film version of *Mary Poppins*)."

Literature also has its share of ridiculously long words, including the twenty-seven-letter *honorificabilitudinitatibus* in Shakespeare's *Love's Labour's Lost* and a hundred-letter nonsense word in James Joyce's *Finnegans Wake: bababadalgharaghtakamminar-ronnkonnbronntonnerronntuonnthunntrovarrhounawnskawntoohoo-hoordenenthurnuk*. Don't ask me how to pronounce that one, but I *can* help you pronounce the name of this lake in Massachusetts, which has forty-five letters: *Chargoggagoggmanchauggagoggchaubunagunga-maugg*. Here's how it goes: chahr-GAW-guh-GAWG-man-CHAW-guh-GAWG-chaw-buh-nuh-GUHNG-guh-MAWG.

Blender Bender

Q. *What do you call words that are created by blending two words, like* brunch *from* breakfast *and* lunch*?*

A. Linguists call them blend words, but the more colorful term is *portmanteau words* or *portmanteaus*, from the large, old-fashioned suitcase of that name. *Portmanteau* was first proposed by Lewis Carroll in 1872 in *Through the Looking-Glass*, a book that features a number of Carroll's own portmanteau inventions, including *slithy*

but I was too driven for that. 🖙

(*lithe* and *slimy*), galumph (*gallop* and *triumph*), and chortle (*chuckle* and *snort*).

Well-established portmanteau words include smog (*smoke* and *fog*), motel (*motor* and *hotel*), and sportscast (*sport* and *broadcast*). Recent blends making a bid for acceptance include rockumentary (*rock* and *documentary*), ragazine (*rag* and *magazine*), sexcapade (*sex* and *escapade*), and brotel (*brothel* and *hotel*). There are even some well-known trademarks that are portmanteau words, e.g., Jazzercise (*jazz* and *exercise*) and Breathalyzer (*breath* and *analyzer*).

Your Words Are Numbered

Q. *The "By the Numbers" feature in the February 14, 2000, edition of* Time *magazine reported the following statistics: "25,000: Number of words in the vocabulary of the average 14-year-old in the U.S. in 1950. 10,000: Number of words in the vocabulary of the average 14-year-old in the U.S. in 1999." What do you make of these numbers and the marked decline that they show?*

A. I'd like to know *Time*'s source for these statistics. Vocabulary is a tricky thing to estimate; even the experts often disagree. I've seen lots of numbers bandied about over the years. *Time*'s numbers seem suspect because most of the estimates that I've seen put the vocabulary of the average educated *adult* at 25,000 to 40,000 words. And that's been the range for a while. Back in 1961, the

⬿ I could have been a mortician

distinguished Columbia professor and linguist Mario Pei wrote that the average person's vocabulary "perhaps embraces 30,000 words."

It's hard to believe that a fourteen-year-old who knew 25,000 words in 1950 would know only 5,000 more words ten years later,

after going to college and perhaps graduate school. And though I don't doubt that the number of words young people command today is fewer than what they knew thirty or forty years ago, I doubt that the decline is as drastic as *Time*'s numbers would have us believe. The 1999 estimate of 10,000 words sounds about right, but I think the 1950 estimate of 25,000 is inflated; my guess would be about 15,000. That still leaves us with a drop of one-third, which is considerable and alarming. What's more, there is no denying that high school students are less interested in reading than they were even a couple of decades ago. As the novelist Norman Mailer reported in an article for *Parade* (January 23, 2005), "In

but it seemed like a dead-end job.

2002, among our teenagers and young adults, the drop from 1982 in books read annually came to more than 25 percent."

I would attribute these drops in vocabulary level and reading to three things that have occurred since 1950: the ubiquitousness of television, and our addiction to it; the disappearance of Latin instruction from the schools; and, in the high school curriculum (and to some extent college as well), the gradual emphasis on contemporary literature to the exclusion of much pre-1900 literature. There's a lot of great contemporary literature, but the older stuff is where most of the challenging words repose.

Are You a Dord?

Q. *What is a* ghost word?

A. For the answer, let us turn to Sidney I. Landau's *Dictionaries: The Art and Craft of Lexicography* (pp. 27–28): "A ghost word is a word that has never existed in actual usage but that appears in dictionaries through the lexicographer's error. Ghost words are introduced in dictionaries iatrogenically, so to speak, as diseases are sometimes introduced in well patients by the physician's treatment. Once a term is in a dictionary it acquires the quiet authority of print and may spread to other innocent dictionaries, thus acquiring more authority, until it appears, by virtue of its ubiquitous representation, to be firmly established in the language."

The only ghost word I know of is in my favorite dictionary, *Webster's New International,* second edition, first published in

FASCINATING FACT 25

"The average American adult reads one book a year, and reads it with the skills and comprehension of a seventh grader ... The average American child spends 78 minutes a week reading, 102 minutes a week on homework and study, and 12 *hours* a week watching television."—from *School of Dreams,* by Edward Humes

I could have been a tennis player

BANNED BOOKS

The first banned book we know of was the Bible, which was censored by the ancient Romans. It continues to be challenged, usually in public schools, not only on the ground that it teaches religion but also on the ground that it is sacred and should be taught only by those qualified to reveal its truth.

"God forbid that any book should be banned," wrote the British novelist and journalist Rebecca West. "The practice is as indefensible as infanticide." Yet every year, scores of books are challenged and sometimes banned from public libraries and schools across the United States.

Here are some of the most frequently banned books in recent years:

The Adventures of Huckleberry Finn
The Diary of a Young Girl (Anne Frank)
Brave New World
The Catcher in the Rye
A Farewell to Arms
The Good Earth
The Grapes of Wrath
Nineteen Eighty-Four
Of Mice and Men
One Flew Over the Cuckoo's Nest
Fahrenheit 451
Black Like Me
Our Bodies, Ourselves
The Scarlet Letter
I Know Why the Caged Bird Sings
Slaughterhouse Five
To Kill a Mockingbird
Black Boy and *Native Son*
The Canterbury Tales
Soul on Ice
Catch-22
The Crucible
Deliverance
Lord of the Flies
Manchild in the Promised Land
The Sun Also Rises

1934. The word is *dord,* and it is defined as "a term in physics and chemistry for density." It should have been printed as an abbreviation, "*d* or *D,*" but some copyeditor apparently screwed up and changed it to *dord.*

but it wasn't my kind of racket. 🖘

FASCINATING FACT 🎐

The simple word *set* has more discrete meanings than any other word in the language. The unabridged second edition of *The Random House Dictionary* (1987) has 119 definitions for *set*, and the second edition of the *Oxford English Dictionary* (1989) devotes twenty-five three-column pages to the word. *Bryson's Dictionary of Troublesome Words* (2002) claims that *set* "has 126 meanings as a verb, 58 as a noun, and 10 as a participial adjective." 🎐

License to Quell

Q. *I'm wondering, if a driver's license allows you to drive, and a business license allows you to do your business, does a poetic license allow you to go from bard to verse?*

A. You've come to the right place, pun pal, because your humble author has an Official Poetic License issued by the Board of Inverse Proportion.

What are the benefits? A poetic license lets you have your trochaic and eat it too. It gets you out of all sorts of enjambments. With it, you can be spondee-aneous. You can tell people, "Iamb what iamb, and that's what iamb." You never have to feed the meter. And wherever you go, you can take out your poetic license and show everybody what sonnet. But there's also a down side to having a poetic license. With a poetic license,

> *Your poetry will never be the best,*
> *Because you are a poet anapest.*
> *Your doggerel will always be*
> *A stain upon some poetry.*

ANSWERS TO THE
BODACIOUS BRAINTEASERS

Colorful Language

1. Baa, baa, black sheep 2. the yellow brick road 3. *Rhapsody in Blue* 4. *The Scarlet Letter* 5. the Black Hole of Calcutta 6. the Red Baron 7. Harvard Crimson and Yale Blue 8. purple haze 9. the Emerald Isle 10. *A Clockwork Orange* 11. black bile 12. Agent Orange 13. brownshirt 14. purple prose 15. the Green Mountain State 16. pink elephants 17. Gray Panthers 18. yellow journalism 19. William of Orange 20. gray eminence or, if you prefer French, *éminence grise*

The Brobdingnagian Rubicund Saxiphage

1. A watchdog. 2. It's time to get a new fence. 3. Because it's too far to walk. 4. To make a hog of himself. 5. When they beat eggs. 6. Bad men. 7. A big red rock-eater. 8. If you don't know, then I wouldn't want to send you to get eggs.

Author Anagrams

1. Dr. Seuss 2. A. A. Milne 3. E. B. White 4. Lewis Carroll 5. Edward Lear 6. Beatrix Potter 7. Toni Morrison 8. William Shakespeare

Tasty Toponyms

1. Welsh 2. French 3. Lima 4. Spanish, Denver, or western 5. New England or Manhattan 6. London 7. Swedish 8. Hollandaise 9. Canadian 10. Newton 11. Jerusalem 12. Alaska 13. Bombay or Peking 14. Belgian 15. Monterey 16. Italian 17. Neapolitan 18. English 19. Brazil 20. Genoa

Are You an Idiom Savant?

1. truth 2. blue moon 3. there's fire 4. or high water 5. punch 6. line, and sinker 7. of the tracks 8. deserves another 9. cats and dogs 10. college

try (*or* heave ho) 11. thicker than water 12. of an eye 13. in the rough
14. in a china shop 15. the nose on your face (*or* day) 16. one's welcome
17. in love and war 18. in sheep's clothing 19. on a log 20. the baby with
the bathwater 21. the catbird seat 22. to nuts 23. in Denmark 24. one's
loins 25. with faint praise 26. must go on 27. while the sun shines
28. the music 29. gift horse in the mouth 30. riot act

Are You Brandiloquent?

1. Xerox 2. Kleenex 3. Band-Aid 4. Q-Tips 5. Jell-O 6. Rollerblade
7. Ping-Pong 8. Styrofoam 9. Popsicle 10. Scotch tape 11. Hi-Liter
12. Levi's 13. Frisbee 14. Walkman 15. aspirin 16. zipper 17. thermos
18. escalator 19. TV dinner 20. yo-yo 21. cornflakes 22. trampoline
23. pogo stick 24. kerosene 25. linoleum

Pompous Proverbs

1. Birds of a feather flock together. 2. Dead men tell no tales. 3. The pen
is mightier than the sword. 4. Do not cry over spilled milk. 5. Too many
cooks spoil the broth. 6. Pride comes before a fall. 7. Cleanliness is next
to godliness. 8. All that glitters (originally *glisters*) is not gold. 9. Charity
begins at home. 10. People who live in glass houses shouldn't throw
stones. 11. Where there's smoke, there's fire. 12. You can't teach an old dog
new tricks. 13. Nothing ventured, nothing gained. 14. The grass is always
greener on the other side. 15. Beauty is only skin deep.

Tea-Totally

1. anxiety 2. thrifty 3. liberty 4. sobriety 5. velvety 6. naughty
7. puberty 8. intensity 9. priority 10. prosperity 11. seniority 12. infinity
13. immunity 14. velocity 15. celebrity and publicity 16. mediocrity
17. audacity 18. chastity 19. joviality and jocularity 20. mendacity
21. domesticity 22. sagacity or perspicacity 23. verbosity and loquacity

Etc. = Et Cetera = And So On

1. *manuscriptum* = manuscript 2. *postscriptum* = postscript 3. *exempli gratia*
= for example 4. *id est* = that is 5. *nota bene* = take careful note 6. *et alii* (or

et alia) = and others (normally used of people, not things) 7. *circa* = about, approximately (used of dates) 8. *ibidem* = in the same place (refers to a single work cited in the footnote or endnote immediately preceding) 9. *confer* = compare, see by way of comparison (*cf.* should not be used when only "see" is meant) 10. *quod vide* = which see 11. *supra* = above 12. *et sequentes* = and the following 13. *videlicet* = namely 14. *floruit* = flourished — used when you don't known someone's precise birth and death dates, as in "the ancient Greek philosopher Herodatus (fl. 5th century B.C.)" 15. *quod erat demonstrandum* = which was to be demonstrated (Euclid appended these letters to his theorems to indicate that he had proved each proposition.)

Famous First Lines

1. Geoffrey Chaucer, General Prologue to *The Canterbury Tales* 2. John Milton, *Paradise Lost* 3. Edmund Spenser, *The Faerie Queene* 4. William Shakespeare, Sonnet 18 5. William Wordsworth, "Intimations of Immortality" 6. Edgar Allan Poe, "Annabel Lee" 7. Walt Whitman, "Song of Myself" 8. W. B. Yeats, "The Second Coming" 9. T. S. Eliot, "The Love Song of J. Alfred Prufrock" 10. Robert Frost, "Mending Wall" 11. Dylan Thomas, "Fern Hill" 12. Allen Ginsberg, "Howl"

Nursery Rhyme Names

1. Jack and Jill 2. Old Mother Hubbard 3. Little Bo-peep 4. Jack Sprat 5. the cat, the fiddle, the cow, the dog, the dish, and the spoon 6. Little Miss Muffet 7. Humpty Dumpty 8. Peter, Peter, pumpkin eater 9. Little Jack Horner 10. Jack 11. Little Tom Tucker 12. Mistress Mary (or Mary, Mary), quite contrary 13. Little Boy Blue 14. Old King Cole 15. Simple Simon 16. Wee Willie Winkie

It's Greek to Thee

1. photograph 2. apostrophe 3. catastrophe 4. agoraphobia 5. hoi polloi 6. marathon 7. sarcastic 8. cynic 9. gymnasium 10. pedagogue 11. ostracism 12. apocryphal

Think King

1. the lion 2. Elvis 3. Budweiser 4. Martin Luther King 5. King Arthur
6. B. B. King 7. Larry King 8. Stephen King 9. Billie Jean King 10. Don
King (a flamboyant boxing promoter who rose to fame managing
Muhammad Ali) 11. Benny Goodman 12. the King James (or Authorized)
Version (published in 1611) 13. Nat King Cole 14. Kingsley Amis
15. Louis XIV of France (he adopted the sun as his emblem) 16. King
Kong 17. Kinko's (did this one fool you?)

What Is Waspleg*?*

The seven deadly sins: wrath, avarice, sloth, pride, lust, envy, and gluttony.

All-American Eponyms

1. Webster (from Noah Webster, 1758–1843, lexicographer and proponent
of the American language) 2. John Hancock (first signer of the Declaration
of Independence) 3. teddy bear (named after Theodore Roosevelt)
4. sideburns (from General Ambrose Everett Burnside, who suffered
defeats at Fredericksburg and Petersburg) 5. Gallup poll (from Dr. George
Horace Gallup, professor of journalism at Northwestern, who introduced
the poll in the 1930s) 6. Ferris wheel (from George Washington Gale
Ferris, an engineer from Illinois. Ferris introduced his wheel at the World's
Columbian Exposition in Chicago in 1893. It was 140 feet high, 250 feet
in diameter, weighed over 1,200 tons, and had 36 cars for 1,440 people —
40 people each.) 7. poinsettia (from Joel Roberts Poinsett, 1779–1851, an
American diplomat who sent specimens of it from Mexico while serving as
the U.S. ambassador in the late 1820s. He did not discover the plant, and
apparently did not introduce it to the U.S., but perhaps because he was
well known his name became attached to it.) 8. maverick (In 1845, Texas
lawyer Samuel Augustus Maverick, a signer of the Texas Declaration of
Independence and hero of the Mexican-American War, acquired a herd of
cattle as payment for a debt. He had little interest in the enterprise, and so
he, or his careless farmhands, let many of his cattle go unbranded. These
unbranded cattle became known as mavericks.) 9. gerrymander (from

Elbridge Gerry, governor of Massachusetts, 1812) **10.** Rube Goldberg (a comic strip artist and political cartoonist in the first half of the twentieth century who was famous for drawing outrageously complicated machinery designed to perform a simple task) **11.** salmonella (from pathologist Daniel Elmer Salmon, 1850–1914) **12.** Horatio Alger story (Alger, 1834–1899, was one of the most prolific American writers, cranking out 120 novels and many articles and stories.) **13.** Gibson (after Charles Dana Gibson, an American artist best known for his drawings of beautiful young women in long flowing dresses, known as the Gibson girls, published on the covers of national magazines from the 1890s to about 1920. As the story goes, the bartender at the New York Players Club ran out of olives and instead garnished Gibson's martini with a pearl onion.) **14.** BVDs or beeveedees (from the initials of the three men—Bradley, Voorhees, and Day—who founded the company in 1876)

Don't Be a Scaredy Cat

1. don't count your chickens before they hatch **2.** happy as a lark **3.** it's raining cats and dogs **4.** birds of a feather flock together **5.** live high off the hog **6.** get one's/your goat **7.** cook your goose **8.** proud as a peacock **9.** more fun than a barrel of monkeys **10.** one-horse town **11.** cash cow **12.** queen bee **13.** two shakes of a lamb's tail **14.** cat-and-mouse game **15.** charley horse **16.** bats in the belfry **17.** elephants never forget

Blenderous Words

1. simultaneous and broadcast **2.** cremated and remains **3.** stagnation and inflation **4.** television and evangelist **5.** guess and estimate **6.** pal and alimony **7.** information and commercial **8.** Spanish and English **9.** slum and landlord **10.** futile and utilitarian **11.** weather and forecast **12.** documentary and drama **13.** *français* (French) and *anglais* (English) **14.** quasi- and stellar **15.** jocose and serious

SOURCES CITED

The American Heritage Dictionary of the English Language, fourth edition. Boston: Houghton Mifflin Company, 2000.

Ammer, Christine. *Seeing Red or Tickled Pink.* New York: Dutton, 1992.

Augarde, Tony. *The Oxford Guide to Word Games.* Oxford and New York: Oxford University Press, 1984.

Barnhart, Robert K., and Sol Steinmetz, eds. *The Barnhart Dictionary of Etymology.* New York: The H. W. Wilson Company, 1988.

Bartlett, John Russell. *Dictionary of Americanisms.* Hoboken, NJ: J. Wiley & Sons, 2003. (First published in 1848.)

Barzun, Jacques. *Simple and Direct: A Rhetoric for Writers.* New York: Harper & Row, Publishers, 1985.

Bernstein, Theodore M. *The Careful Writer: A Modern Guide to English Usage.* New York: Atheneum, 1983. (Originally published in 1965.)

Bierce, Ambrose. *The Devil's Dictionary.* New York: Dover Publications, 1958.

Blood, Peter, and Annie Patterson, eds. *Rise Up Singing: The Group Singing Songbook.* Bethlehem, PA: The Sing Out Corporation, 1992.

Bollard, John K., ed. *Pronouncing Dictionary of Proper Names,* second edition. Detroit: Omnigraphics, Inc., 1988.

Brewer, E. Cobham. *The Dictionary of Phrase and Fable.* New York: Avenel Books, 1978.

Bryson, Bill. *Bryson's Dictionary of Troublesome Words.* New York: Broadway Books, 2002.

———. *The Mother Tongue: English and How It Got That Way.* New York: William Morrow and Company, 1990.

Burchfield, R. W., ed. *The New Fowler's Modern English Usage,* third edition. Oxford: Clarendon Press, 1996.

The Century Dictionary, revised and enlarged edition. New York: The Century Co., 1914.

Chapman, Robert L. *Dictionary of American Slang,* third edition. New York: HarperCollins, 1995.

——. *Thesaurus of American Slang.* New York: Harper & Row, 1989.

The Chicago Manual of Style, fifteenth edition. Chicago and London: The University of Chicago Press, 2003.

Cooper, Samuel. *Dictionary of Literary Terms.* Canada: Key Book Publishing Company, 1970.

Copperud, Roy H. *American Usage and Style: The Consensus.* New York: Van Nostrand Reinhold, 1980.

Cralle, Trevor. *The Surfin'ary: A Dictionary of Surfing Terms and Surfspeak.* Berkeley, CA: Ten Speed Press, 1991.

Dalzell, Tom. *Flappers 2 Rappers: American Youth Slang.* Springfield, MA: Merriam-Webster, 1996.

Dickson, Paul. *Dickson's Word Treasury.* New York: John Wiley & Sons, 1992.

——. *Labels for Locals.* Springfield, MA: Merriam-Webster, 1997.

——. *The New Dickson Baseball Dictionary.* San Diego: Harcourt Brace & Company, 1999.

——. *War Slang.* New York: Pocket Books, 1994.

Ehrlich, Eugene, and Raymond Hand. *NBC Handbook of Pronunciation,* fourth edition. New York: Harper & Row, 1984.

Encarta World English Dictionary. New York: St. Martin's Press, 1999.

Evans, Bergen. *Comfortable Words.* New York: Random House, 1962.

Evans, Bergen, and Cornelia Evans. *A Dictionary of Contemporary American Usage.* New York: Random House, 1957.

Follett, Wilson. *Modern American Usage.* New York: Hill & Wang, 1966.

Fowler, H. W. *A Dictionary of Modern English Usage.* Oxford: Clarendon Press, 1961. (First published in 1926.)

Gallant, Frank K. *A Place Called Peculiar.* Springfield, MA: Merriam-Webster, 1998.

Garner, Bryan A. *A Dictionary of Modern Legal Usage.* New York, Oxford: Oxford University Press, 1995.

——. *Garner's Modern American Usage.* New York: Oxford University Press, 2003.

Goldstein, Norm, ed. *The Associated Press Stylebook and Briefing on Media Law.* Cambridge, MA: Perseus Publishing, 2000.

Green, Jonathon. *The Cassell Dictionary of Slang.* London: Cassell, 1998.

———. *Cassell's Rhyming Slang.* London: Cassell & Co., 2000.

Hale, Constance, and Jessie Scanlon. *Wired Style: Principles of English Usage in the Digital Age.* New York: Broadway Books, 1999.

Hall, Joan Houston, ed. *Dictionary of American Regional English (DARE),* vols. 1–4. Cambridge, MA, and London: The Belknap Press of Harvard University Press, 1985–2002.

Hellweg, Paul. *The Insomniac's Dictionary.* New York: Ivy Books, 1986.

Hendrickson, Robert. *The Dictionary of Eponyms: Names That Became Words.* New York: Dorset Press, 1972.

———. *Grand Slams, Hat Tricks and Alley-oops: A Sports Fan's Book of Words.* New York: Prentice Hall General Reference, 1994.

———. *QPB Encyclopedia of Word and Phrase Origins.* New York: Facts on File, 1997.

Hitt, Jack. *In a Word: A Dictionary of Words That Don't Exist, but Ought To.* New York: Dell Laurel, 1992.

Humes, Edward. *School of Dreams.* Orlando, FL: Harcourt, Inc., 2003.

Johnson, Edward D. *The Handbook of Good English.* New York: Washington Square Press, 1991.

Landau, Sidney I. *Dictionaries: The Art and Craft of Lexicography.* New York: Charles Scribner's Sons, 1984.

Lass, Abraham, and Betty Lass. *Dictionary of Pronunciation.* New York: Quadrangle/The New York Times Book Co., 1976.

Lederer, Richard. *Crazy English.* New York: Pocket Books, 1989.

Lighter, J. E., ed. *Random House Historical Dictionary of American Slang,* vol. 1, *A–G,* and vol. 2, *H–O.* New York: Random House, 1994, 1997.

Lipton, James. *An Exaltation of Larks,* second edition. New York and London: Penguin Books, 1977.

McKean, Erin. *More Weird and Wonderful Words.* Oxford and New York: Oxford University Press, 2003.

McQuain, Jeffrey. *Never Enough Words.* New York: Random House, 1999.

Mencken, H. L. *The American Language,* fourth edition. New York: Alfred A. Knopf, 1937.

Merriam-Webster's Collegiate Dictionary, eleventh edition. Springfield, MA: Merriam-Webster, 2003.

Merriam-Webster's Dictionary of English Usage. Springfield, MA: Merriam-Webster, 1994.

Merriam-Webster's Encyclopedia of Literature. Springfield, MA: Merriam-Webster, 1995.

Microsoft Encarta College Dictionary. New York: St. Martin's Press, 2001.

Morris, Evan. *The Word Detective.* Chapel Hill, NC: Algonquin Books of Chapel Hill, 2000.

Morris, William, and Mary Morris. *Harper Dictionary of Contemporary Usage,* second edition. New York: Harper & Row, 1985.

———. *Morris Dictionary of Word and Phrase Origins,* second edition. New York: HarperCollins, 1988.

Morton, Mark. *Cupboard Love: A Dictionary of Culinary Curiosities.* Winnipeg, Canada: Bain & Cox, 1996.

The New Oxford American Dictionary. New York: Oxford University Press, 2001.

The New York Public Library Desk Reference, third edition. New York: Macmillan, 1998.

Oxford English Dictionary, second edition. Oxford: Clarendon Press, 1989. (Often referred to as the *OED.*)

Popcorn, Faith, and Adam Hanft. *Dictionary of the Future.* New York: Hyperion, 2001.

The Random House Dictionary of the English Language, second edition, unabridged. New York: Random House, 1987.

Random House Webster's College Dictionary. New York: Random House, 2001.

Rawson, Hugh. *Devious Derivations.* New York: Crown Publishers, 1994.

Room, Adrian. *Brewer's Dictionary of Modern Phrase and Fable.* London: Cassell & Co., 2000.

Rosten, Leo. *The Joys of Yinglish.* New York: Plume, 1989.

Safire, William. *On Language.* New York: Avon Books, 1980.

Schur, Norman W. *British English, A to Zed.* New York: HarperPerennial, 1987.

Siegal, Allan M., and William G. Connolly. *The New York Times Manual of Style and Usage,* revised and expanded edition. New York: Times Books, 1999.

Smitherman, Geneva. *Black Talk: Words and Phrases from the Hood to the Amen Corner,* revised edition. Boston: Houghton Mifflin Company, 2000.

Stevens, Payson R., Charles M. Levine, and Sol Steinmetz. *Meshuggenary: Celebrating the World of Yiddish.* New York: Simon & Schuster, 2002.

Stimpson, George. *A Book About a Thousand Things.* New York and London: Harper & Brothers Publishers, 1946.

Thorne, Tony. *The Dictionary of Contemporary Slang.* New York: Pantheon Books, 1990.

Trench, Richard Chenevix. *On the Study of Words,* second edition. New York: Redfield, 1854.

Twain, Mark. *Mark Twain's Autobiography.* New York and London: Harper & Brothers Publishers, 1924.

Wallraff, Barbara. *Word Court.* New York: Harcourt, 2000.

Webster's New International Dictionary, second edition. Springfield, MA: G. & C. Merriam Company, 1934. (Sometimes referred to as *Webster 2.*)

Webster's New World College Dictionary, fourth edition. New York: Macmillan USA, 1999.

Webster's Third New International Dictionary. Springfield, MA: G. & C. Merriam Company, 1961.

Wright, Larry. *Happy As a Clam and 9,999 Other Similes.* New York: Prentice Hall General Reference, 1994.

INDEX

Made in the USA
Middletown, DE
23 December 2014